"十三五"江苏省高等学校重点教材

高等院校研究性学习英语系列教材

# 英语语言学实用教程

（第二版）

*English Linguistics: A Practical Coursebook*

陈新仁 • 编著

苏州大学出版社
Soochow University Press

图书在版编目(CIP)数据

英语语言学实用教程 / 陈新仁编著. —2 版. —苏州：苏州大学出版社，2017.6（2021.6重印）
"十三五"江苏省高等学校重点教材　高等院校研究性学习英语系列教材
ISBN 978-7-5672-1733-1

Ⅰ.①英… Ⅱ.①陈… Ⅲ.①英语－语言学－高等学校－教材 Ⅳ.①H31

中国版本图书馆 CIP 数据核字(2016)第 105817 号

| | |
|---|---|
| 书　　名 | 英语语言学实用教程（第二版） |
| 编　　著 | 陈新仁 |
| 责任编辑 | 杨　华 |
| 出版发行 | 苏州大学出版社（Soochow University Press） |
| 社　　址 | 苏州市十梓街 1 号　邮编：215006 |
| 印　　刷 | 常州市武进第三印刷有限公司 |
| 网　　址 | www.sudapress.com |
| 邮购热线 | 0512-67480030 |
| 销售热线 | 0512-65225020 |
| 开　　本 | 787 mm×1 092 mm　1/16　印张：19　字数：428 千 |
| 版　　次 | 2017 年 6 月第 1 版 |
| 印　　次 | 2021 年 6 月第 3 次印刷 |
| 书　　号 | ISBN 978-7-5672-1733-1 |
| 定　　价 | 48.00 元 |

凡购本社图书发现印装错误，请与本社联系调换。服务热线：0512-67481020

# 前　言

　　本教材是笔者在 2007 年出版的《英语语言学实用教程》基础上修订、增补而来的新版本，期待赢得更多读者的更多关注和喜爱，更希望能对普及英语语言学知识、提升英语研究能力尽绵薄之力。

　　我们知道，语言是我们生活的一部分，是人类拥有的一种独特资源。英语是一门国际性语言，在中国拥有广大的学习者。把握语言、学好英语对于每个英语专业学生来说都意义重大。

　　我们同样知道，"英语语言学概论"是高校英语专业课程设置中的一门必修课，其目的在于揭示语言的基本规律，系统描述英语的结构层次、构成规则、使用原则、社会变异、文化属性、认知属性等，从而深化学生对语言的认识，提高英语学习效率。

　　众所周知，国内为"英语语言学概论"课程编写的教材有多种版本。总体来看，这些教材采用典型的理论课程教材编写思路，理论性、系统性强。然而，过强的理论性容易引发"一言堂""填鸭式"的教学程式，容易让课堂陷入沉闷，学生提不起兴趣，教师难以获得教学成就感。为此，笔者多年前广泛、深入研究了国内外大量语言学入门教材，研读了一些理论课程的教学研究成果，另辟蹊径，引入先进的研究型教学理念，以学生需求为导向，以师生互动为手段，以促进英语学习和培养学生的研究性思维和能力为目标，博采众长，推陈出新，从内容组织到编排方式都进行了大胆的革新，为英语专业学生和教师提供了一个全新的选择——《英语语言学实用教程》。

　　此次第二版增加了 3 个单元，将第一版最后有关语言学研究方法的 2 个单元改为供学习者自学用的附录。调整后的 15 个单元布局如下：第 1 单元为绪论，介绍自然语言的属性、功能、谱系、习得等；第 2 单元至第 14 单元从语音、结构、语义、语用、修辞、认知、语体等角度系统解析英语；第 15 单元介绍影响中国学生英语学习的各种因素，剖析中国学生在学习和使用英语方面存在的问题和原因。此外，笔者对第一版部分单元的 Pre-Class Reading 内容进行了一定程度的充实，同时调整了 In-Class Activities 中的部分讨论题，删减了一些开放性过强或实用性不足的讨论题，一些讨论题中换用了应用性更强的例子，撤换或调整了一些单元中的 Presentation Topics，删去了课后 Exercises 中一些开放性过强的题目及难度较大的 Comment Work 部分，充实了部分单元的 Term Definition，更新了全书的 Glossary 和 References。

　　第二版保持了原教材的特色，主要包括以下几点。

- 面向中国学生和教师。从中国学生学习英语、使用英语的实际出发,根据课程教学大纲,结合中国学生的实际需求,提供精选的、难度适中的语言理论知识。为中国教师着想,以讨论性、开放性活动组织教学内容,便于教师开展活泼、生动的课堂教学,获取良好的教学效果。
- 面向英语的语言学。从各种渠道选取大量有趣、典型、题材各异的英语素材,全方位探索英语的基本规律,体现真正的"英语"语言学,同时适当联系汉语,增进学生对英语个性的把握,从而服务于英语学习和交际。
- 面向教学全过程。课前部分有适量的浅易阅读材料(Pre-Class Reading),为课堂讲解、讨论作铺垫,并通过一些真伪习题予以检查阅读情况;课内有充足的包含语言学知识点的开放性互动话题(In-Class Activities),融理论知识的讲解和应用于课堂活动中。在多数单元中,提供了3个操作性强、可供学生进行课外合作性学习、课内团队汇报的话题(Presentation Topics)。课后设计了丰富多样的探索性、研究性习题(Exercises),以巩固、深化相关单元的学习效果。教师可以根据学生水平和课时情况,有选择地使用教材中提供的讨论内容和练习。另外,为了拓宽学有余力者的语言学知识面,在一些单元中还提供了2篇精选的、配有思考题的原汁原味读物(Recommended Readings)。
- 注重语言理论与语言事实的结合。以语言现象为驱动,采集大量鲜活、一手的英语语料,贴近生活,力避空洞、抽象的概念讲解,力戒理论与实践的脱节,以语言事实演绎语言理论,以语言理论解读语言事实,让学生直接感受本课程的适用性、实用性和趣味性。
- 注重语言学知识传授与语言研究能力培养的结合。从课堂讨论到练习设计,注重培养学生的批判性思维,并讲解语言研究方法论,促进学生研究能力的发展。
- 注重传统语言学理论知识与现代语言学前沿成果的结合。本教材在保留传统语言学基本内容的基础上,密切跟踪、反映当代语言学的最新发展,深入浅出地吸纳了认知语言学、语用学、会话分析、二语习得等领域的最新成果,如原型理论、隐喻理论、构式语法、词汇语用学、语块理论等。同时,引进语料库语言学的研究手段,为开展英语教学和研究提供服务。

修订成书之际,本人衷心感谢曾经在南京大学外国语学院英语系工作过的美籍专家唐斯诺博士(Dr. Don Snow)帮助审校第一版的全部书稿,感谢苏州大学外国语学院徐健博士为本书付出的辛劳,对来自多所高校第一线并给本书修订工作提出宝贵意见的老师表示衷心的感谢,感谢苏州大学出版社对本书修订与出版给予的支持。

由于编者水平有限,书中难免存在瑕疵和谬误,敬请读者和同行赐教。

编 者
2017年5月于南京大学

# 目 录　Contents

## Unit 1　Some Preliminaries about Language

Pre-Class Reading ································································ (1)
   1.1　The languages of the world ············································ (1)
   1.2　The functions of language ·············································· (4)
   1.3　The defining features of language ····································· (5)
   1.4　The origin of language ··················································· (6)
   1.5　The acquisition of language ············································ (7)
   1.6　Linguistics: The science of language ································· (9)
In-Class Activities ································································· (10)
Exercises ············································································ (13)

## Unit 2　The Sounds of English

Pre-Class Reading ································································ (16)
   2.1　Speech organs ····························································· (16)
   2.2　Speech sounds ···························································· (17)
   2.3　Phones, phonemes and allophones ··································· (18)
   2.4　Classifying English vowels ············································· (20)
   2.5　Classifying English consonants ········································ (21)
   2.6　English syllables ·························································· (22)
   2.7　Stress, tone and intonation in English ······························· (22)
   2.8　Phonological rules in English ·········································· (24)
   2.9　Rhythm in English ······················································· (25)

In-Class Activities ································································· (26)
Exercises ····································································································· (28)

## Unit 3  The Units of English

Pre-Class Reading ····························································································· (32)
   3.1   English morphemes ························································· (32)
   3.2   English words and idioms ················································· (33)
   3.3   English clauses and sentences ·········································· (35)
   3.4   Constructions in English ····················································· (36)
In-Class Activities ································································································ (37)
Presentation Topics ···························································································· (41)
Exercises ················································································································ (41)
Recommended Readings ···················································································· (45)

## Unit 4  The Structures of English (I)

Pre-Class Reading ····························································································· (49)
   4.1   Grammatical knowledge ······················································· (49)
   4.2   Sentence patterns in English ··········································· (51)
   4.3   The hierarchical structuring of English sentences ··············· (52)
   4.4   Surface structure and deep structure ································ (53)
In-Class Activities ································································································ (56)
Presentation Topics ···························································································· (59)
Exercises ················································································································ (59)
Recommended Readings ···················································································· (62)

## Unit 5  The Structures of English (II)

Pre-Class Reading ····························································································· (66)
   5.1   English paragraphs ······························································ (66)
   5.2   English texts ············································································· (67)
   5.3   Cohesion in English texts ··················································· (67)
   5.4   Thematic progression in English texts ······························· (68)

In-Class Activities ················································ (69)
Presentation Topics ················································ (72)
Exercises ··························································· (72)
Recommended Readings ··········································· (75)

## Unit 6  The Meaning of English (I)

Pre-Class Reading ·················································· (78)
   6.1  The notion of semantics ··································· (78)
   6.2  Semantic properties ······································· (79)
   6.3  Semantic relations ········································ (80)
   6.4  Sense and reference ······································ (82)
In-Class Activities ················································ (83)
Presentation Topics ················································ (87)
Exercises ··························································· (87)
Recommended Readings ··········································· (91)

## Unit 7  The Meaning of English (II)

Pre-Class Reading ·················································· (96)
   7.1  Semantic extension ······································· (96)
   7.2  Sentence semantics ······································· (97)
   7.3  Semantic roles ············································ (98)
In-Class Activities ················································ (99)
Presentation Topics ················································ (101)
Exercises ··························································· (101)
Recommended Readings ··········································· (103)

## Unit 8  The Use of English (I)

Pre-Class Reading ·················································· (108)
   8.1  Study of English in context ······························ (108)
   8.2  Anchoring the use of English in context ················ (109)
   8.3  Using English as a speech act ··························· (110)

    8.4   Using English as a social act ·········································· (112)
    8.5   Presuppositions in the use of English ································ (112)
In-Class Activities ······························································ (114)
Presentation Topics ····························································· (118)
Exercises ············································································· (118)
Recommended Readings ······················································ (122)

## Unit 9　The Use of English (II)

Pre-Class Reading ······························································· (125)
    9.1   Cooperation in using English ·········································· (125)
    9.2   Politeness in using English ············································· (128)
    9.3   Face considerations in using English ······························· (129)
    9.4   Using English as a strategic act ······································· (129)
    9.5   Using English as a cultural act ········································ (130)
In-Class Activities ······························································ (131)
Presentation Topics ····························································· (135)
Exercises ············································································· (135)
Recommended Readings ······················································ (141)

## Unit 10　The Use of English (III)

Pre-Class Reading ······························································· (145)
    10.1   Turn-taking in English conversation ······························· (145)
    10.2   Adjacency pairs in English conversation ·························· (146)
    10.3   Pre-sequences in English conversation ···························· (147)
    10.4   Repairs and interruptions in English conversation ············ (148)
    10.5   Backchannel signals in English conversation ···················· (149)
In-Class Activities ······························································ (150)
Presentation Topics ····························································· (153)
Exercises ············································································· (154)
Recommended Readings ······················································ (156)

## Unit 11　The Use of English (IV)

Pre-Class Reading ······················································ (159)
    11.1　Comparison-based tropes in English ·················· (159)
    11.2　Association-based tropes in English ·················· (161)
    11.3　Repetition-based rhetoric in English ·················· (163)
    11.4　Omission-based rhetoric in English ··················· (163)
    11.5　Contrast-based rhetoric in English ····················· (164)
In-Class Activities ······················································ (165)
Presentation Topics ··················································· (168)
Exercises ·································································· (169)

## Unit 12　The Cognitive Study of English

Pre-Class Reading ······················································ (173)
    12.1　Cognitive approach to language ························ (173)
    12.2　Conceptual metaphors in English ····················· (175)
    12.3　Conceptual metonymies in English ··················· (177)
    12.4　Categorization and prototypes in English ·········· (177)
In-Class Activities ······················································ (179)
Presentation Topics ··················································· (182)
Exercises ·································································· (183)
Recommended Readings ············································ (186)

## Unit 13　The Varieties of English (I)

Pre-Class Reading ······················································ (190)
    13.1　Regional dialects of English ····························· (190)
    13.2　Social dialects of English ································ (192)
    13.3　Styles of English ············································· (193)
    13.4　Genres and registers of English ······················· (194)
In-Class Activities ······················································ (195)
Presentation Topics ··················································· (202)

Exercises ·················································································· (202)
Recommended Readings ··················································· (205)

## Unit 14   The Varieties of English (II)

Pre-Class Reading ······················································· (210)
   14.1   African-American Vernacular English ············· (210)
   14.2   Pidgin English and Creole ······························ (211)
   14.3   British English and American English ············· (212)
   14.4   Bilingualism and diglossia ······························ (213)
   14.5   English as a lingua franca ······························ (214)
In-Class Activities ························································· (215)
Presentation Topics ······················································· (218)
Exercises ······································································ (218)
Recommended Readings ··················································· (221)

## Unit 15   The Acquisition of English

Pre-Class Reading ······················································· (227)
   15.1   Study of English in China ······························ (227)
   15.2   Factors in English learning ···························· (228)
   15.3   Aspects of learners' English ·························· (231)
   15.4   Learners' English errors ································ (232)
In-Class Activities ························································· (234)
Presentation Topics ······················································· (240)
Exercises ······································································ (240)
Recommended Readings ··················································· (245)

## Appendix I   Empirical Studies of English

1. Defining linguistic research ············································· (250)
2. Interview-based studies of English ··································· (256)
3. Questionnaire-based studies of English ···························· (258)
4. Experiment-based studies of English ································ (261)

5. Corpus-based studies of English ……………………………………… (262)

## Appendix II  Conceptual Studies of English

1. Preliminaries of conceptual research ……………………………… (265)
2. Defining terms …………………………………………………………… (266)
3. Classifying objects ……………………………………………………… (268)
4. Formulating rules ………………………………………………………… (270)
5. Constructing models …………………………………………………… (272)

**References** ……………………………………………………………………… (274)
**Glossary** ………………………………………………………………………… (279)

# Unit 1

# Some Preliminaries about Language

* 1.1  The languages of the world
* 1.2  The functions of language
* 1.3  The defining features of language
* 1.4  The origin of language
* 1.5  The acquisition of language
* 1.6  Linguistics: The science of language

> *The question "What is language?" is comparable with—and, some would say, hardly less profound than—"What is life?"*
>
> —John Lyons

## Pre-Class Reading

## 1.1  The languages of the world

People have been called social animals and thinking animals. Understandably, humans are also language animals. The possession of language is an essential trait unique to humans, but absent in other animals. Thanks to language, we are able and apt to think. Thanks to language, we can talk about something in the past or imagine something in the future; we can describe something present, far away or non-existent. Thanks to language, we can express our ideas and emotions, and understand those of others.

There are some 6,800 known languages spoken in the world. In 2003, the total number of languages in the world was estimated to be 6,809, of which 2,261 languages have writing systems (the others are only spoken). 90% of these languages are spoken by less than 100,000 people. There are 357 languages which have less than 50 speakers. The Leco language (Bolivian Andes) has about 20 speakers. Mati Ke (in northern Australia) had 4 speakers in 2003. A total of 46 languages have just a single speaker. The most widely spoken languages include Chinese, English, Russian, French, Spanish, Portuguese, Japanese, Korean, and Italian, with English and French being the working languages of the United Nations Secretariat.

There are over 100 **language families** in the world. Top 10 language families are as follows:

**The Indo-European Family**: The most widely studied family of languages and the family with the largest number of speakers. Languages include English, Spanish, Portuguese, French, Italian, Russian, Greek, Hindi, Bengali; and the classical languages of Latin, Sanskrit, and Persian.

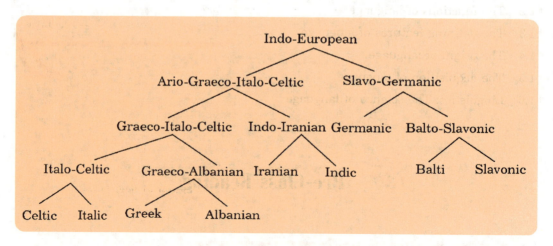

**The Uralic Family**: A family found in Europe (Hungarian, Finnish) and Siberia (Mordvin) with complex noun structures.

**The Altaic Family**: A family spreading from Europe (Turkish) through Central Asia (Uzbek), Mongolia (Mongolian), to the Far East (Korean, Japanese). These languages have the interesting property of vowel harmony.

**The Sino-Tibetan Family**: An important Asian family of languages that includes the world's most widely spoken language, Mandarin. These languages are monosyllabic and tonal.

**The Malayo-Polynesian Family**: A family consisting of over 1,000 languages spread throughout the Indian and Pacific Oceans as well as Southeast Asia. Languages of this family include Malay, Indonesian, Maori and Hawaiian.

**The Afro-Asiatic Family**: This family contains languages of northern Africa and the Middle East. The dominant languages are Arabic and Hebrew.

**The Caucasian Family**: A family based around the Caucas Mountains between the Black Sea and the Caspian Sea. Georgian and Chechen are the main languages. They are known for their large number of consonants.

**The Dravidian Family**: The languages of southern India (in contrast to the Indo-European languages of northern India). Tamil is the best known of these languages.

**The Austro-Asiatic Family**: This family consists of a scattered group of languages in Asia. They are found from eastern India to Vietnam. Languages of this family include Vietnamese and Khmer.

**The Niger-Congo Family**: This family features the many languages of Africa south of the Sahara. They include Swahili, Shona, Xhosa and Zulu.

Over time, many languages have dropped out of use and many others are near extinction today. With the increase of mass communications (rapid flights, radio, television, telephone, and the Internet), many of the smaller languages are in real danger of extinction. Over the last 500 years, 4.5% of the world's described languages have disappeared. Even so, some countries and regions are still rich in **linguistic diversity**. Mexico has 52 languages spoken within its borders. The island of Papua New Guinea has over 700, virtually a different one in each valley. India has over 800 languages in several families (Indo-European, Dravidian, Sino-Tibetan, and Austro-Asiatic).

Many languages today are already placed on the endangered list. Linguists attempt to preserve these languages by studying and documenting their grammars—the phonetics, phonology, and so on—and by recording for posterity the speech of the last few speakers. This is significant, because the grammar of each language provides new evidence about the nature of human cognition. Also, the literature, poetry, ritual speech, and word structure of each language store the collective intellectual achievements of a culture, offering unique perspectives on the human condition. The disappearance of a language is tragic: not only are these insights lost, but the major medium through which a culture maintains and renews itself is gone as well. For this reason, UNESCO (United Nations Educational, Scientific and Cultural Organization) passed a resolution in 1991 stating that "as the disappearance of any one language constitutes an irretrievable loss to mankind, it is for UNESCO a task of great urgency to respond to this situation by promoting ... the description—in the form of grammars, dictionaries, and texts—of endangered and dying languages".

## 1.2 The functions of language

By and large, language is a tool of communication and thinking. Specifically, language can serve the following functions:

**phatic**: as found in greetings, e.g. "Hello!"

**directive**: as found when we get somebody to do something, e.g. "Get out of my way!"

**informative**: as found when we provide some information to others, e.g. "The earth revolves around the sun."

**interrogative**: as found when we want to get some information from others, e.g. "Do you know his hobby?"

**evocative**: as found when we want to know how others feel about somebody or something, e.g. "How do you like Jack?"

**expressive / emotive**: as found when we express some emotion, e.g. "I hate her."

**performative**: (by narrow definition) as found when we use language to bring about a certain event, especially in a ceremony, e.g. "I hereby declare the meeting open."

**recreational**: as found in the use of language to create humor, fun, etc.

**metalinguistic**: as found when we use language to talk about language, e.g. "in other words".

Brown and Yule distinguish between transactional function and interactional (or interpersonal) function. The **transactional function** has to do with what one is seeking to do, whereas the **interactional function** has to do with the social and emotional distance one is conveying. Thus, a directive act like "Get out of my way!" can perform both transactional and interactional functions at the same time. Here, the emotional distance expressed is large, compared with that in "Honey, move a bit."

M. A. K. Halliday puts forward a tripartite classification of language functions, namely the **ideational function** (language can be used to represent the world), the **interpersonal function** (language can be used to encode interpersonal relations) and the **textual function** (language can be used to construct texts). An utterance in context fulfils the three **metafunctions** simultaneously.

Language may serve communicative purposes and play a role in **identity construc-**

tion. The communicative function and identity function are complementary. With their ability to communicate, human beings can build communities, which then provide, among other things, a powerful source of identity for their members. Language can be a tool of inclusion and exclusion. When we meet someone from our hometown, we tend to switch to a common dialect. While treating him or her as an in-group member, we exclude others from our talk. Similarly, when you use "on behalf of the general manager", you are assuming an identity that is not your own in the production of that utterance.

## 1.3 The defining features of language

Language, as a system of communication, falls within the scope of **semiotics**, the science of signs, about which there has been extensive discussion in the past decades. Unlike other systems of communication, language has the following design features:

### A Arbitrariness

As a symbolic unit, a word has both **form** and **meaning**. As a rule, the relation between the form and the meaning, however, is arbitrary. In other words, there is no inherent connection between the form and the meaning. Look at Figure 1.1.

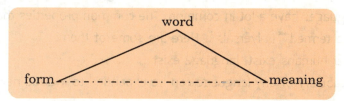

Figure 1.1 The arbitrary nature of language

It is impossible to predict the meaning from the form, or vice versa.

### B Duality of structure/double articulation

Language operates at two levels: at the lower level, language consists of a bunch of meaningless elements; at the higher level, the meaningless elements combine to form meaningful units like words. For example,

l-a-n-g-u-a-g-e (meaningless elements: lower level, secondary) →language (meaningful unit: higher level, primary)

### C Creativity

"Creativity", sometimes also called "productivity", means the property which makes possible the construction and interpretation of new symbols, i.e. of signals that have not been previously encountered.

Most animal communicative systems seem to be highly restricted in terms of the number of different signals that their users can send and receive. With natural language, however, we can construct and understand infinitely many utterances that we have never heard or read before.

Note that the property of creativity is rule-governed. Different languages specify different sets of rules constraining the organization of meaningful units at different levels.

### D  Displacement

Language can be used to talk about what happened in the past, what is happening at present, or what will happen in the future. Also, we can use language to refer to things no matter how far away they are or whether they are present or absent. Animal communication is generally assumed to lack this property.

### E  Cultural transmission

Language is not genetically inherited. Passed from generation to generation, it requires some learning. By contrast, the signals used in animal communication are presumed to be instinctive and not learned. Human infants produce no "instinctive" language if they grow up in isolation from any language-speaking community.

Natural languages have a lot in common. The common properties that all natural languages share are termed "universals". Here are some of them:

(1) Wherever humans exist, language exists.
(2) The vocabulary of any language can be expanded to include new words for new concepts.
(3) All languages change through time.
(4) All grammars contain rules for the formation of words and sentences of a similar kind.
(5) Similar grammatical categories (for example, nouns, verbs) are found in all languages.

## 1.4  The origin of language

How did human language come into being? Some advocated the divine origin of language (as a product of creation), claiming that God created language as well as man. A manifestation of this supposition is the belief in the magic of spells and **language worship**. Later on, some other hypotheses, which were later nicknamed as follows, were proposed either from the perspective of evolution or invention:

**A The bow-wow theory**

Primitive words were imitative sounds; for example, from the barking of dogs, we created a word which meant "dog" or "bark".

**B The pooh-pooh theory**

Language is derived from instinctive cries called forth by intense emotions.

**C The ding-dong theory**

Every substance has a natural resonance when struck. Possibly, when man was struck by an impression (for example, the sight of a sheep), he would emit the appropriate vocal response, that is, the word "sheep".

**D The yo-he-ho theory**

Under heavy external loads, man would emit noises from his vocal tract; these noises became language, so the first words might mean "heave" or "haul".

**E The ta-ta theory**

Man made gestures appropriate to certain situations, for example, waving when taking leave; the tongue might duplicate the manual gesture and utter the sound ta-ta.

**F The ta-ra-ra-boom-de-ay theory**

Language might have arisen from ritual dance and incantation.

To investigate the origin of language, one alternative approach to the study of **primitive languages** is through the study of how children learn languages. Since no primitive languages have ever been found, either in the very earliest written records or in the least accessible corners of the globe, how children acquire language has become an important issue in recent years, though it cannot tell us anything directly about the origin of language. Recently new approaches have been suggested, e.g. the study of the anatomical and psychological attributes necessary for the production of human language and the differences between animal communication and human language.

## 1.5 The acquisition of language

Any new-born normal infant will start its process of language learning once it is exposed to some **language environment**. The acquisition of one's **mother tongue**, sometimes called **L1 acquisition**, is said to have the following features:

(1) universally successful;
(2) no explicit instruction (teacher, textbook, school, syllabus, etc.);

(3) rapid (0-4 years old);

(4) conditional (i. exposure; ii. critical period—1.5-4 years old; iii. no mental deficiency).

L1 acquisition generally falls into several stages:

(1) babbling period: birth—around 6 months, some sounds produced;

(2) syllabic speech period: around 8 months, syllables like "mama" replace babbled sounds;

(3) single-word stage: around 1 year old, first words, no grammar; carry out simple commands;

(4) onset of speech: 18 months, more words (3-50 words);

(5) two-word utterances stage: 2 years old, can name most things around; begin one's own creation of two-word phrases (early stage of grammar), pivot words + open words, e.g. "Mummy sock";

(6) full-understanding stage: 2.5 years old, e.g. "daddy kick ball";

(7) near adult-speech: 3 years old; overgeneralization of inflections, e.g. "goed" (instead of "went");

(8) adult speech: 4 years old.

A child can simultaneously acquire two or more languages without an accent, on condition that he acquires them before he is 3 or 4 years old. Around the age of puberty (10-13 years old), the child loses his ability to learn a second language without an accent.

Some points deserve our attention:

(1) vocabulary acquisition lasts throughout life;

(2) complicated constructions like passives are acquired late (around 10 years old);

(3) appropriate use of language comes later.

Appropriate use of language refers to the use of language appropriately in accordance with **social conventions** (e.g. **politeness**), and **conversational routines** (e.g. **role plays**, **turn-taking**, etc.). The acquisition of the rules leads to the development of **pragmatic competence**. In this respect, parental instruction is necessary (usually starting from 3 years old).

Some scholars suggest that children are able to learn language because adults speak to them in a special "simplified" language sometimes called **motherese**, **care-takerese**, or **child directed speech** (CDS) (more informally, baby talk). Adults typically talk to young children in a special way. We tend to speak more slowly and more clearly, we exaggerate our intonation, and our sentences are generally short and simple.

One theory of child language acquisition argues that children learn to produce "correct" sentences because they are positively reinforced when they say something right and negatively reinforced when they say something wrong. For example:

Child: Nobody don't like me.
Mother: No, say "Nobody likes me".
Child: Nobody don't like me.
(*dialogue repeated eight times*)
Mother: Now, listen carefully, say "Nobody likes me".
Child: Oh, nobody don't likes me.

## 1.6 Linguistics: The science of language

The scientific study of language makes what we call **linguistics**. Unlike children or adults learning a native or foreign language, which involves the accumulation of words and rules and development of language skills, linguists study language in a systematic way to reveal rules, patterns, and principles that underlie the organization and use of language.

Linguistics comprises the following branches: Core branches such as **phonetics** and **phonology**, **morphology**, **syntax**, **semantics**, and **pragmatics**; Peripheral branches such as **sociolinguistics**, **psycholinguistics**, **neurolinguistics**, **anthropological linguistics**, **language pedagogy**, **first/second language acquisition**, **clinic linguistics**, **computational linguistics**, etc. While the core branches fall primarily within the scope of **theoretical linguistics**, the peripheral ones are basically under the umbrella of **applied linguistics**.

Modern linguistics is characterized by the following preferences: **synchronic approach** over **diachronic approach** (that is, linguists give priority to the study of language as it stands at the moment rather than focus on its different states in the past); **descriptivism** over **prescriptivism** (that is, linguists theorize about language on the basis of describing it rather than squeeze one language into prior rules or principles from another); **spoken language** over **written language**. We owe these preferences to **Ferdinand de Saussure**, founder of modern linguistics.

### Check your understanding

State whether each of the following statements is True or False.
(1) There is universal agreement about the origin of language.
(2) Pet dogs can speak human language.

(3) All human infants can speak some language.
(4) By creativity we mean the creative use of language as often practiced by poets.
(5) With different cultures there will be different languages.
(6) Not all uses of language are meant to convey new information.

## In-Class Activities

1. "Language", like "*yuyan*" in Chinese, is used for different meanings in different contexts, as shown below:
   A. Chinese is a <u>language</u>.
   B. Linguistics is the systematic study of <u>language</u>.
   C. Both Jane and John like Shakespeare's <u>language</u>.
   D. the <u>language</u> of bees

   (1) What does "language" mean in each of the contexts?
   (2) Is there any other context in which the use of the word means something else?

2. There is a well-known story in *the Bible* that reflects the importance of language in human society. According to *the Old Testament*, mankind spoke only one language until Nimrod began to build a tower that was to reach heaven. The Lord said, "Behold, they are one people, and they have all one language, and nothing that they propose to do will now be impossible for them. Come, let us go down, and there confuse their language, that they may not understand each other's speech."

   (1) What if there were no language?
   (2) What if there were only one language the world over?
   (3) What can we learn from this Bible story?

3. The arbitrary nature of language does not suggest that individuals can use a language arbitrarily. In fact, once the members of a community agree on the meaning of words, they are supposed to abide by the convention. Look at the following cartoon:

Unit 1   Some Preliminaries about Language        11

ask

Can one really invent a language of one's own? If not, why?

4. Before the middle of the eighteenth century, theories of the beginning of language were widely discussed. According to these early theories, man was created almost instantaneously and speech was provided to him as a divine gift at the moment of creation. So goes the story of the Garden of Eden. God created Adam and speech simultaneously. God spoke with Adam and Adam answered him. The language they used was Hebrew.

Andreas Kemke, a Swedish philologist, asserted that in the Garden of Eden, God spoke Swedish, Adam spoke Danish, and the serpent spoke French. Goropius Becanus, a Dutch theorist, asserted that the language of the Garden was Dutch. The Egyptians considered themselves the oldest civilization, and therefore the original language was Egyptian.

On the assumption that babies, if left alone, will grow up speaking "the original" language, Psammetichus had two babies taken at random from an ordinary family and given to a servant to raise them. He ordered the servant not to speak a word to the babies. When they were two years old, the children one day abruptly greeted the servant with "Bekos!" The servant immediately reported this to Psammetichus. The king checked with his counselors, who informed him that "bekos" meant "bread" in Phrygian. So in true "scientific" spirit, Psammetichus announced that Phrygian was the original language.

## ask

(1) Is there any basic flaw in this experiment?

(2) Do you think we really can answer the question about the beginning of language? Why or why not?

5. Below are samples of speech from children at three different stages in their acquisition process.

   Child A: You want to eat?
   I can't see my book.
   Why you wake me up?

   Child B: Where those dogs goed?
   You didn't eat supper.
   Does lions walk?

   Child C: No picture.
   Where momma boot?
   Want cake.

## ask

(1) Can you identify the most likely order (from least to most advanced) of these samples?

(2) What features in each child's utterances can you use as evidence to support your ordering?

6. The following data (from Fromkin and Rodman 1983) might give some hints about first language acquisition:

### Episode 1

Adult: He's going out.
Child: He go out.
Adult: That's an old-time train.
Child: Old-time train.
Adult: Adam, say what I say: Where can I put them?
Child: Where I can put them?

### Episode 2

Child: My teacher holded the baby rabbits and we patted them.

Unit 1  Some Preliminaries about Language     13

Adult: Did you say your teacher held the baby rabbits?
Child: Yes.
Adult: What did you say she did?
Child: She holded the baby rabbits and we patted them.
Adult: Did you say she held them tightly?
Child: No, she holded them loosely.

**ask**

(1) It is often assumed that children imitate adults in the course of language acquisition. Can imitation account for the above production on the part of the child?
(2) What distinguishes the child's production from that of the adult?

Find in the library or online some information about the following themes:
(1) Esperanto
(2) phatic communion
(3) Ferdinand de Saussure
(4) language acquisition device (LAD)
(5) Innate Hypothesis

### Task 2  Term Definition

Different linguists may offer different definitions, as cited below. How are the definitions different? Search for at least two more definitions.

**language**: Language is a purely human and non-instinctive method of communicating ideas, emotions and desires by means of voluntarily produced symbols. (Edward Sapir)

**language**: From now on I will consider a language to be a set (finite or infinite) of sentences, each finite in length and constructed out of a finite set of elements.

(Noam Chomsky)

**parole**: the written and spoken language produced in everyday life (Ferdinand de Saussure)

**langue**: the abstract, systematic rules and conventions of a signifying system (Ferdinand de Saussure)

## Task 3　Study Questions

1. What do you think is essential to the emergence of language?

2. Can our pets learn human languages? Why or why not?

3. Naturally occurring "experiments" with so-called "wolf-children", "Mowgli", "bear-children" or "monkey-children" and other such feral youngsters have been widely reported for hundreds of years. None of these children could speak or understand speech and, indeed, most efforts to teach them language ended in failure. How would you account for the failure?

4. The following are some instances of using English for communication. What specific function does each use of English serve in the following pictures?

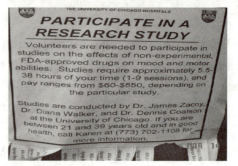

Unit 1  Some Preliminaries about Language

5. The following two transcriptions (taken from Bellugi, 1970) are fragments of conversations between the same mother and child. The first one took place when the child was 24 months old, and the second three months later.

| | |
|---|---|
| Eve: Have that? <br> M: No, you may not have it. <br> Eve: Mom, where my tapioca? <br> M: It's getting cool. You'll have it in just a minute. <br> Eve: Let me have it. <br> M: Would you like to have your lunch right now? <br> Eve: Yeah. My tapioca cool? <br> M: Yes, it's cool. <br> Eve: You gonna watch me eat my lunch? <br> M: Yeah, I'm gonna watch you eat your lunch. <br> Eve: I eating it. <br> M: I know you are. | M: Come and sit over here. <br> Eve: You can sit down by me. That will make me happy. Ready to turn it. <br> M: We're not quite ready to turn the page. <br> Eve: Yep, we are. <br> M: Shut the door, we won't hear her then. <br> Eve: Then Fraser won't hear her too. Where he's going? Did you make a great big hole there? <br> M: Yes, we made a great big hole in here; we have to get a new one. <br> Eve: Could I get some other piece of paper? |

(1) What are some of the changes which appear to have taken place in the child's ability to use English during that period?

(2) What do these changes suggest about the order of language acquisition?

6. Not only are many languages dying today, many dialects are also disappearing from the planet. For example, according to a report once circulated on the Internet, many parents discourage their children from speaking their local dialect. They would rather their children took hold of every chance to learn English, because the latter will give them an edge in future competition. Given this situation, what measures do you suggest for protecting dialects as well as languages?

## Task 4  Mini-Project

Randomly select ten most commonly used words and ten infrequently used words from an English vocabulary list. Compare and find if there is a possible correspondence between the size of words and the frequency of usage (e.g. the more common the word, the smaller it is). If so, can you work out any plausible explanation?

# Unit 2

# The Sounds of English

* 2.1 Speech organs
* 2.2 Speech sounds
* 2.3 Phones, phonemes and allophones
* 2.4 Classifying English vowels
* 2.5 Classifying English consonants
* 2.6 English syllables
* 2.7 Stress, tone and intonation in English
* 2.8 Phonological rules in English
* 2.9 Rhythm in English

> *The English have no respect for their language, and will not teach their children to speak it. They cannot spell it because they have nothing to spell it with but old foreign alphabet of which only the consonants—and not all of them—have any agreed speech value.*
> 
> —Victoria Fromkin et al.

## Pre-Class Reading

## 2.1 Speech organs

As advanced animals, human beings are endowed with flexible and adaptable **speech organs** or **vocal tracts**. These organs, involved in the production of **speech sounds**, include:

(1) **breathing organs**—initiators of the airstream, including lungs, bronchial tubes,

and windpipe.

(2) **larynx**—the organ that makes the airstream vibrate, and consists of vocal bands/cords, and glottis.

(3) **pharynx**, **oral cavity** and **nasal cavity**—resonating cavities, organs where the airstream vibrates.

The following diagram presents the structure of the speech organs and corresponding types of consonants:

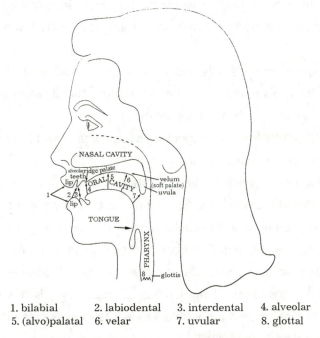

1. bilabial  2. labiodental  3. interdental  4. alveolar
5. (alvo)palatal  6. velar  7. uvular  8. glottal

Figure 2.1  Speech organs and types of consonants

## 2.2  Speech sounds

Human beings can make a number of speech sounds by using the speech organs. To make a speech sound in English, breath is expelled from the lungs through the larynx (the "voice box") into the mouth or the oral cavity and the breath is emitted either from the mouth, the nose, or both. The manner in which it is expelled or released determines what sort of sound will be heard. There may be a point of constriction in the mouth and what takes place at the point of constriction, such as the partial or complete interruption of air, aids in determining the kind of sound that is made.

**Vowels** and **consonants** are two basic kinds of speech sounds we produce in English as well as in other languages. A third set generally called **semivowels**, including /w/ and /j/, is neither totally consonantal nor totally vocalic, but shares some characteristics of both.

Vowels and consonants differ along the following lines.

(1) Functionally, vowels are the basis of **syllables** (most syllables contain at least one vowel).

(2) Physically, vowels are musical, whereas consonants are mostly noisy.

(3) Articulatorily, in pronouncing vowels, the airstream is not obstructed, and speech organs are tense. In pronouncing consonants, however, the airstream from the lungs through the mouth or the nose is totally or partially obstructed somewhere along the path.

The study of speech sounds falls under the scope of both **phonetics** and **phonology**. Specifically, phonetics deals mainly with the description, classification and transcription of speech sounds. It has three sub-branches, namely:

(1) **articulatory phonetics**, which studies speech organs and how speech sounds are made (or articulated) by the vocal organs;

(2) acoustic phonetics, which studies the physical properties of speech sounds;

(3) **auditory phonetics**, which studies the perception of speech sounds.

Phonology is concerned with the exploration of the patterns governing sound combinations. For instance, the sequential combination of sounds in English into words is rule-governed. A possible word in English is one that contains phonemes in sequences that obey the phonotactic constraints of the language. Thus, "lig" is possible in English but "lgi" is not. The conditions on the possible sequences of phonemes in a given language are part of a study called **phonotactics**.

## 2.3 Phones, phonemes and allophones

The smallest perceptible discrete segment of sound in a stream of speech is called a **phone** (Greek for "sound, voice"). Thus, all of the four segments of the utterance [h aʊ ɑː juː] ("How are you?") are phones. Technically, a phone is

(1) a phonetic unit;
(2) not distinctive of meaning;
(3) physical as perceived;
(4) marked with [ ].

An English letter, say "t", can occur in different positions of words, as realized in "tape", "stay", "later", and "let". Its phonetic realizations in these different positions seem to be identical sounds. The fact, however, is that they are phonetically different in effect, however slightly. Nevertheless, to capture the overwhelming similarity among them, we may treat them as representing a larger abstract unit, which we call a **phoneme**. Thus, a phoneme is realized by a "family" of sounds, all of which are phonetically similar but actually slightly different. The family of sounds, which are predictable **phonetic variants** of the same phoneme, are technically called the **allophones** ("allo" comes from Greek "allos", meaning "other") of the phoneme. Accordingly, the phoneme /t/ has four allophones depending on where we hear it. When it occurs in the initial position of a word, we get [tʰ], characterized by **aspiration** or a strong puff of air. When the phoneme /t/ follows /s/ and precedes a vowel, as in "stay", we get [t], with almost no puff of air. Thirdly, when the phoneme occurs between vowels, as in "later", we get [τ], which is not very distinct from [d] as in "ladder". Finally, when the phoneme occurs in the final position of a word, as in "let", we get an unreleased sound [t˺]. In spite of these variations and perhaps others, all the variations combine into one class that we call the phoneme /t/. We derive the abstract phoneme /t/ but usually ignore (or are not aware of) these allophonic variations.

The phoneme is the minimal unit in the sound system of a language. It is

(1) a **phonological unit** of description in a language;

(2) contrastive in a language and therefore distinctive of meaning;

(3) abstract, not physical;

(4) marked with /    /.

In order to discover the phonemes used in the sound system of a language, scholars once designed a method based on the notion of **minimal pairs**, like "pat" vs. "fat". Three requirements were proposed for identifying a minimal pair: (1) the two words are different in meaning; (2) the two words are different because of just one phoneme; and (3) the phonemes that make the two words different occur in the same phonetic environment. By **phonetic environment** we mean the sound(s) preceding and that/those following it, e.g. the phonetic environment of [ɪ] in [pɪt] is [p_t] and that of [p] is [#_ɪt] (# stands for a word or syllable boundary). The contrasting sounds in words forming a minimal pair are said to be in **contrastive distribution**, as in [bɪt] vs. [beɪt] and [pɪt] vs. [bɪt].

With phonemes, we establish the systems of sounds in a language. Each language can be shown to operate with a relatively small number of phonemes (15-80). Virtually no two languages seem to have exactly the same phonemic system. The following table lists all the phonemes used in English.

Table 2.1  English phonemic system

| | Consonants | | Vowels | | | Consonants | | Vowels | |
|---|---|---|---|---|---|---|---|---|---|
| 1 | /p/ | pill | /iː/ | beat | 13 | /v/ | vast | /eɪ/ | bay |
| 2 | /b/ | bill | /ɪ/ | pit | 14 | /θ/ | thin | /aɪ/ | buy |
| 3 | /t/ | tin | /e/ | pet | 15 | /ð/ | then | /ɔɪ/ | boy |
| 4 | /d/ | din | /æ/ | pat | 16 | /s/ | sink | /aʊ/ | cow |
| 5 | /k/ | cut | /ɑː/ | part | 17 | /z/ | zinc | /əʊ/ | boat |
| 6 | /g/ | got | /ɒ/ | pot | 18 | /ʃ/ | ship | /ɪə/ | beer |
| 7 | /m/ | meat | /ɔː/ | port | 19 | /ʒ/ | vision | /eə/ | bare |
| 8 | /n/ | neat | /ʊ/ | put | 20 | /h/ | hat | /ʊə/ | tour |
| 9 | /ŋ/ | sing | /uː/ | boot | 21 | /tʃ/ | chin | /aɪə/ | fire |
| 10 | /l/ | lake | /ʌ/ | but | 22 | /dʒ/ | gin | /eɪə/ | player |
| 11 | /r/ | rate | /ɜː/ | bird | 23 | /w/ | wet | /aʊə/ | power |
| 12 | /f/ | fast | /ə/ | ago | 24 | /j/ | yet | | |

A phoneme can be further analyzed into a set of **distinctive features**. For example, /p/ is defined as composed of such distinctive features as [plosive] + [bilabial] + [breathed] because each of them can distinguish /p/ from some other phonemes. However, the property of aspiration contained in the allophone [pʰ] does not distinguish meaning and therefore is not a distinctive feature in this case.

## 2.4 Classifying English vowels

The classification of English vowels may be conducted according to various criteria, as listed below:

(1) the height of the tongue (high, mid, low);
(2) the position of the highest part of the tongue (front, central, back);
(3) the degree of lip-rounding (rounded, unrounded);
(4) the length of articulation (long, short);
(5) the tenseness of the speech organ (tense, lax);
(6) the purity of the vowel (pure, gliding).

Following these dimensions, as partly captured by Figure 2.2 (which covers **cardinal vowels** only), it is easy to describe and distinguish English vowels.

e.g. /iː/ high, front, tense    /ɪ/ high, front, lax    /ɑː/ low, back, tense

/æ/ low, front, lax     /ʌ/ mid, central, lax     /ɔː/ mid, back, rounded, tense
/ʊ/ high, back, rounded, lax

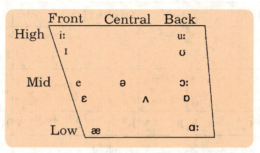

Figure 2.2  Cardinal vowels in English

## 2.5  Classifying English consonants

English consonants may be classified into sets or classes on the basis of three phonetic criteria or features:

(1) **Manner of articulation** (the kind of sound produced in the mouth or the kind of obstruction which the air undergoes). Air may be partially or completely obstructed.

(2) The **point or place of articulation** (the important parts of the vocal tract which are used in making the sound). These include the lips, various parts of the tongue, the teeth, the alveolar ridge (the ridge of gum behind the upper teeth), the soft and hard palates, the vocal cords, and the glottis.

(3) The presence or absence of **voicing**. The larynx contains two cords, or bands, which may close off air completely, or may be kept open, permitting them to vibrate while allowing air to pass through. Certain English consonants are **voiced** (involving vibration of vocal bands) while others are **voiceless**.

Table 2.2 summarizes the classification of English consonants based on the criteria above:

Table 2.2  Classification of English consonants

|  | bilabial | labio-dental | dental | alveolar | post-alveolar | palatal | velar | glottal |
|---|---|---|---|---|---|---|---|---|
| plosive | p  b |  |  | t  d |  |  | k  g |  |
| nasal | m |  |  | n |  |  | ŋ |  |
| fricative |  | f  v | θ  ð | s  z | ʃ  ʒ |  |  | h |

(*To be continued on the next page*)

|  | bilabial | labio-dental | dental | alveolar | post-alveolar | palatal | velar | glottal |
|---|---|---|---|---|---|---|---|---|
| affricate |  |  |  | (ts) (dz) | (tr) (dr) | tʃ  dʒ |  |  |
| lateral/ liquids |  |  |  | l | r |  |  |  |
| semi-vowel/ glides | w |  |  |  |  | j |  |  |
|  | B   V | B   V | B   V | B   V | B   V | B   V | B   V | B   V |

Note: B stands for breathed or voiceless, and V for voiced.

## 2.6 English syllables

Speech sounds in English are organized into larger segments or units called syllables. /let/, for example, consists of one syllable (Consonant Vowel Consonant, or CVC for short), and so does /steɪ/(CCV), whereas /rɪˈɡɑːd/ consists of two syllables (CV-CVC).

In English, every syllable has a **nucleus**, which is usually a vowel (but which may be a **syllabic liquid** or **nasal**, as in /ˈlɪtl/ and /ˈlɪsn/). The nucleus may be preceded by one or more phonemes called the **syllable onset** and followed by one or more segments called the **coda**, as shown in Figure 2.3:

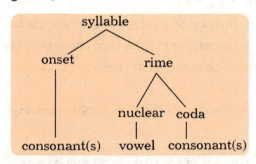

Figure 2.3  The structure of an English syllable

## 2.7 Stress, tone and intonation in English

When a word has more than one syllable, one of them will be pronounced with more prominence, i.e. **stress**, than the other(s). English is a **stress-timed language**. The use of stress follows, to a large extent, a certain pattern. For example, the stress in **disyllabic** (two-syllable) nouns usually falls on the first syllable, as in "English" and "pattern". The second syllable may receive the stress if it contains a long or gliding vowel nucleus, as in "regard". In words with three or more syllables the position of the main stress can vary. It is either on the second syllable from the right (the **penultimate syllable**) or on the third from the right (the **antepenultimate syllable**), as shown below:

| **Penultimate Syllable** | **Antepenultimate Syllable** |
| --- | --- |
| example | America |
| population | generality |
| electric | consonant |

The difference in stress placement in these words is not random. Rather, stress will be on the penultimate syllable if that syllable consists of either a long vowel (as in "example") or any vowel followed by at least two consonants (as in "electric"). These two types of syllables are both designated as strong syllables. A weak syllable, on the other hand, consists of a short (or lax) vowel followed by at most one consonant; for example, all of the syllables in "America" are weak. In words of at least three syllables the stress will be on the penultimate syllable unless that syllable is weak. If the penultimate syllable is weak, stress will be on the next syllable to the left, i.e. the antepenultimate syllable.

A distinction is drawn between **primary stress** and **secondary stress** (and even **tertiary stress**). The primary stress, or **main stress**, goes along with the most highly stressed vowel, indicated by an acute accent ( ´ ) over the vowel whereas the secondary stress goes to some vowel preceding the most stressed vowel, indicated by a grave accent( ` ), as marked in "rèsignátion" and "sỳstemátic". Another way of assigning stresses goes like this: [ˌɪntrəˈdjuːs].

When reading a phrase like "a red line", the head word "line" is stressed. Yet, when reading a compound word like "blackbird" and "greenhouse", the stress goes to the modifier component "black" or "green".

Apart from words and phrases, sentences also have the pattern of stress. Usually, **open-class words** like nouns, verbs, adjectives and adverbs are stressed whereas **closed-class words** like articles, prepositions, pronouns, and the infinitive marker "to" are not stressed except for the sake of contrast (as in "I, not you, am responsible for the accident").

Different rates of vibration produce different frequencies, which are termed pitches.

**Pitch** variations are distinctive of meaning. In some languages like Chinese, pitch variations are called **tones**. Languages using tones are **tone languages**.

When pitch and stress are tied to the sentence, they result in **intonation**, which also distinguishes meaning. For example, the sentence "What's in the tea, honey?" may, depending on the kind of intonation used, be a query to someone called "honey" regarding the contents of the tea (**falling intonation** on "honey"), or may be a query regarding whether the tea contains honey (**rising intonation** on "honey"). English is an **intonation language**.

## 2.8 Phonological rules in English

Native speakers have internalized abstract principles about the conditions or rules that shape the combination of sounds in their language.

**Sequential rules** are language-specific, as in the case of /ŋ/, which does not occur initially in English but may be allowed in some other languages. Here is another example. If three consonants should cluster together at the beginning of an English word, the combination should follow the sequence below:

(1) The first phoneme must be /s/;
(2) The second phoneme must be /p/, /t/, or /k/;
(3) The third phoneme must be /l/, /r/, or /w/.

A sound may change by assimilating/copying a feature of a sequential/neighboring sound; e.g. [ɪn] is realized as [ɪm], [ɪr] and [ɪl] respectively in "impossible", "irresistible", and "illegal". This is what we call the **assimilation rule**. Assimilation, particularly noticeable in ordinary conversational speech, occurs in a variety of contexts. For example, when you tell someone "I can go", the influence of the following velar [g] will almost certainly make the preceding nasal sound [n] come out as [ŋ] (a velar) rather than [n] (an alveolar). Notice also that the vowel in "can" has also changed to **schwa** [ə] from the isolated-word version [æ] through the process of **weakening**.

A certain sound in words like "sign", "design" and "resign" may be deleted even though it may be orthographically represented, while their corresponding nominal forms, namely "signature", "designation" and "resignation", involve the articulation of the sound. The process involved here is the **deletion rule**.

A word that is found in actual use by speakers of English is the union of a possible word with a meaning. Possible words without meaning are sometimes called **nonsense**

**words**. They are also referred to as accidental gaps in the **lexicon**, or **lexical gaps**. Thus, words such as "creek" and "cruck" are such accidental gaps in the lexicon of English.

## 2.9 Rhythm in English

**Rhythm** is an important aspect of English. It is analyzed first in terms of **intonation units**. For instance, the sentence below contains two intonation units:

① [Jane loves John], [doesn't she?]

We read the first intonation unit with a falling tone and the second unit with a rising tone.

An intonation unit can then be analyzed into **feet**, if the stressed syllables in the unit fall at approximately regular intervals. Thus the following sentence is a single intonation unit consisting of three feet.

② The ˈman / is ˈwalking / in the ˈgarden /.

The term "foot" is an extension of the term "**meter**" in a poetic line, that is, patterning of stressed and unstressed syllables. Four common patterns are listed below:

**iambic**: an unstressed + stressed (˘ˈ) pattern(translated as 抑扬格/短长格)
**trochaic**: an stressed + unstressed (ˈ˘) pattern(translated as 扬抑格/长短格)
**dactylic**: a pattern of (ˈ˘˘) (translated as 扬抑抑格/长短短格)
**anapestic**: a pattern of (˘˘ˈ) (translated as 抑抑扬格/短短长格)

In traditional studies of **metrical verse structure**, the many regular patterns of stressed/unstressed syllable sequence were given a detailed classification, as listed below:

A line containing two feet of any kind is **dimeter**.

A line containing three feet is **trimeter**.

A line containing four feet is **tetrameter**.

A line containing five feet is **pentameter**.

The following example demonstrates the case of **iambic** pentameter:

③ The Sound | must seem | an Ec | cho to | the Sense.

### Check your understanding

State whether each of the following statements is True or False.
(1) [iː] and [ɪ] are allophones of the same phoneme.

(2) Not all English phonemes have allophones.
(3) The same set of vowels is used in all languages.
(4) All syllables must contain at least one vowel.
(5) The marking of word stress is arbitrary for the most part in English.
(6) English is a tone language.

**In-Class Activities**

1. Allophones as the realizations of the same phoneme are technically said to be in **complementary distribution**; in other words, they are found in different phonetic environments. For instance, the allophones of the phoneme /l/, clear [l] and dark [ɫ], occur as follows:

   Clear [l]: occurs before vowels or after initial consonant(s) like /b/, /s/, /k/, /g/, /f/, /p/, /sp/.

   Dark [ɫ]: occurs elsewhere.

   (1) Characterize how the allophones of the phoneme /k/ are complementarily distributed.
   (2) Is there any other way of characterizing the complementary distribution of clear [l] and dark [ɫ]?

2. Suppose the distribution of [r] and [l] in the following words is characteristic of Korean:

   | | | | |
   |---|---|---|---|
   | rupi | "ruby" | mul | "water" |
   | kiri | "road" | pal | "leg" |
   | saram | "person" | səul | "Seoul" |
   | ratio | "radio" | ipalsa | "barber" |

   (1) Are [r] and [l] in complementary distribution? In what environment does each occur?
   (2) Do they occur in any minimal pairs?
   (3) Suppose that [r] and [l] are allophones of one phoneme. State the rule

Unit 2　The Sounds of English 　27

that can derive the allophonic forms.

3. Study the following dialect of English carefully. There seems to be a predictable variant [ʌɪ] of the diphthong [ay].
    A. [bʌɪ] bite
    B. [tay] tie
    C. [rayd] ride
    D. [fayl] file
    E. [tʌɪp] type
    F. [taym] time
    G. [lʌɪf] life
    H. [rayz] rise

(1) Can you give more examples of assimilation?
(2) Can you find any exceptions?
(3) What phonetic segments condition this change?

4. If two sounds can occur in the same environment and the substitution of one sound for another does not cause a change of meaning, they are said to be in **free variation**. For example, "economics" can be read as both [ˌiːkəˈnɒmɪks] and [ˌekəˈnɒmɪks]. Here, /iː/ and /e/ are in free distribution.

(1) Can you give more examples of free variation?
(2) Why do you think such a phenomenon exists in a language like English?

5. Some phonetic transcriptions below are English words, some are not existing words but are possible words or nonsense words, and others are definitely "foreign" or impossible because they violate English sequential constraints.

| Word | Possible | Foreign | Reason |
|---|---|---|---|
| Example: | | | |
| [pɑːk]   park | | | |
| [tɪf] | √ | | |
| [lkɪb] | | √ | Initial [l] must precede a vowel. |

A. [ŋɑːf]
B. [skiː]

C. [knaɪt]
D. [meɪj]
E. [blaft]

(1) Which of the five transcriptions are possible words in English?
(2) Which are not? Why?

6. **Slips of the tongue**, or **speech errors**, are common in daily conversation. Some of these tongue slips are called **spoonerisms**, named after William Archilbald Spooner, a distinguished head of an Oxford College in the early 1900s who reportedly referred to Queen Victoria as "That queer old dean" instead of "that dear old queen". Here are more examples:

| Intended Utterance | Actual Utterance |
| --- | --- |
| gone to seed | god to seen |
| [gɔːn tə siːd] | [gɒd tə siːn] |
| stick in the mud | smuck in the tid |
| [stɪk ɪn ðə mʌd] | [smʌk ɪn ðə tɪd] |
| speech production | preach seduction |
| [spiːtʃ prəˈdʌkʃən] | [priːtʃ sɪˈdʌkʃən] |

(1) What factors may lead to slips of the tongue?
(2) What interesting things do speech errors tell us about language and its use?

Find in the library or online some information about the following themes:

(1) RP
(2) Daniel Jones
(3) Prague School
(4) elision
(5) liaison

Unit 2　The Sounds of English

## Task 2　Term Definition

Study the following definitions and then discuss how they combine to help you understand the terms.

**phone**: a discriminable speech sound [Ronald Wardhaugh]

**phone**: A phone is a minimal distinct speech sound, e.g. [f]. Also called a segment. [Stuart Poole]

**phoneme**: a minimal significant contrastive unit in the phonological system of a language [Ronald Wardhaugh]

**phoneme**: A phoneme is a sound that is semantically or functionally distinctive in a language system. [Stuart Poole]

**allophone**: a positional variant of a phoneme [Ronald Wardhaugh]

**allophone**: An allophone is a variant form of a phone that is dependent on context and cannot be functionally significant. [Stuart Poole]

**allophone**: the version of phoneme as actually realized phonetically in speech [Henry Widdowson]

## Task 3　Study Questions

1. Study the following picture carefully:

(1) Does the string of sounds mean anything to you?

(2) What does the picture suggest to you about the role of consonants and vowels in English?

2. In English, the vowel /ɪ/ becomes almost as long as /iː/ under certain conditions. Consider the examples listed below:

　　A. [hɪs]　　　　B. [riːb]　　　　C. [diːg]　　　　D. [pɪt]
　　E. [hiːd]　　　　F. [mɪθ]　　　　G. [liːm]　　　　H. [kɪt]

(1) List the phonemes that condition the change.

(2) State the rule that seems involved.

3. The use of plural "-s" in English has three different, but very regular, phonological alternatives. One adds:

/s/ to words like ship, bat, book and cough;

/z/ to words like cab, lad, cave, rag and thing;

/ɪz/ to words like bus, bush, judge, church and maze.

(1) Can you work out the set of sounds which regularly precedes each of these alternatives?

(2) What features does each of these sets have in common?

Similarly, in English, the past tense marker for regular verbs -ed is pronounced as /t/, /d/ or /ɪd/. For example, "crashed" has final /t/, "heated" has final /ɪd/. Look at the following data.

A. brushed    B. heaped    C. kicked    D. petted
E. played     F. lagged    G. killed    H. heeded
I. thrived    J. perished

(3) Is there any pattern regarding the different pronunciations of the past tense marker?

(4) Do you think that one of these phonological forms for "-ed" is more basic, with the others being derived from it in a regular way? Which, and how?

4. Below are three columns of words with different patterns of stress:

| A | B | C |
|---|---|---|
| perish | maintain | collapse |
| edit | impose | exhaust |
| consider | appear | elect |
| imagine | cajole | erupt |
| cancel | canteen | lament |

(1) How is stress distributed in each column?

(2) In Column B, what kinds of vowels appear in the last syllable? How does the syllabic structure of Column C differ from A and B?

5. The following is a list of words that are spelt in a similar way:

fuddy—duddy      hocus—pocus      namby—pamby
fuzzy—wuzzy      hurly—burly      razzle—dazzle
hanky—panky      lovey—dovey      roly—poly
helter—skelter   mumbo—jumbo      super—duper

(1) What similarity can you spot among the words listed?

(2) What effects may such words have in common when they are put into use?

6. Write the phonetic transcription for each of the following words.
   - (1) admirable
   - (2) advertising
   - (3) advisable
   - (4) demonstrate
   - (5) duration
   - (6) employee
   - (7) ignorant
   - (8) inspiration
   - (9) massage
   - (10) mechanism
   - (11) parachute
   - (12) pertain
   - (13) portray
   - (14) suburban
   - (15) mastery
   - (16) photographer

7. Read the following words or phrases and point out the phonological processes that yield assimilation.
   - (1) pat /pæt/     pan /pān/     sat /sæt/     Sam /sām/
   - (2) since /sɪns/  sink /sɪŋk/   hint /hɪnt/   dink /dɪŋk/
   - (3) five pits /faɪfpɪts/    love to /lʌftə/

 Task 4  Mini-Project

Record two fragments of native speakers' conversation, one by a man and the other by a woman. Compare the data in terms of pronunciation and intonation.

# Unit 3

# The Units of English

*3.1 English morphemes
*3.2 English words and idioms
*3.3 English clauses and sentences
*3.4 Constructions in English

> *From now on I will consider a language to be a set (finite or infinite) of sentences, each finite in length and constructed out of a finite set of elements.*
> —Noam Chomsky

## Pre-Class Reading

## 3.1 English morphemes

The smallest units of meaning in English are not words, but **morphemes**. Many words, such as "suitable", can be broken down into component morphemes. Thus, "suitable" has two morphemes, one being "suit" and the other "-able".

Morphemes can be classified into different categories:

(1) **bound morphemes** (like "-able", "-ful", "re-") and **free morphemes** (like "suit", "play");

(2) **affix morphemes** (like "-ful", "re-") and root morphemes (like "-ceive", "suit");

(3) **derivational morphemes** (like "-able", "-ful", "re-") and **inflectional morphemes** (like "-est", "-ed"), the former conveying **lexical meaning** while the latter

convey **grammatical meaning**.

A complex word is not a simple sequence of morphemes, but has an internal hierarchical structure. For example, the word "unsuitable" is composed of three morphemes, namely "un-", "suit", and "-able". The root is the verb "suit", to which we add the suffix "-able", resulting in an adjective, "suitable", to which we add the prefix "un-", thus forming a new adjective, "unsuitable". The hierarchical organization of the word "unsuitable" is represented in Figure 3.1:

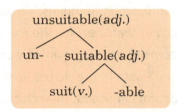

Figure 3.1 The hierarchical structure of the word "unsuitable"

## 3.2 English words and idioms

Speakers of English tend to assume that words are the basic units of language: our dictionaries are based on them; we write and read in units called words. Nevertheless, "word" is hard to define consistently in English. Here intuitive judgment is evoked for the sake of convenience. In English, words fall into two types, i.e. open classes and closed classes. The former include **nouns**, **verbs**, **adjectives**, and **adverbs**, whereas the latter include **pronouns**, **prepositions**, **auxiliary verbs**, **modal verbs**, **particles**, and **determiners**.

English boasts a variety of devices for forming new words, often on the basis of existing ones. The most commonly used ones are **affixation**, as found in "unsuccessful" and "learner", **conversion** or **functional shift**, as found in "increase" and "hand" (used both as nouns and verbs), and **compounding** or **composition**, as found in "makeup" and "greenhouse". There are some less widely used devices, too. For example, the word "smog" represents the **blending** of "smoke" and "fog". The word "edit" illustrates the **back-formation** from the pre-existing word "editor" by deleting the assumed suffix "-or". "NATO" is an **acronym** for "North Atlantic Treaty Organization". "USA" is a case of **initialism** for "The United States of America". The word "fridge" is a case of **clipping** or **shortening** from the word "refrigerator". The word "sandwich", originally the name of a person, is now a common noun after undergoing the process of **coinage**. Finally, words can also be created by virtue of **analogy**, as indicated by "zipper-gate", "Irangate" and "football-gate", all derived from "Watergate".

Words combine into **phrases**, most of which are free combinations like "a dark room" and "read the passage carefully". Phrases, which lack **subject-predicate structure**, may be of various kinds, such as nominal, verbal, adjectival, adverbial, and prepositional.

Some phrases, for various reasons, are more or less tight **collocations** (like "a handsome car", "a pretty girl") or closed **idioms** (like "in the end" and "leave off"). Idioms generally have semantic unity and function as nouns, verbs, adjectives and so forth. Idioms differ from compound words in that they, for the most part, allow a certain amount of internal modification. The nominal idiom "man-of-war", for example, pluralizes as "men-of-war", instead of "man-of-wars". The verbal idiom "take off" can change into "took off" when its past tense form is needed. In addition, verbal idioms like "take off" consist of a verb and what is usually termed a "particle". Compare:

① a. The plane took off at 9:00.
   b. He took a book off the shelf.

Clearly, the "off" in the idiom belongs to the verb preceding it while the "off" in the phrase belongs to both the verb and the noun following it.

Verb-particle idioms have become extremely common in English during the last three centuries or so. Such idioms are more common in American English than in British English. Those consisting of three rather than two parts, like "miss out on" and "meet up with", are almost exclusively American in origin. Some of these verbal idioms add a time-dimension to the action named, especially those formed with "up". For example, "drink up" and "burn up" mean "to completely drink/burn" or "drink/burn to the end".

A lexical item does not always coincide with a word. In the case of derivative morphemes, a lexical item may be less than a word. In the case of idioms, it may be considerably more than one word.

Today, people often talk about **prefabricated chunks**, or **lexical bundles**, which may cover such units as collocations, idioms, and even more open units that often occur together. "For example", "think of", "on the whole" are such chunks. Native speakers retain many prefabricated lexical items in their memory. They are stored as a whole in people's memory and retrieved for use as a whole. The volume of chunks learners possess and familiarity with them have an effect on learners' fluency of language use. Preliminary identification of utterances as chunks has often rested on an intuitive approach, which is quite common in the literature. There are also some principled criteria as listed below:

1) at least two words in length;
2) fluently articulated, without pause in between;
3) not produced based on grammatical rules;
4) used repeatedly and often in the same form.

## 3.3 English clauses and sentences

A **clause** in English is one unit of organization that contains a subject-predicate structure. A clause may be **finite** or **non-finite**. In the latter case, the subject of the predicate is implicit but inferable from the sentence containing the clause, such as an infinite clause, an "-ing" or "-ed" **participle clause**.

An English **sentence** may be one that contains only one clause. It is then a **simple sentence**. Often, an English sentence contains more than one sentence. We have a **compound sentence** when two or more clauses are conjoined by "and", "or", "so", or "for" (e.g. "Linguistics is interesting but some people may find it abstract"). We have a **complex sentence** when one or more subordinate clauses are embedded into a **main** or **matrix clause** to communicate purpose, reason, time, place, manner, or concession (e.g. "I like linguistics because I find it interesting"). We have a **compound complex sentence** when a complex sentence is conjoined with a simple clause or another complex sentence (e.g. "Linguistics is sometimes difficult because it involves some abstract terms, but it is also useful because it can help us explain a lot of language phenomena.").

Functionally, English sentences can be classified into **declarative sentences**, **imperative sentences**, **exclamatory sentences** and **interrogative sentences**. Interrogative sentences can be further categorized into (simple) **Yes-No questions** (e.g. "Are you from China?"), **WH-questions** (e.g. "What's your birth date?"), **tag questions** (e.g. "You've been here before, haven't you?"), **alternative questions** (e.g. "Are you coming tomorrow morning or afternoon?"), and **rhetorical questions** ("Don't you know I trust you?").

A sentence in English can be divided into two major parts: the subject and the predicate [which may contain a **predicate verb** plus an **object**, **adverbial(s)**, a **complement**].

The notion of subject may be classified into three types: **grammatical subject** (the major nominal part corresponding to the predicate), **logical subject** (the doer or executor of the action concerned), and **psychological subject** (the first major component of the sentence, like a nominal phrase, an adverbial phrase, or a prepositional phrase). For instance,

② John (grammatical subject, psychological subject, logical subject) robbed the City Bank last night.

③ The City Bank (grammatical subject, psychological subject) was robbed by John (logical subject) last night.

④ Last night (psychological subject) John (grammatical subject, logical subject) robbed the City Bank.

## 3.4 Constructions in English

Rather than treating sentences as uniformly formed by virtue of generative rules, a new perspective known as **construction grammar** argues that there is no principled divide between lexicon and rules and language is a **repertoire** of more or less complex patterns—**constructions**—that integrate form and meaning in conventionalized and often **non-compositional** ways (that is, we cannot derive the meaning of a construction from the meaning of the individual words that make up the construction). "Form" in constructions may refer to any combination of syntactic, morphological, or prosodic patterns and "meaning" is understood in a broad sense that includes all we intend to communicate. The following are some commonly discussed constructions:

⑤ a. Jane gave John an apple. (*ditransitive construction*)
   b. Jane gave an apple to John. (*dative construction*)
   c. It was Jane that John saw. (*It-cleft construction*)
   d. Jane, John saw her. (*left dislocation construction*)
   e. Jane John saw. (*topicalization construction*)
   f. Jane kissed John unconscious. (*resultative construction*)

According to construction grammar, basic sentences of English are instances of constructions, form-meaning correspondences that exist independently of the words in the sentences. A construction is held to exist if one or more of its properties are not strictly predictable from knowledge of other constructions in the grammar. For example,

⑥ John baked Jane a cake.

This sentence does not mean:

   a. John baked the cake so that Jane wouldn't have to bake it.
   b. John baked the cake as a demonstration of cake-baking.
   c. John baked a cake for himself because Jane wanted him to have one.

Unit 3  The Units of English      37

Unless we associate the "intended transfer" aspect of meaning to the construction, we are supposed to say that "bake" itself means something like "X intends to cause Y to receive Z by baking". The construction in which we find "bake" assigns an additional meaning of "transfer" to the word.

State whether each of the following statements is True or False.
(1) All words in English have a hierarchical structure.
(2) Clipping is one of the three most important devices of word-formation in English.
(3) Idioms in English are modifiable in some grammatical ways.
(4) The presence of constructions is unique to English.
(5) Every English sentence has a subject.

1. Some languages have not only prefixes and suffixes, but also **infixes**, morphemes that are inserted into other morphemes. Bontoc, spoken in the Philippines, is such a language, as illustrated by the following:

| Nouns/Adjectives | | Verbs | |
|---|---|---|---|
| fikas | "strong" | fumikas | "to be strong" |
| kilad | "red" | kumilad | "to be red" |
| fusul | "enemy" | fumusul | "to be an enemy" |

(1) What is the infix used in the above language data?
(2) What is the verb form in Bontoc for "to be poor", given that "pusi" means "poor"?

2. In some languages, a new word can be formed by **reduplication**—through the repetition of part or all of a word. The following examples from Samoan exemplify this kind of morphological rule.

| matua | "he is old" | matutua | "they are old" |
|---|---|---|---|
| malosi | "he is strong" | malolosi | "they are strong" |

| | | | |
|---|---|---|---|
| punou | "he bends" | punonou | "they bend" |
| atamaki | "he is wise" | atamamaki | "they are wise" |
| savali | "he travels" | pepese | "they sing" |

**ask**

(1) What is the Samoan for: (a) "they travel", and (b) "he sings" respectively?

(2) Formulate a morphological rule regarding how to form the plural verb form from the singular verb form in Samoan.

3. English has a couple of affixes that serve to express the opposition of meaning, of which "un-" figures prominently. Observe the following sets of English words (words marked with * are not allowed in English):

| | |
|---|---|
| happy—unhappy | sad— *unsad |
| friendly—unfriendly | hostile— *unhostile |
| wise—unwise | foolish— *unfoolish |
| selfish—unselfish | selfless— *unselfless |
| polite—impolite | rude— *unrude |
| attractive-unattractive | ugly— *unugly |
| safe-unsafe | dangerous— *undangerous |

**ask**

(1) What other affixes are there in English that function as markers of negation?

(2) What pattern underlies the use of "un-" in the data above?

(3) Why are "ungood" and "unbig" not found in English, although George Orwell coined "ungood" in his novel *Nineteen Eighty-Four*? Do you think they are accidental gaps in the lexicon of English?

(4) Read the following extract from Lewis Carroll's *Through the Looking-Glass*. How do you think Humpty Dumpty would explain the word "un-birthday" to Alice?

"They gave it me," Humpty Dumpty continued, "for an un-birthday present."

"I beg your pardon?" Alice said with a puzzled air.

"I'm not offended," said Humpty Dumpty.

"I mean, what is an **un-birthday** present?"

Unit 3  The Units of English   39

(5) The fact that "un-" can be both a verb prefix and an adjective prefix may explain the occurrence of the ambiguous word "unlockable". Can you imagine two situations corresponding to the two senses of the word? Can you give more examples like "unlockable"?

4. The suffix "-able" in English roughly means "able to be X-ed", where X is the meaning of the stem verb. For example, "teachable" means "able to be taught". In deriving new words via "-able", however, there seems to be some constraint on what is permitted. For example, if we wish to express the idea that man is mortal, we cannot say "Man is dieable", because we cannot say "Man is able to be died". Indeed, if we compare the columns below, a generalization may emerge:

| A: Verbs that take "-able" | B: Verbs that don't take "-able" |
|---|---|
| learn | go |
| wash | cry |
| separate | sleep |
| mend | rest |
| debate | walk |
| use | sit |

(1) How are the verbs in Column A different from those in Column B?
(2) Can we use "able to be X-ed" to paraphrase "perishable"?
(3) A further complication with "-able" is that in words like "unthinkable", the suffix means more than "able to be X-ed". Why? Can you think of more words of this type?
(4) Now, let's look at another complication. None of the following words are permitted. What does this suggest about the use of the suffix "-able"?
　　* chairable　　　* hairable　　　* deskable
　　* oldable　　　　* redable　　　 * underable

5. "Re-" as an English prefix is said to mean "again" in some words like "replay" and "revisit". Now consider the following four lists of words carefully.

**List A**

| redo | rebuild | regain | reuse |
| replay | repaint | redraw | redecorate |

**List B**

| *rego(= go again) | *resit(= sit again) | *recry | *resleep |

**List C**

| renew | refine | refresh | relax |

**List D**

| return | reflect | repay | recall |

(1) Note the contrast between List A and List B. Could you think of any reason that can explain why the set of words in List B are impossible words in English?

(2) How are the "re-" words in List C and List D different from those in List A?

(3) Some "re-" prefixed words may mean more than the mere addition of the meaning of "re-" and the meaning of its base. For example, "rewrite" means "write something again, especially in a different or improved form". Can you give more examples like "rewrite"?

6. **Elliptical sentences** are widely found in public signs as well as in daily use of English.

Elliptical sentences are also frequently found in newspaper headlines. The following are some from *The Washington Post*.

(1) U.S. at Odds with Allies on Mideast Conflict

(2) 3 Arrested in New Orleans Hospital

(3) Blast Kills 53 in Iraqi Holy City

(4) Optimism on Both Sides of Gay Marriage Debate
(5) Mission Applauded as Shuttle Returns

(1) Can you write the public signs in complete forms?
(2) What rules are there when we write elliptical English newspaper headlines?

1. Word classes in English advertisements
2. The formation of English neologisms
3. Chunks in English research paper abstracts

Find in the library or online some information about the following themes:
(1) neologism
(2) allomorph
(3) formulaic sequence/chunk
(4) collocation
(5) inflection

Study the following definitions and then discuss how they combine to help you understand the terms.

**lexeme**: A lexeme is an item of vocabulary which may consist of one or more than one word, e.g. "concede, give in". The term is often used to denote the basic uninflected form of an item; the lexeme "give" can, for example, be realized by such words as "gives" and "gave". [Stuart Poole]

**lexeme**: a word or phrase that is a meaningful unit [Ronald Wardhaugh]

**lexeme/lexical item**: a separate unit of meaning, usually in the form of a word (e.g. "dog"), but also as a group of word (e.g. "dog in the manger") [Henry Widdowson]

**lexicon**: the vocabulary of a language [Ronald Wardhaugh]

**word**: a morpheme or combination of morphemes which native speakers regard as a minimal pronounceable meaningful unit [Ronald Wardhaugh]

**idiom**: An idiom is a phrase which can only be understood as a unit, not as a summation of the meaning of each constituent word; "kick the bucket", for example, contains little that would suggest dying. [Stuart Poole]

**idiom**: morphemes or words which have a particular meaning by virtue of their occurrence in a certain construction; for example, "put up with" and "kick the bucket" [Ronald Wardhaugh]

## Task 3  Study Questions

1. Point out the word-formation process that applies to each of the following words.
   worsen   edit   brunch   laptop   televise   airsick   WTO   Xerox   dust (v.)
   endearment   peddle   tec   laser   urinalysis   FIFA   nylon   prof
   plane (v.)   swindle   bike   daughter-in-law

2. How are the open-class words and the closed-class words different from each other?

3. What are the inflectional morphemes in the following phrases?
   (1) the government's policies
   (2) the latest news
   (3) Isn't it snowing!
   (4) two frightened cows

4. Which of the following contains verb phrase idioms? For each idiom, provide a paraphrase with one word instead of the idiom.
   (1) a. John went in for stamp collecting.
       b. Jane went in for a check-up.
   (2) a. John came down with the guns.

b. Jane came down with the flu.
(3) a. John came up with the guns.
   b. Jane came up with a brilliant idea.
(4) a. That music doesn't exactly turn me on.
   b. Jane didn't turn on the tap.
(5) a. John passed over the house.
   b. The president passed over the peace proposal.
(6) a. John ran after dinner.
   b. John ran after Jane.

5. In English, some intransitive verbs can be converted into a special type of transitive verbs called causative verbs. Here are some examples:
   (1) John **grows** tomatoes. (Compare: Tomatoes **grow**.)
   (2) John **galloped** the horse. (Compare: The horse **galloped**.)
   (3) John **ran** the machine. (Compare: The machine **ran**.)
   (4) John **walked** the dog. (Compare: The dog **walked**.)
   **Can you give more examples?**

6. The distinction between auxiliary verbs and main verbs is a basic one in English. Auxiliary verbs are fronted to form questions whereas main verbs cannot be fronted in this fashion. The following sentences illustrate three additional differences between main verbs and auxiliary verbs. What are these differences?
   (1) Mary will not know the answer.
   (2) Jon will leave the room.
   (3) He will eat supper, won't he?

7. A very large part of language is made up of prefabricated chunks, or ready-made expressions, phraseological units which do not have to be generated every time they are used. Read the following spoken data of a Chinese student. Can you point out the chunks used in it? Can you classify them into some types?

   It is the most unforgettable birthday um … that I … and I can not forget it for forever. Um … it it was when I was a freshman. It is the first year um … I left my family and spend my birthday alone. Um … I remember clearly um … that day I strode gloomily at campus along for a long time um. And um … um … I I felt very … I I felt … I felt very gloomy because no one, um no one except my parents um remember my birthday and, and, wan and wanted to um … and wanted to stay with me for my birthday. Um … um … I did, I did not went back I did not go back to the dormitory um ... until um ... until seven o'clock in the evening. Um ... the light, the light in the dormitory was off. Obviously, um there was no ... there was nobody staying in the dormitory. Um ... but now um ... it may ... it ... it ... seemed um ... it seemed that it doesn't matter. Um ... And I open the door um ... and I found except darkness there was nothing. Suddenly a song "Happy birthday to you" sound. I felt, I felt very astonished. Then, the light was turned on. Some familiar faces um ... um full of full of sweet smiles towards me. Um they were my dorm they were my dorm mates ... Yes, they still remembered um ... my birthday, my birthday. And in fact they have ... they indeed prepared for it two days ago. They bought er ... a very beautiful cake for me, and that night um ... we sang, we danced and ... and had that delicious cake. I felt very happy, and and later I ... I made a call to my parents that told them that I has spent a very unforgettable birthday with my roommates.

8. The following is an excerpt from James Joyce's *Ulysses*. What has been deleted in many of its sentences? What effect does Joyce achieve by using this deletion?

   No, not like that. A barren land, bare waste. Vulcanic lake, the dead sea: no fish, weedless, sunk deep in the earth. No wind would lift those waves, grey metal, poisonous foggy waters. Brimstone they called it raining down: the cities of the plain: Sodom. Gomorrah. Edom. All dead names. A dead sea in a dead land, grey and old. Old now. It bore the oldest, the first race. A bent hag crossed from Cassidy's clutching a naggin bottle by the neck. The oldest people. Wandered far away over all the earth, captivity to captivity, multiplying, dying, being born everywhere. It lay there now. Now it could bear no more. Dead.

## Task 4　Mini-Project

Do you want to know how big the size of your English vocabulary is? Here is a way to estimate the number of words in your mental lexicon. Consult any standard dictionary and then do the following:

(1) Count the number of entries, usually bold-faced, on a typical page.

(2) Multiply the number of words per page by the number of pages in the dictionary.

(3) Pick five pages in the dictionary at random, say, pages 5, 65, 115, 175, 235. Count the number of words on these pages.

(4) Count how many of these words you know.

(5) Calculate the average percentage of the words on the five pages you know.

(6) Multiply the words in the dictionary by the percent you arrived at in (5). You know approximately that many English words.

Reading 1

## Rule Productivity

Some morphological rules are productive, meaning that they can be used freely to form new words from the list of free and bound morphemes. The suffix "-able" appears to be a morpheme that can be conjoined with any verb to derive an adjective with the meaning of the verb and the meaning of -able, which is something like "able to be" as in accept + able, blam(e) + able, pass + able, change + able, breath + able, adapt + able, and so on. The meaning of "-able" has also been given as "fit for doing" or "fit for being done". The productivity of this rule is illustrated by the fact that we find -able affixed to new verbs such as *downloadable* and *faxable*.

There is a morpheme in English meaning "not" that has the form un- and that, when combined with adjectives like *afraid, fit, free, smooth, American,* and *British,* forms the antonyms, or negatives, of these adjectives. Note that unlike -able, un- is not fully productive. We find *happy* and *unhappy, cowardly* and *uncowardly,* but not *sad* and *\*unsad, brave* and *\*unbrave,* or *obvious* and *\*unobvious.* The starred forms that follow may be merely accidental gaps in the lexicon. If someone refers to a person as being unsad we would know that the person referred to was "not sad", and an unbrave person would not be brave. But, as the linguist Sandra Thompson points out, it may be the case that the "*un*-Rule" is most productive for adjectives that are themselves derived from verbs, such as *unenlightened, unsimplified, uncharacterized, unauthorized, undistinguished,* and so on.

Morphological rules may be more or less productive. The rule that adds an -er to verbs in English to produce a noun meaning "one who performs an action (once or habitually)" appears to be a very productive morphological rule. Most English verbs accept this suffix: *examiner, exam-taker, analyzer, lover, hunter, predictor,* and so forth (-or and -er have the same pronunciation and are the same morpheme even though they are spelled differently). Now consider the following:

| | | |
|---|---|---|
| sincerity | from | sincere |
| warmth | from | warm |

moisten     from     moist

The suffix *-ity* is found in many other words in English, like *chasity, scarcity,* and *curiosity*; and *-th* occurs in *health, wealth, depth, width, growth*. We find *-en* in *sadden, ripen, redden, weaken, deepen*. Still, the phrase "the fiercity of the lion" sounds somewhat strange, as does the sentence "I'm going to thinnen the sauce". Someone may use the word *coolth*, but, as Thompson points out, when words such as *fiercity, thinnen, fullen,* and *coolth* are used, usually they are either errors or attempts at humor. It is possible that in such cases a morphological rule that was once productive (as shown by the existence of related pairs like *scarce/scarcity*) is no longer so. Our knowledge of the related pairs, however, may permit us to use these examples in forming new words, by analogy with the existing lexical items. Other derivational morphemes in English are not very productive, such as the suffixes meaning "diminutive", as in the words *pig + let* and *sap + ling*.

In the morphologically complex words that we have seen so far, we can easily predict the meaning based on the meaning of the morphemes that make up the word. *Unhappy* means "not happy" and *acceptable* means "fit to be accepted". However, one cannot always know the meaning of the words derived from free and derivational morphemes by knowing the morphemes themselves. The following *un-* forms have unpredictable meanings:

| | |
|---|---|
| unloosen | "loosen, let loose" |
| unrip | "rip, undo by ripping" |
| undo | "reverse doing" |
| untread | "go back through in the same steps" |
| unearth | "dig up" |
| unfrock | "deprive (a cleric) of ecclesiastic rank" |
| unnerve | "fluster" |

Morphologically complex words whose meanings are not predictable must be listed individually in our mental lexicons. However, the morphological rules must also be in the grammar, revealing the relation between words and providing the means for forming new words.

(Victoria Fromkin et al., *An Introduction to Language*, p. 88)

 Food for Thought

(1) Why are some morphological rules more productive than some others?
(2) Are there similar cases in Chinese where affixes are applied with exceptions?

## Reading 2

### Size and Variability of the Lexicon

The size of the lexicon varies a good deal from language to language, but in no language do we expect to find individual speakers who know the whole lexicon. You can open a major English dictionary at almost any page and find entries unfamiliar to you. One reason for this is that most languages have specialized vocabularies that relate to particular fields of knowledge or activity in the culture, like medicine, law, sports, weather, or trading, and that are mainly used by people with special expertise in the field. Thus, when we list in the lexicon all the lexical items in a language and the principles on which new ones can be coined, we are not representing the competence of any real speaker. Rather, we are representing the competence of a hypothetical and idealized speaker. Moreover, in the lexicon of a real speaker, we will find a marked difference in size between the speaker's "use" vocabulary, that is, the lexical items that he or she uses in composing utterances, and the speaker's "recognition" vocabulary, that is, the lexical items that he or she understands in deciphering utterances. In any real speaker, the latter is by far the larger; however, the lexicon of the grammar does not reflect this distinction.

The lexicon of English is very large; indeed, it is now probably the largest of all languages. There are some 450,000 entries in *Webster's Third New International Dictionary* (1961). The reasons for the size of the English lexicon are many, but two are of particular importance. First, from the very beginning of the Old English period, English has constantly borrowed vocabulary from other languages. English vocabulary was heavily influenced by Latin, both under the influence of the Church in the early period of Christianization in the late sixth century and under the influence of classicism in the Renaissance. It was also heavily influenced by Scandinavian languages owing to large settlements in eastern and northern England in the eighth to tenth centuries, and especially by French after the Norman Conquest in 1066. While foreign words sometimes supplanted native ones, more frequently they were simply added to the vocabulary, with the result that we have native "hound" from Old English "hund" (dog), besides "dog" from Scandinavian; likewise, we have native "fatherly" besides Latinate "paternal". Even though they may have been basically synonymous at the time of the borrowing, native and borrowed words soon differentiate in meaning, as in the case of both pairs cited above. Sometimes they come to be associated with different levels of formality, as is the case with "help" and "assist", or "fatherly" and "paternal" (note also the pejorative "paternalistic"). Not all languages have tolerated borrowing as much as English has. In German, for example, until recently there had been a preference for coining new words from native bases, rather than borrowing.

Another reason for the size of the English lexicon is the rapid expansion of knowledge and technology that English-speaking countries have experienced in the last few hundred years. As a result of this expansion, specialized vocabularies in English are relatively numerous and relatively large—every scientific discovery or technological innovation, every new theory or methodology gives rise to new vocabulary. Much of the technical vocabulary in English is actually not from native word stock but rather is coined from Greek and Latin morphemes. This, in part, reflects the longstanding tendency in the West to select Latin and Greek for erudite subjects, but also a deliberate policy to create a relatively international vocabulary that is not markedly English.

(Elizabeth Traugott and Marry Pratt, *Linguistics for Students of Literature*, pp. 103-104)

Food for Thought

(1) Do you think the huge English lexicon is a burden for the learners of the language?
(2) What do you think of the Chinese language which seems to work on a rather limited number of characters, as opposed to English? Is a small vocabulary an advantage or disadvantage? Why?

# Unit 4

# The Structures of English (I)

* 4.1  Grammatical knowledge
* 4.2  Sentence patterns in English
* 4.3  The hierarchical structuring of English sentences
* 4.4  Surface structure and deep structure

> *If language were just "words, words, words", it would do us little good except in the rather limited linguistic functions of naming. There are some languages, such as trade languages and pidgins, that have quite small vocabularies, sometimes not more than three or four thousand words. And they are languages because they have rules for putting words, or rather, lexical items, together in specific ways. In other words, they have sentence structure, or syntax.*
> 
> —Elizabeth Traugott and Mary Pratt

## Pre-Class Reading

## 4.1  Grammatical knowledge

Every competent speaker of English has some implicit knowledge about the language. Such knowledge can be seen to operate in the production of grammatical sentences and making grammatical judgments. We may call this type of knowledge **linguistic knowledge**, which is subconscious and is not the result of any formal teaching, but is a kind of "**mental grammar**". A second kind of "grammar", which we may term "**prescriptive grammar**", involves so-called "**linguistic etiquette**", that is, the identification of the "proper" or "best" structures to be used in a language. A third type of "grammar" is "**descriptive grammar**", which involves the study and analysis of the structures found in a language, usually with the aim of establishing a description of the grammar of English, for example, as distinct from the grammar of Chinese or any other language. To illustrate the first type of grammar, we may consider the following situations.

When native speakers of English encounter the following sentences,

① a. Loves Jane John.
   b. Visiting guests can be boring.

they know that ①a is ungrammatical and ①b is ambiguous.

Also, native speakers of English know they may choose between ②a and ②b without basically changing the meaning they intend to convey:

② a. Jane invited John to her party.
   b. John was invited by Jane to her party.

Moreover, native speakers of English may find it natural that their language allows them to construct and understand infinitely long sentences within certain constraints. They may create, and understand, something like the following children's rhyme:

This is the farmer sowing the corn,
that kept the cock that crowed in the morn,
that waked the priest all shaven and shorn,
that married the man all tattered and torn,
that kissed the maiden all forlorn,
that milked the cow with the crumpled horn,
that tossed the dog,
that worried the cat,
that killed the rat,
that ate the malt,
that lay in the house that Jack built.

Thus, knowing the grammar of a language consists of the following abilities, i.e. the abilities to:

—distinguish grammatical from ungrammatical strings;
—detect structural ambiguity;

—judge whether two sentences are paraphrases made possible by transformations; and
—construct and understand new sentences never heard of or written before.

## 4.2 Sentence patterns in English

English sentences seem to be built on five basic components: subject (S), predicate verb (V), object (O), complement (C) and adverbial (A). Altogether, seven major **sentence patterns** are found in English: SV, SVC, SVO, SVOO, SVOC, SVA, and SVOA, as illustrated below:

③ a. Jane arrived. (SV)
　b. Jane looks fine. (SVC)
　c. Jane loves John. (SVO)
　d. Jane gave John a kiss. (SVOO)
　e. Jane called John honey. (SVOC)
　f. Jane weighs 100 pounds. (SVA)
　g. Jane put her hand on John's shoulder. (SVOA)

Note that in each of these sentence types, none of the components is optional. Thus, ④ does not belong to SVA because "early" is optional as far as the **grammaticality** and **meaningfulness** of the sentence are concerned.

④ Jane arrived early. (SV)

Every language seems to contain sentences that include a subject (S), an object (O), and a predicate verb (V), although not all sentences have all the three elements. Languages have been classified according to the basic or most common order in which these constituents occur in sentences. There may be six possible combinations—SOV, SVO, VSO, VOS, OVS, OSV—permitting six possible language types. Here are examples of some of the languages in these classes.

　**SVO**: English, French, Swahili, Hausa, Thai
　**VSO**: Tagalog, Irish, (Classical) Arabic, (Biblical) Hebrew
　**SOV**: Turkish, Japanese, Persian, Georgian
　**OVS**: Apalai (Brazil), Barasano (Colombia), Panare (Venezuela)
　**OSV**: Apurina and Xavante (Brazil)
　**VOS**: Cakchiquel (Guatemala), Huave (Mexico)

The most frequent **word orders** in languages of the world are SVO, VSO, and SOV, while languages with OVS, OSV, and VOS as basic word orders are much rarer.

## 4.3 The hierarchical structuring of English sentences

An English sentence is apparently a string of words grouped together. Naturally, word order plays a crucial role in determining the grammaticality and meaning of the sentence—"*Loves John Jane" is not grammatical; "John loves Jane" does not mean the same thing as "Jane loves John". But there are also cases in which a change in the word order of a sentence will not change its meaning. For example, "John arrived yesterday" means very much the same as "Yesterday John arrived".

The apparent linear grouping of a sentence does not mean that there is no internal structure within the sentence. Look at the following sentence:

⑤ The mother of the boy and the girl arrived.

The sentence has two readings:

a. The mother of both the boy and the girl arrived.
b. The girl and the mother of the boy arrived.

**Immediate Constituent Analysis (IC analysis** for short) using a **tree diagram** can bring out such syntactic ambiguity:

For the first reading:

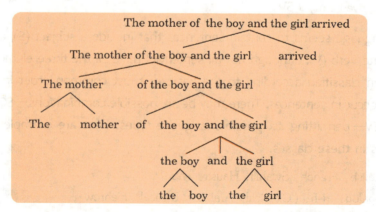

For the second reading:

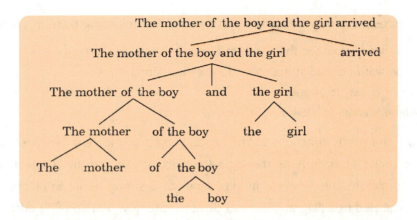

## 4.4 Surface structure and deep structure

Apart from IC analysis, another major approach that helps to reveal the complex structuring of English sentences is **Transformational Generative Grammar** (**TG grammar** for short). A major distinction proposed by the theory in its early version (called "**Standard Theory**"), but rejected in its more mature and latest versions (namely "**Government and Binding Theory**", "**Principles and Parameters Theory**", and "**Minimalist Program**") is drawn between **surface structure** and **deep** (or **underlying**) **structure** (note that the "**S-structures**" and "**D-structures**" used in the late stages mean somewhat differently). Thus, the sentence "The mother of the boy and the girl arrived" has one surface structure but two deep structures, which leads to its two interpretations.

Whereas IC analysis cannot uncover the basic syntactic difference between the following sentences, TG grammar can. Take another example:

⑥ a. Jane tempted John to sign the contract.
b. Jane wanted John to sign the contract.

The differences between the two sentences are shown as follows:

| Tempt | Want |
| --- | --- |
| (1) Jane tempted John to sign the contract. | (1) Jane wanted John to sign the contract. |
| (2) *What Jane tempted was for John to sign the contract. | (2) What Jane wanted was for John to sign the contract. |
| (3) John was tempted to sign the contract by Jane. | (3) *John was wanted to sign the contract by Jane. |
| (4) Jane tempted John. | (4) *Jane wanted John. (unless "want" takes on a different meaning) |
| (5) *Jane tempted something. | (5) Jane wanted something. |

Similar differences may be further illustrated in the following pairs of sentences.

⑦ a. The team promised the coach to exercise during vacation.
　b. The team persuaded the coach to exercise during vacation.
⑧ a. Jane is easy to please.
　b. Jane is eager to please.

In ⑦a, "the team" functions as the logical subject of the verb "exercise". However, in ⑦b "the coach" functions as the logical subject of exercise. In ⑧a, somebody may find it easy to please Jane, whereas in ⑧b, Jane has a strong desire to please somebody.

Using a labeled tree diagram, we can demonstrate how ⑧a and ⑧b differ from each other. (Note that, for simplicity, the analysis is not performed down to the last detail, as conventionally indicated by the use of triangular shapes.)

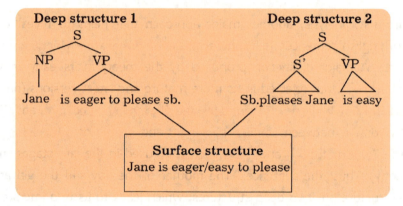

Sentences are believed to be generated by virtue of two basic types of rules: **phrase structure rules** and **transformational rules**. While we analyze a sentence statically as captured by the tree diagram on the left below, we can also see a sentence as generated in accordance with some rules as indicated by the diagram on the right. Compare the following diagrams:

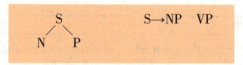

These rules are what we call phrase structure rules. The rule here reads, "a sentence consists of a noun phrase followed by a verb phrase". In addition to rules of this type which generate structures, we can also have lexical rules which indicate the words to be used for **constituents**. For example:

N→{Jane, John ...}

Unit 4  The Structures of English (I)

which means that N is rewritten as "Jane", or "John". We can thus create a set of extremely simple (and necessarily incomplete) phrase structure rules that can be used to generate a large number of English sentences:

S→NP VP
NP→{(Art) (Adj) N}
VP→V (NP) (AP)
N→{Jane, John, contract}
V→{love, tempt, persuade, please}
Adj→{easy, eager}
Art→{a, an, the}

Common transformational rules (T-rules for short) in English include **deletion**, **copying**, **addition**, and **reordering**. For example, in transforming an active voice sentence into a passive voice one, as in ⑨, such rules as reordering and addition are involved.

⑨ a. John kissed Jane.
   b. Jane was kissed by John.

In its initial stages, as indicated by the left diagram below, TG theory attributes all the meaning of a sentence to its deep structure. This has raised a lot of disputes, because the transformation from the deep structure to the surface structure may bring about some changes in the meaning. So, in the later version (namely Government and Binding Theory), the meaning of a sentence is determined by the **logical form** of a sentence derived from its surface structure, as indicated by the right diagram below.

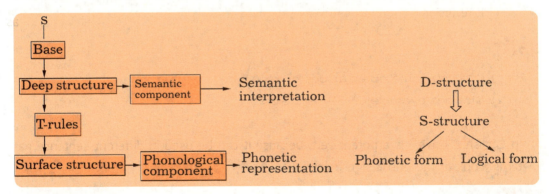

Another important change in the late stages of TG Grammar is that all the earlier transformational rules are reduced into one single rule termed "**move α**". For an element to move from one position to another, some conditions, technically named "principles", must be satisfied.

## Check your understanding

State whether each of the following statements is True or False.
(1) Word order plays an important role in the organization of English sentences.
(2) All ambiguous sentences result from our failure to use proper organization.
(3) With transformations, we can organize a sentence the way we like.
(4) Like English, modern Chinese is an SVO language.

## In-Class Activities

1. Natural language is said to differ from animals' communication systems along many lines. For example, it is characterized by its recursive property; in other words, there is no limit to the potential length of sentences, and the set of sentences of any language is infinite. There are a variety of means that enable **recursion**. Here are the illustrations for some of them in English:

   A. Jane visited John's brother's wife's mother's father's cousin's friend's store. (NP recursion)
   B. The very seedy battered rundown old red wooden shack fell down. (AP recursion)
   C. Jane wants to begin to try to learn to write novels in English. (VP recursion)
   D. John likes the brightness of the coloring of the lettering on the cover of Jane's report. (PP recursion)

   **ask**

   (1) Can you name other modes of recursion?
   (2) Give one example of VP recursion.

2. In English, "leave" is a potent verb because it can be used in different sentence patterns. Look at the public sign below.

   **ask**

   (1) Is the sign ambiguous? If so, use paraphrases to show the different readings.

Unit 4　The Structures of English (I) 　　57

(2) Is the ambiguity involved the same kind as that in "The mother of the boy and the girl arrived"?

(3) Newspaper headlines and advertisements often deliberately employ ambiguity to attract customers or readers. How are the following ambiguous?
 1) A New Model for Getting Rich Online
 2) Two Philippine Ships Collide-One Dies.
 3) Eye Drops off Shelf.
 4) Wanted: A man to Wash Dishes and Two Young Waitresses.

(4) Is the following public sign ambiguous?

3. In the text, seven basic sentence patterns are introduced in English. Now consider the following sentences:
   A. There will be a discussion this afternoon.
   B. It is surprising that you should arrive so late.

   (1) Are these sentence patterns found in English but not in Chinese?
   (2) Can you think of any other sentence patterns in English that are not shared by Chinese?

4. There are many sorts of **discontinuous organization** in English. For instance, in the sentence "I want to see with my own eyes the new changes that have taken place there", the object of "see" is delayed by "with my own eyes". Another type of **dis-**

**continuous structuring** results from what is called particle movement. For example, we may say both "look up a word" and "look a word up", in which "up" is a particle rather than a preposition. In "look a word up", "up" is moved away from the verb and becomes discontinuous. Note that particle movement is obligatory in some special condition in English. Look at the following data:

A. John wrote down the number. /John wrote the number down.
   * John wrote down it.
B. Jane stood up John. /Jane stood John up.
   * Jane stood up him.
C. John kicked out Jane. /John kicked Jane out.
   * John kicked out her.

### ask

(1) What similarities do those sentences in the second category share?
(2) What is the special condition that necessitates particle movement?

5. Here is a phrase-structure rule involving the convention that parentheses mean "optional element", and each line contained in braces can occur separately to the right of the arrow.

$$VP \rightarrow V \begin{Bmatrix} (NP)(PP) \\ S \end{Bmatrix}$$

### ask

(1) Can you write out four different phrases in English illustrating each of the VP types?
(2) Can you use the abbreviatory convention above to integrate the following sets of rules into a single rule?
   1) A→B  C           2) W→X  Y
      A→C                 W→Y
                          W→X  Y  Z

6. Newspaper headlines seem unique in terms of their syntactic properties. Examine the following headlines collected randomly from *The Washington Post*.
   A. Mexico Vote Tally Gives Free-Trader a Narrow Victory

Unit 4　The Structures of English (I)

B. Israeli Tanks Meet Fierce Resistance
C. Ruling Keeps DeLay on Ballot
D. Favoritism Trial Hurts Chicago Mayor
E. Discovery Docks with Space Station
F. Russia's Signal to Stations Is Clear: Cut U. S. Radio
G. Mayor's Stadium Proposal Advances
H. Dumfries Regrets Raid on Homeless
I. A Driven President Faces a World of Crises
J. Consultant Breached FBI's Computers

(1) How many sentence types are covered by the data?
(2) Which type occurs most frequently?

1. Inversion in English poems
2. Ellipsis in English public signs
3. Interrogative sentences in English advertisements

 Task 1　Reference Search

Find in the library or online some information about the following themes:
(1) complement
(2) particle
(3) ambiguity
(4) Leonard Bloomfield
(5) Noam Chomsky

## Task 2  Term Definition

Study the following definitions and then discuss how they combine to help you understand the terms.

**constituent**: A unit of grammatical structure, e.g. the sentence "The lights went out" consists, at one level, of two constituents, the noun phrase ("the lights") and the verb phrase ("went out"). [Henry Widdowson]

**constituent**: one of the parts of a construction [Ronald Wardhaugh]

**constituent structure**: a mapping of a sentence or a part of a sentence into its constituents [Ronald Wardhaugh]

**constituent structure**: Constituent structure is the hierarchical relationship between words, phrases and sentences. [Stuart Poole]

**clause**: A clause is a sequence of words that incorporates a subject and a predicate. It may be a whole sentence (e.g. "He will do it today") or parts of a sentence (e.g. "... that he will do it today"). [Stuart Poole]

**clause**: a construction containing a subject and a finite verb [Ronald Wardhaugh]

**sentence**: a basic or primitive unit in language: the initial S of a generative-transformational grammar [Ronald Wardhaugh]

**sentence**: The largest STRUCTURAL UNIT in terms of which the GRAMMAR of a LANGUAGE is organised. TRADITIONAL grammar defined the sentence as "the expression of a complete thought". Most linguistic definitions of the sentence show the influence of the American linguist Leonard Bloomfield, who pointed to the structural autonomy, or independence, of the notion of sentence: it is "not included by virtue of any grammatical construction in any larger linguistic form". [David Crystal]

**bind/bound**: To say that one constituent $x$ binds (or serves as the binder for) another constituent $y$ (and conversely that $y$ is bound by $x$) is to say that $x$ determines the semantic (and grammatical) properties of $y$. For example, in "John wants to PRO leave", "John" binds "PRO". [Andrew Ratford]

## Task 3  Study Questions

1. It is important that the rules of syntax specify all and only the grammatical sentences of the language. Why is it important to say "only"? That is, what would be wrong with grammar that specified as grammatical sentences all of the truly grammatical ones plus a few that were not grammatical?

2. Analyze how the following sentences are incorrect according to English grammar.
   (1) Snowing outside.
   (2) Jane loves John, she calls him every day.
   (3) There are two boys play football on the ground.
   (4) Jane is very kind to John, for example, she prepares dinner for him whenever she can.
   (5) Diligent is very important to succeed.
   (6) John find the two books very interesting.
   (7) John is a great leader, however, he is sometimes too strict.
   (8) Although Jane loves John, but she never says "I love you" to him.
   (9) The reason Jane loves John is because he is kind to her.
   (10) —Have you seen John lately, Jane?
        —Not seen.
   (11) Finish the job in two days is impossible.
   (12) Why Jane didn't go to Beijing with John?

3. Paraphrase each of the following sentences in two different ways to show that you understand the ambiguity involved:
   (1) Smoking grass can be nauseating.
   (2) John finally decided on the boat.
   (3) Jane's appointment was shocking.
   (4) Old men and women are hard to live with.
   (5) The governor is a dirty street fighter.
   (6) I cannot recommend him too highly.

4. Give the passive version of the following sentences.
   (1) Phil watered the garden too much.
   (2) Bill expected me to leave soon.
   (3) The doctor expected the technician to develop the X-rays fast.
   (Note that there are three possibilities for passivizing this sentence, depending on whether the main clause or the subordinate clause is passivized, or both.)

5. Explain why the following exchange is humorous.
   Tourist: Can you tell me how long cows should be milked?
   Farmer: The same as short ones, of course.

6. Draw a tree diagram to illustrate the structure of the following sentence:

Who was the first to reach school yesterday?

## Task 4　Mini-Project

Native speakers are said to have intuitive knowledge about their language. Does the knowledge vary from person to person? Design some questions pointing to one's grammatical knowledge as introduced in this unit. Then interview a few small groups of people with different ages, genders, and professions or education backgrounds (grouping may allow overlaps), checking the amount and type of grammatical knowledge they have.

Reading 1

### Immediate Constituent Analysis

This type of sentence-analysis became popular in American structuralism. With this method, any sentence can be regarded as a string of morphemes, for example "The-lone-ly-police-man-ate" ( = {EAT} + {PAST})-a-boil-ed-egg. Such morphemes can be called the ultimate constituents of the sentences. But some morphemes "cohere" or belong more closely to each other than to other morphemes: for example, "lone-" and "-ly" being more closely together than either does to "-ed". The test of such mutual coherence is whether or not such a group is syntactically replaceable by a single element: "lone-ly" could be replaced by the monomorphemic "sad". (It is not necessary that the replacement should have the same meaning.) Often, but not always, words are the result of the first grouping of ultimate constituents, such as "lonely".

This process may be repeated successively until the entire original sentence is reduced to a sentence of a favourite type. Thus "police-man" may be replaced by "man"; "lone-ly" and "boil-ed" by "sad" and "large" respectively; then "the man" by "John" and "a(n) egg" by "chocolate"; finally "ate chocolate" by "sang". Thus the utterance is seen to belong to the favourite sentence-type "John sang".

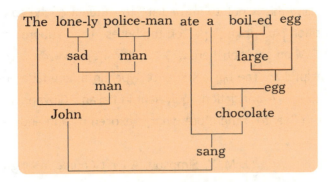

Such a procedure reveals a hierarchically ordered set of structures. The sentence is seen to fall into two main parts: "The lonely policeman" and "ate a boiled egg", each being ultimately reducible to one word. Each main part then falls into two parts: on the one hand, "The" and "lonely policeman", on the other hand "ate" and "a boiled egg", and so on, until we arrive at the ultimate constituents.

It is convenient to define a sentence or any significant group of words or morphemes as a construction. A constituent is a construction or a word or morpheme that enters into a larger construction. An immediate constituent (or IC) is one of the constituents of which any given construction is directly formed. Thus "The lonely policeman" and "ate a boiled egg" are the ICs of the sentence above.

An endocentric construction may be replaced by one of its immediate constituents ("lonely policeman" by "policeman") or by a member of the same major word-class as one of its immediate constituents ("the man" by "John"; both are nouns, though in different sub-classes). A co-ordinative endocentric construction is one in which both or all of the immediate constituents may replace the whole construction; thus "ladies" and "gentlemen" may be replaced by either "ladies" or "gentlemen". A subordinative endocentric construction is one in which only one of the immediate constituents can stand for the whole: "bald gentleman". A subordinative endocentric construction is one in which only one of the immediate constituents can stand for the whole: "bald gentleman" can be replaced by "gentleman" but not by "bald". In a subordinative endocentric construction, the immediate constituent that can stand for the whole construction is the head "gentleman"; that which cannot is the modifier: "bald" is the modifier to the head "gentleman".

An exocentric construction is one which cannot be replaced syntactically by any of its immediate constituents, or by a member of the same major word-class as one of its immediate constituents. Thus, "on the buses" cannot be replaced by anything but an adverb (e.g. "there"), and this is not an immediate constituent of the construction. Phrases consisting of preposition plus noun (e.g. "on the buses") and subordinate clauses in English are exocentric: "When she got there...", "... that he had won a Nobel prize"; "Because she was so helpful..." The basic sentence-types in a language are also exocentric, for instance "John sang". A translation equivalent in Italian "Giovanni canto" is endocentric, being reducible to "canto"; therefore what is exocentric and endocentric depends on the language.

(J. M. Y. Simpson, *A First Course in Linguistics*, pp. 115-117)

 Food for Thought

(1) What advantages and disadvantages does immediate constituent analysis have?
(2) What methodological implications can you draw from this type of analysis?

## Generative Grammar

Since the 1950s, particularly developing from the work of the American linguist Noam Chomsky, there have been attempts to produce a particular type of grammar which would have a very explicit system of rules specifying what combinations of basic elements would result in well-formed sentences. (Let us emphasize the word "attempts" here, since no fully worked-out grammar of this or any other type yet exists.) This explicit system of rules, it was proposed, would have much in common with the types of rules found in mathematics. Indeed, a definitive early statement in Chomsky's first major work betrays this essentially mathematical view of language: "I will consider a language to be a set (finite or infinite) of sentences." (Chomsky, 1957:13)

This mathematical point of view helps to explain the meaning of the term *generative*, which is used to describe this type of grammar. If you have an algebraic expression like $3x + 2y$, and you can give x and y the value of any whole number, then that simple algebraic expression can generate an endless set of values, by following the simple rules of arithmetic. When $x = 5$ and $y = 10$, the result is 35. When $x = 2$ and $y = 1$, the result is 8. These results will follow directly from applying the explicit rules. The endless set of such results is "generated" by the operation of the explicitly formalized rules. If the sentences of a language can be seen as a comparable set, then there must be a set of explicit rules which yield those sentences. Such a set of explicit rules is a generative grammar.

## Some Properties of the Grammar

A grammar of this type must have a number of properties, which can be described in the following terms. The grammar will generate all the well-formed syntactic structures (e.g. sentences) of the language and fail to generate any ill-formed structures. This is the "all and only" criterion (i.e. all the grammatical sentences and only the grammatical sentences).

The grammar will have a finite (i.e. limited) number of rules, but will be capable of generating an infinite number of well-formed structures. In this way, the productivity of language (i.e. the creation of totally novel, yet grammatical, sentences) would be captured within the grammar.

The rules of this grammar will also need the crucial property of recursion, that is, the capacity to be applied more than once in generating a structure. For example, whatever rule yields the component "that chased the cat" in the sentence "This is the dog that chased the cat", will have to be applied again to get "that killed the rat" and any other similar structure which could continue the sentence "This is the dog that chased the cat that killed the rat …"

You can do the same recursive thing with phrases specifying a location, beginning with "The book was on the table". This sentence tells us where the book was. "Where was the table?" "Near the window?" "Okay, where was the window?" "In the hallway?" Okay. Putting this type of recursive effect into a single sentence will lead us to: "The book was on the table near the window in the hallway beside the …" There is, in principle, no end to the recursion which would yield ever-longer versions of this sentence, and the grammar must provide for this fact.

Basically, the grammar will have to capture the fact that a sentence can have another sentence inside it, or a phrase can have another phrase of the same type inside it. This grammar should also be capable of revealing the basis of two other phenomena: first, how some superficially distinct sentences are closely related, and second, how some superficially similar sentences are in fact distinct.

(Adapted from George Yule, *The Study of Language*, pp. 101-102)

 Food for Thought

(1) Is language fully analogous to mathematics?
(2) Is the generative model of grammar applicable to the analysis of Chinese?

# Unit 5

## The Structures of English (II)

* 5.1  English paragraphs
* 5.2  English texts
* 5.3  Cohesion in English texts
* 5.4  Thematic progression in English texts

> *For some, conversation is like a dance, with the conversational partners coordinating their movements smoothly. For others it's like traffic crossing an intersection, involving lots of alternating movement without any crashes.*
> —George Yule

 **Pre-Class Reading**

## 5.1 English paragraphs

A typical English **paragraph** employs a **topic sentence**, which states the controlling idea of the paragraph. The topic sentence usually occurs at the beginning of the paragraph, although occasionally it may also be found at the end of the paragraph or even in the middle of it. To develop the idea given in the topic sentence, one needs to provide specific details, either to explain or verify the point. Thus, we have **supporting sentences**. For a long paragraph, it might be advisable to use a sentence to sum up or reinforce the main point of the paragraph.

To develop a paragraph, one may employ such means as **exemplification**, instantiation, **comparison or contrast**, **cause-effect reasoning**, **definition**, **analogy**, and **enumeration**. A paragraph can be long or short. Writings of different styles, say narrative and argumentative, may differ widely in the organization of paragraphs. One may find a single-sentence paragraph in a novel, often used to convey a special effect.

## 5.2 English texts

A well-written **text** is not a simple amalgam of paragraphs. It must be properly organized around a central purpose or coherent topic. As there are different purposes of writing complete essays, there are different forms of texts. The four major forms are **narration**, **description**, **exposition**, and **argumentation**. Yet a basically argumentative essay, for instance, may make use of local narration.

Different forms of writing are developed in different ways. An English narrative story runs, by default, in **chronological order**. There are deviations, though. For example, we can use **flashbacks** or we can report the activities of different characters separately. In all cases, the choice of a primary **perspective** or **point of view** is central. Usually, narration is complete when it covers the various stages of the principal event.

By comparison, an English argumentative essay contains three major parts: introduction, main body and conclusion. It is consistent if it develops a unique yet subjective **thesis** on the basis of adequate **evidence**. Argumentation, in general, is built on explicit organization.

## 5.3 Cohesion in English texts

A text is not a mess of sentences lumped together. Rather, it is unified in meaning (topic-relatedness or **coherence**) and tied up or organized in form (**cohesion**).

Logically, the use of such expressions as "because", "however", "by contrast", and "firstly" indicates how the previous sentence(s) is connected with the current or even following sentence(s). Grammatically, the use of ellipsis, **reference** like "he" and "it", and **substitution** like "so", "do", and "the former" helps to establish **cross-reference** across sentences. Lexically, the repetition of the same word(s) or the use of synonyms, antonyms, meronyms, hyponyms, and summary terms contributes to the connectedness of the neighboring sentences.

Reference deserves further elaboration here. The first distinction can be drawn between **exophoric reference** and **endophoric reference**. While the former points to a relation between an entity in the situational context and a linguistic item in the text (as in "He is the man you want to see!" said when the mentioned person comes up to the speaker), the latter refers to the relation between two linguistic items in the same text.

For endophoric reference, further distinction is available between **anaphoric reference** and **cataphoric reference**. The former involves a relation between a preceding referential expression or an **antecedent** and the current **pronominal item** (as in "John loves Jane. He takes great care of her. This is known to all."), whereas the latter denotes a relation between the current pronominal item and the later occurring expression (as in "This is what John does for Jane: he sends a bunch of roses to her every day.").

## 5.4 Thematic progression in English texts

The way a sentence is organized in a certain word order implies the choice of a **focus**, **point of departure**, or **perspective**. Compare the following sentences:

① John loved Mary.
② Mary was loved by John.

Clearly, though the two sentences are paraphrases, they are different in their focus or point of departure. By moving Mary from the position of object of the verb to the first part of the sentence, our attention is focused on who it was that John loved. This can also be done for contrastive purposes, as in:

③ It was Mary that John loved, not Jane.

In English, sentences can be thought of as being divided into a **topic**—what is being talked about—and a **comment**—what is being said about the topic. The topic often corresponds to the structural or grammatical subject of a sentence. The topic of a sentence is also called the **old information**, because it represents something already under discussion. The comment, on the other hand, is the **new information**, because it represents information added to the **discourse**. The tendency for old information to occur first in a sentence may be universal.

Another pair of terms used sometimes interchangeably with "topic" and "comment" is "**theme**" and "**rheme**". By analyzing the modes of **thematic progression**, that is, the pattern of theme and rheme variation, we can find how an author develops his or her writing. The following types are found to be common ways of development:

| Type 1 | Type 2 | Type 3 |
|---|---|---|
| Theme 1→rheme 1 ↘<br>Theme 2→rheme 2 ↘<br>Theme 3 → rheme 3 | Theme 1→rheme 1<br>↓<br>Theme 2→rheme 2<br>↓<br>Theme 3→rheme 3 | Theme 1→rheme 1<br>↙      ↘<br>Theme 2→rheme 2    Theme 3→rheme 3 |

In actuality, texts we encounter may involve more complex patterns of thematic progression, but these three types provide the basic ones on which we depend for analysis.

## Check your understanding

State whether each of the following statements is True or False.
(1) Every English paragraph contains a topic sentence, supporting details and a summary sentence.
(2) One may tell a story when arguing for a thesis.
(3) In order for two neighboring sentences to be cohesive, one must use some explicit device to conjoin them.
(4) Good texts always follow the same pattern of thematic progression.

## In-Class Activities

1. By "anaphora" we mean reference through the use of pronominal forms to something that has already been mentioned in the preceding text. Study the picture on the right.

**ask—**

   (1) What does "it" refer to?
   (2) What is omitted in the sentence?

2. English texts can be further categorized into different genres (to be detailed in Unit 13), each with its content components and organizational patterns. Public notices, given their characteristic content, have their unique style in terms of the way they are organized. Study the following sign:

(1) What components make up the public notice?

(2) How is the public sign organized?

(3) How is it different from a similar sign in the Chinese context?

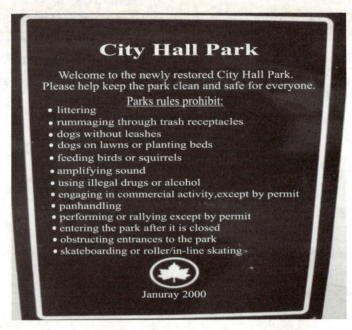

3. A coherent text depends heavily, though not necessarily, on an explicit use of cohesive devices. Read the following excerpt from the first chapter of Mark Twain's *Life on the Mississippi*.

(1) The Mississippi is well worth reading about. (2) It is not a commonplace river, but on the contrary is in all ways remarkable. (3) Considering the Missouri its main branch, it is the longest river in the world—four thousand three hundred miles. (4) It seems safe to say that it is also the crookedest river in the world, since in one part of its journey it uses up one thousand three hundred miles to cover the same ground that the crow would fly over in six hundred and seventy-five. (5) It discharges three times as much water as the St. Lawrence, twenty-five times as much as the Rhine, and three hundred and thirty-eight times as much as the Thames. (6) No other river has so vast a drainage-basin: it draws its water supply from twenty-eight States and Territories; from Delaware, on the Atlantic seaboard, and from all the country between that and Idaho on the Pacific slope—a spread of forty-five degrees of longitude. (7) The Mississippi receives and carries to the Gulf water from fifty-

four subordinate rivers that are navigable by steamboats, and from some hundreds that are navigable by flats and keels. (8) The area of its drainage-basin is as great as the combined areas of England, Wales, Scotland, Ireland, France, Spain, Portugal, Germany, Austria, Italy, and Turkey; and almost all this wide region is fertile; the Mississippi valley, proper, is exceptionally so.

(1) Point out the cohesive devices used in the paragraph.

(2) Which type of cohesive devices is used most often?

4. Language users, poets in particular, are sometimes "creative" in the sense that they may flout regular sentences or text patterns of organization in order to achieve unusual effects. Here is an imaginative poem by Roger McGough.

|  | 40-Love |  |
| --- | --- | --- |
| middle |  | aged |
| couple |  | playing |
| ten |  | nis |
| when |  | the |
| game |  | ends |
| and |  | they |
| go |  | home |
| the |  | net |
| will |  | still |
| be |  | be |
| tween |  | them |

(1) What is the theme the poet seems to convey?
(2) How does the layout of the poem best reveal the theme?

5. In writing novels, an author has at his or her disposal a variety of ways to achieve psychological description or thought presentation. Here are some of them: a. **direct speech**; b. **indirect speech**; c. **free direct speech**; d. **free indirect speech**; and e. **direct narration**. To illustrate, compare the following:
(1) She thought, "He is a good boy."
(2) She thought that he was a good boy.

(3) He is a good boy, she thought.

(4) He was a good boy, she thought.

(5) She considered him a good boy.

(1) What are the differences among the 5 versions?

(2) Find two more examples of each from novels by such authors as James Joyce, Henry James, and William Faulkner.

## Presentation Topics

1. The structure of an English poster for a public lecture

2. The structure of a thesis defense

3. The structure of an invitation letter

## Exercises

### Task 1  Reference Search

Find in the library or online some information about the following themes:

(1) cohesion

(2) coherence

(3) M. A. K. Halliday

(4) theme and rheme

(5) texture

### Task 2  Term Definition

Study the following definitions and then discuss how they combine to help you understand the terms.

**discourse**: a group of sentences related in some sequential manner [Ronald Wardhaugh]

**discourse**: the use of language in speech and writing to achieve pragmatic meaning; cf.

# Unit 5　The Structures of English (II)

text [Henry Widdowson]

**text**: The product of the process of discourse. In written language, the text is produced by one of the parties involved (the writer) and is a part of the communication. In spoken language, the text will only survive the discourse if it is specially recorded. [Henry Widdowson]

**text**: Any passage, spoken or written, of whatever length, that does form a unified whole. ... it is a semantic unit: a unit not of form but of meaning ... a text does not CONSIST OF sentences; it is REALIZED BY, or encoded in, sentences. [Michael Halliday & Ruqaiya Hasan]

**utterance**: a spoken sentence or part of a sentence [Ronald Wardhaugh]

**utterance**: An instance of language behaviour (in speech or writing), i.e. of parole or performance. It can be considered either as an act of speech, the physical manifestation of the medium, and the concern of phonetics, or as a mode of use in the performance of a speech act, and therefore the concern of pragmatics. [Henry Widdowson]

 Task 3　Study Questions

1. What differences and similarities exist between conversation and written discourse(text)?

2. What is the typical global or macro structure of a data-driven MA thesis/a note of thanks/a resume?

3. The following texts were written by a group of second-graders:
    A. One day some people moved in a house. The army ant gobbled up the house. So the people had to start all over again.
    B. Once there was a parrot and she laid an egg. The egg didn't hatch and the mother parrot, whose name was Sheila, started crying. One day Sheila heard a peck-peck and the baby bird walked out. The mother bird was very happy.
    C. Once upon a time there was a lady bug who was busy eating aphids. There are plants in the garden. The lady bug is always in the garden. Every day the lady bug eats aphids. The lady bug is always on plants. The lady bug is always catching aphids.
    D. Once there was a shark and there was another shark and they ate fishes and they got so fat that they exploded. The sea got so hot that it got on fire and all the fish died and sharks and plants died and the sea was not there.
    E. One day I planted a seed and I waited and waited and waited until I was an old man.

Then it grew a little bit and I died.

(1) A story can be divided into orientation, evaluation, complicating action, and resolution. Analyze the texts in terms of these categories (not all of these will be present in all texts).

(2) Are there any examples here that are not narrative (i.e. that do not use temporally ordered narrative clauses)?

(3) Causal and/or chronological sequence in a text may not be explicitly specified. Give two examples where they are established by implication.

4. An ad is a short discourse. Study the following ad and analyze the way it is constructed. Discuss the perspective employed and its effect on communication.

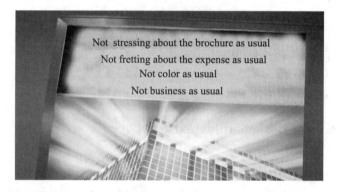

5. Analyze the sentences of the following passage in terms of their thematic structure. Discuss the way in which the author chooses the themes for the sentences.

For the Greeks, beauty was a virtue: a kind of excellence. Persons then were assumed to be what we now have to call—lamely, enviously—whole persons. If it did occur to the Greeks to distinguish between a person's "inside" and "outside," they still expected that inner beauty would be matched by beauty of the other kind. The well-born young Athenians who gathered around Socrates found it quite paradoxical that their hero was so intelligent, so brave, so honorable, so seductive—and so ugly. One of Socrates' main pedagogical acts was to be ugly—and teach those innocent, no doubt splendid-looking disciples of his how full of paradoxes life really was.

6. Point out the cohesive devices used in the following passage.

They may have resisted Socrates' lesson. We do not. Several thousand years later, we are more wary of the enchantments of beauty. We not only split off—with the greatest facility—the "inside" (character, intellect) from the "outside" (looks); but we are actually surprised when someone who is beautiful is also intelligent, talented, good.

### Task 4  Mini-Project

Record an English dialogue program and a Chinese dialogue program. Make a contrastive study of the global and local organization of the data.

### Reading 1

#### Cohesion

Halliday & Hasan take the view that the primary determinant of whether a set of sentences do or do not constitute a text depends on cohesive relationships within and between the sentences, which create **texture**: "A text has texture and this is what distinguishes it from something that is not a text. ... The texture is provided by the cohesive RELATION." (1976:2) Cohesive relationships within a text are set up "where the INTERPRETATION of some element in the discourse is dependent on that of another. The one PRESUPPOSES the other in the sense that it cannot be effectively decoded except by recourse to it" (1976:4). A paradigm example of such a cohesive relationship is given (1976:2):

(1) Wash and core six cooking apples. Put them into a fireproof dish.

Of this text they say: "It is clear that *them* in the second sentence refers back to (is ANAPHORIC to) the *six cooking apples* in the first sentence. This ANAPHORIC function of *them* gives cohesion to the two sentences, so that we interpret them as a whole; the two sentences together constitute a text." (1976:2)

Halliday & Hasan outline a taxonomy of types of cohesive relationships which can be formally established within a text, providing cohesive "ties" which bind a text together.

(Extracted from Gillian Brown and George Yule, *Discourse Analysis*, p. 191)

### Food for Thought

(1) How do you define "cohesion"?

(2) What does "texture" mean?
(3) Does cohesion alone guarantee coherence?

## Coherence

The key to the concept of coherence is not something which exists in the language, but something which exists in people. It is people who "make sense" of what they read and hear. They try to arrive at an interpretation which is in line with their experience of the way the world is. Indeed, our ability to make sense of what we read is probably only a small part of that general ability we have to make sense of what we perceive or experience in the world. When we read a text, we try to make the text "fit" some situation or experience which would accommodate all the details. If we work at it long enough, we may indeed find a way to incorporate all those disparate elements into a single coherent interpretation. In doing so, we would necessarily be involved in a process of filling in a lot of "gaps" which exist in the text. We would have to create meaningful connections which are not actually expressed by the words and sentences. This process is not restricted to trying to understand "odd" texts. In one way or another, it seems to be involved in our interpretation of all discourse.

It is certainly present in the interpretation of casual conversation. We are continually taking part in conversational interactions where a great deal of what is meant is not actually present in what is said. Perhaps it is the ease with which we ordinarily anticipate each other's intentions that makes this whole complex process seem so unremarkable. Here is a good example, adapted from Widdowson (1978):

**Her**: That's the telephone.
**Him**: I'm in the bath.
**Her**: O.K.

There are certainly no cohesive ties within this fragment of discourse. How does each of these people manage to make sense of what the other says? They do use the information contained in the sentences expressed, but there must be something else involved in the interpretation. It has been suggested that exchanges of this type are best understood in terms of the conventional actions performed by the speakers in such interactions. Drawing on concepts derived from the study of speech acts, we can characterize the brief conversation in the following way:

Unit 5　The Structures of English (II) 　　77

She makes a request of him to perform an action
He states reason why he cannot comply with the request
She undertakes to perform the action

If this is a reasonable analysis of what took place in the conversation, then it is clear that language-users must have a lot of knowledge of how conversational interaction works which is not simply "linguistic" knowledge. Trying to describe aspects of that knowledge has been the focus of research by an increasing number of discourse analysts.

(Adapted from George Yule, *The Study of Language*, pp. 141-142)

 Food for Thought

(1) Are some texts more coherent than others?
(2) Are there any external criteria for measuring the coherence of texts?
(3) How do you define coherence?

# Unit 6

## The Meaning of English (I)

* 6.1  The notion of semantics
* 6.2  Semantic properties
* 6.3  Semantic relations
* 6.4  Sense and reference

> *The Greek word (from which we get "semantics") conveys the idea of importance. The Chinese equivalent is also used to mean interest. This suggests that the subject touches on questions of why people bother to use language in the first place, and why we bother to listen to them.*
> — Howard Gregory

 **Pre-Class Reading**

## 6.1  The notion of semantics

Learning a language involves learning the "agreed-upon" **meanings** of certain strings of sounds and learning how to combine these meaningful units into larger units that also convey meaning. If you chance upon a sentence like the following,

① Colorless green ideas sleep furiously

you may feel puzzled. Why would one write such a nonsensical sentence? This sentence, not used for communication, is actually an invention by the linguist Noam Chomsky who would argue that a sentence, while grammatical, can be meaningless. Linguists today generally agree that a good sentence has to be well-formed not only in structure, but in meaning or logic as well.

The study of the meaning aspect of language constitutes the branch of linguistics termed as **semantics**. In its full scope, it not only deals with how a well-formed sentence is with regard to its meaning, as mentioned above, but also with other meaning-related issues, as illustrated below.

## 6.2 Semantic properties

By and large, we may view words as units comprising universal **semantic properties** or **features**. If we reflect upon sentence ①, we may come to understand why it is semantically ill-formed. For instance, "ideas", which are abstract, cannot have the property of "green". Similarly, they cannot be said to "sleep" since they are inanimate, unlike animals or creatures. On a different plane, the word "colorless" is incongruent with "green" as the latter entails the presence of color. Also, the verb "sleep" is incongruent to some degree with "furiously" since the latter implies an active state of mind. Lack or misuse of certain features will lead to semantically ill-formed phrases, clauses, or sentences.

The analysis of words into a combination of semantic features has another advantage. On the basis of more or less shared semantic features we can make all sorts of word groupings. For example, the following words, with the exception of "computer", can be grouped together because they share the property of [HUMAN]:

    student, doctor, scholar, teacher, plumber, computer, professor

Also, by analyzing words into a cluster of semantic properties, we can see more visually how words relate to or contrast with each other.

    woman—[ +HUMAN ] [ −MALE ] [ +ADULT ]
    man—[ +HUMAN ] [ +MALE ] [ +ADULT ]
    boy—[ +HUMAN ] [ +MALE ] [ −ADULT ]
    girl—[ +HUMAN ] [ −MALE ] [ −ADULT ]

(Note: " + " indicates the presence of the feature while " − " denotes the absence of the feature.)

Technically, the process that breaks down the meaning of a word into its minimal distinctive features or properties using feature symbols (**metalanguage**) is called **componential analysis**. The following are some common semantic features (capitalized words) used for analysis:

| General terms | [ +MALE ] / [ +ADULT ] | [ +FEMALE ] / [ +ADULT ] | |
|---|---|---|---|
| human | man | woman | [ +HUMAN ] |
| horse | stallion | mare | [ +EQUINE ] |
| sheep | ram | ewe | [ +OVINE ] |
| cattle | bull | cow | [ +BOVINE ] |
| pig | boar | sow | [ +PORCINE ] |
| dog | dog | bitch | [ +CANINE ] |
| hare | buck | doe | [ +LEPORINE ] |
| deer | buck | doe | [ +CERVINE ] |
| cat | tom | queen | [ +FELINE ] |

**Componential analysis** can also be applied to the study of English verbs. For example,

darken, kill, uglify ... [ CAUSE ]
bring, fall, walk, run ... [ MOTION ]
hit, kiss, touch ... [ CONTACT ]
build, imagine, make ... [ CREATION ]
see, hear, feel ... [ SENSE ]

## 6.3 Semantic relations

Componential analysis is instrumental in revealing **semantic relations**, relations that exist between or among words in terms of meaning. For example, if two or more words, like "broad" and "wide", "answer" and "reply", share all the semantic properties to a significant degree, they are said to be **synonymous**. If two words, say "long" and "short", are contradictory with regard to one or more important semantic properties, they are said to be **antonymous**. If two or more words, such as "teacher", "lawyer", and "worker", include the same important semantic property as another word, i.e. "occupation", the former are said to be the **(co-) hyponyms** of the latter, which is technically a **superordinate**.

**Synonymy** can be partial or almost total. For example, "ripe" and "mature" are synonymous in very limited cases, whereas "broad" and "wide" are synonymous in most cases. However, it needs to be borne in mind that since no two words contain exactly the same number or type of semantic properties (if such properties also include formality, collocation, and affect), there is no pair of words that are absolutely interchangeable or synonymous. In certain respects, "tall" and "high" appear to be synonymous; in others, they are rather different. For example, we can say "tall building", "high building", "tall person", but not "high person".

**Antonyms** can be categorized into three types, namely **gradable antonyms** (e.g. tall—short, strong—weak), **complementary antonyms** (e.g. dead—alive, married—single), and **converse antonyms** or **relational opposites** (e.g. husband—wife, child—parent).

In the case of **hyponymy**, different languages may overlap to a great extent in that they possess equivalents of superordinates and their hyponyms. But languages can also differ in this regard point. For instance, there may be more hyponyms in one language than in another for the same kind of superordinate, as in the case of address terms. The English term "cousin" corresponds to a variety of terms denoting cousin relationships in Chinese.

The very many words in English are not unrelated to each other. Rather, they form different **semantic fields**. Those that belong to the same semantic category, like color words, fall into the same semantic field. Here are some more examples of semantic fields:

a. vegetable: cabbage, spinach, cucumber, cauliflower, pepper, onion, tomato, etc.
b. furniture: table, stool, bench, cupboard, wardrobe, bed, sofa, tea table, etc.

Verbs of the same category can also form semantic fields. For instance,

c. movement: run, walk, scramble, stroll, saunter, wander, stride, strut, pace, parade, tramp, ramble, race, dash, etc.
d. laugh: giggle, guffaw, heehaw, sneer, simper, smirk, etc.

Clearly, the word denoting the semantic field is a superordinate term, whereas those denoting items in the field are its hyponyms.

Finally, let's have a look at the semantic relation of **meronymy**, from "meros" (part) + "nym" (name), that is, the part-whole relationship between lexical items. For example, a "finger" is a part of a "hand", a "hand" is a part of an "arm", and an "arm" is a part of a "body". Therefore, "finger" is a **meronym** of "hand", "hand" is a meronym of "arm", and "arm" is a meronym of "body". We can identify this relationship by using the following formulae:

A        An  X              is a part of a Y
         A page             is a part of a book.

|   | A nose | is a part of a face. |
|---|--------|---------------------|
| B | A Y    | has an X            |
|   | A book | has pages.          |
|   | A face | has a nose.         |

The following are some common types of meronymy:

a. component—object  (branch—tree, page—book)
b. member—collection  (tree—forest, fish—shoal)
c. portion—mass  (slice—cake, strand—hair)
d. place—area  (Beijing—China)

## 6.4 Sense and reference

All words in a language have **senses**, lexical or grammatical. They are assigned some meaning systematically, each being more or less unique in the lexical or grammatical system of the language. A word like "dog" has some **lexical sense(s)**, while a function word like the infinitive marker "to" has a **grammatical sense**. Synonymous words have more or less the same senses.

Some, but not all, words make **reference** to the real or possible world. Thus, reference is the relation between words and entities in the world. Words like "dog", "moon" and "ghost" denote some entities outside the language system whereas grammatical words generally do not have reference. Interestingly, some words or expressions with different senses, like "morning star" and "evening star", may have the same **referent**. In writing, people often use a variety of expressions to refer to the same object or person for artistic effects.

### Check your understanding

State whether each of the following statements is True or False.
(1) A grammatical sentence is also meaningful.
(2) Some words are always superordinates while some others are always hyponyms.
(3) Synonyms are those words that can be used interchangeably in all contexts.
(4) Antonyms have opposite meanings.
(5) All English words have their referents.

Unit 6　The Meaning of English (I)

## In-Class Activities

1. The fact that we can understand the "meaning" of a sentence does not mean that the sentence is semantically well-formed. Look at the following sentences.
   A. The hamburger ate the man.
   B. The television drank my water.
   C. His dog writes poetry.

   (1) Do you find the sentences above sound queer? If yes, give your explanation for their oddness.
   (2) Is the public sign in the picture below semantically problematic?

   (3) In Chinese, we may say "晒太阳""救火""吃火锅", and the like. How are they semantically problematic?

2. When applying componential analysis, we need to know that for a term void of a particular feature like [MALE], we often use the notation [ – MALE] instead of [FEMALE].

   (1) How can the following words be analyzed into semantic features? What feature is common to them?
   lamb, calf, piglet, puppy, kitten
   (2) Complete the following data by (a) devising a category that distinguishes the word "bus" from the word "car", and (b) giving the appropriate symbol for the words "bicycle" and "motorcycle".

|  | [POWERED] | [CARRY PEOPLE] | [FOUR-WHEELED] |
| --- | --- | --- | --- |
| bus | + | + | + |
| car | + | + | + |
| van | + | − | + |
| bicycle |  |  |  |
| motorcycle |  |  |  |

3. Contemporary English seems very **redundant** sometimes. Look at the following sentences.

   A. You will receive a free gift.

   B. That was an unexpected surprise.

   In sentence (A), we might complain that if it is a gift, it is necessarily free, so it is redundant to use both words. Likewise, in sentence (B), since a surprise is surely unexpected, it seems repetitious to modify "surprise" with "unexpected". The following are further such examples:

   C. We should provide advance warning next time.

   D. I'll make your visit my first priority.

   E. We got the house for a cheap price.

   F. There was a general consensus on the issue.

**ask**

   (1) Do you agree with the idea that the sentences above are redundant?

   (2) Given the fact that these sentences are used for the sake of communication, can you figure out the reason for such combinations?

   (3) Can you give more examples of a similar nature?

4. One particular point we find interesting about gradable antonyms is that generally one member of the pair is used more often than the other in certain constructions. Technically, the frequently used one is called the "**unmarked**" member. For example, we usually ask "How old is Jane?" if we want to know Jane's age, but not the **marked** form "How young is Jane?" This is taken as evidence that "old" is the unmarked member of the old-young pair. Additional evidence is the common practice of saying that someone is "five years old" rather than "five years young" in talking about age.

Unit 6  The Meaning of English (I)    85

# ask

(1) Can you determine the "unmarked" member in each of the following pairs?

small—big         cheap—expensive       wide—narrow
near—far          many—few              easy—difficult
early—late        dangerous—safe        full—empty

(2) Can you think of any special situations where the "marked" member is appropriately used?

5. It is not hard to find, from any dictionary, that English words are for the most part **polysemous**: the same form having at least two meanings. These meanings are intrinsically or etymologically related. Usually, one meaning is more basic, with other meanings derived from it directly or indirectly. Some words, like "bank", "bark", or "trunk" are not exactly polysemous. Rather, the distinct unrelated meanings are associated with the same forms quite by accident. This phenomenon is described as **homonymy**. It may take other forms: **homography**, the same spelling with different pronunciations and distinct meanings, as regards "lead" ([liːd] vs. [led]); **homophony**, the same pronunciation with different spellings and distinct meanings, as pertains to "sweet" vs. "suite". Now, read the following conversation.

"How is bread made?"
"I know that!" Alice cried eagerly. "You take some flour —"
"Where do you pick the flower?" the White Queen asked. "In a garden or in the hedges?"
"Well, it isn't picked at all," Alice explained. "It's ground —"
"How many acres of ground?" said the White Queen.

(1) Which words are being played on in the conversation?
(2) Are they cases of **polysemy** or homonymy?
(3) How about the word "carry" in the following picture?

**6.** Antonyms are frequently used in English proverbs. Here are some examples:
Short pleasure, long lament.
Rich men feed, and poor men breed.
Penny wise, pound foolish.
Offence is the best defence.

**ask**

(1) Why is it common to use antonyms in proverbs?
(2) Can you give two more proverbs involving the use of antonyms?

**7.** The meaning of a word is often determined by its **collocates**, i.e. words they collocate with in its environment. They give rise to some associations on account of its mutual expectancy. For example, cows may "wander", but not "stroll". One "trembles" with fear, but "quivers" with excitement. Similarly, "pretty" and "handsome" are different in terms of the range of words they usually collocate with:
pretty {girl, woman, flower, etc.}
handsome {boy, man, car, vessel, etc.}

**ask**

(1) How does "make" differ from "do" in terms of collocation? Give some examples to illustrate their differences.
(2) Which verbs collocate with "effect" and "role"?
(3) What implications does collocation have for our learning of English?

Unit 6  The Meaning of English (I)

8. Naming is seldom an arbitrary practice. Read the following fragment of conversation from Lewis Carroll's *Through the Looking-Glass*:

"My name is Alice."

"It's a stupid name enough!" Humpty Dumpty interrupted impatiently. "What does it mean?"

"Must a name mean something?" Alice asked doubtfully.

"Of course it must," Humpty Dumpty said with a short laugh. "My name means the shape I am—and a good handsome shape it is, too. With a name like yours, you might be any shape, almost."

(1) Does your name have a meaning?

(2) Do you agree that naming plays an important role in economic life? Use an example to illustrate.

## Presentation Topics

1. The naming of people in English
2. Types of synonyms in English
3. The meaning of "meaning"

## Exercises

### Task 1  Reference Search

Find in the library or online some information about the following themes:

(1) Frank Palmer
(2) denotation
(3) meaning
(4) grammatical meaning
(5) anomaly

## Task 2  Term Definition

Study the following definitions and then discuss how they combine to help you understand the terms.

**denotation**: all the entities which can be described by an expression X [Howard Gregory]

**sense**: Sense relates to the complex system of relationships that hold between the linguistic elements themselves (mostly the words); it is concerned only with intra-linguistic relations. [Frank Palmer]

**sense**: The sense of an expression may be defined as the set, or network, of sense relations that hold between it and other expressions of the same language. [John Lyons]

**reference**: Reference deals with the relationship between the linguistic elements, words, sentences, etc. and the non-linguistic world of experience. [Frank Palmer]

**reference**: the relationship by which language hooks onto the world [John Saeed]

**implication**: a relation between two statements such that if the first is true, the second must be true [Howard Gregory]

**entailment**: A relationship between sentences so that if a sentence A entails a sentence B, then if we know A we automatically know B. Or alternatively, it should be impossible, at the same time, to assert A and deny B. [John Saeed]

**contradiction**: a pair of sentences which are opposites, in the sense that one must be false if the other is true and vice versa [Howard Gregory]

## Task 3  Study Questions

1. Look at the following sentences, and then answer the questions that follow:

    A. Lightning willingly hit the boy.

    B. My cat studied linguistics.

    C. A table was listening to some music.

    (1) How would you describe the oddness of these sentences in terms of semantic features?

    (2) Semantic violations are frequent in poetry. For example, we may say "a week/hour/century ago", but usually do not say "a table/dream/mother ago". However, Dylan Thomas does write "a grief ago". How would you account for the effect of such usage?

    (3) Can you find more similar use of language in English literature?

2. Look at the following picture.

   While "listen" and "hear" are semantically related, we usually say "we listen and we hear". Why is this order reversed in the picture?

3. Study the following pairs of words. What is the basic lexical relation between these pairs of words?
   (1) shallow    deep          (2) mature    ripe
   (3) suite      sweet         (4) table     furniture
   (5) single     married       (6) move      run

   For "mature" and "ripe", give an example where one can be used for collocation but not the other. For "suite" and "sweet", give another pair with a similar semantic relation. For "move" and "run", give more words that are in the same semantic relation to "move" as "run".

4. The following are more pairs of antonyms:
   alive—dead      male—female       boy—girl
   east—west       true—false        hit—miss
   (1) Which pairs of the antonyms are complementary opposites?
   (2) How do you account for the following usages or misuses?
       half dead/alive           * very dead/alive
       more dead than alive      * A is more dead than B.

5. The following sentences are redundant in a semantic sense. Specify how each is so.
   (1) Could you repeat that word again?
   (2) They had already heard the name before.
   (3) And that was his final conclusion.
   (4) The church was in close proximity.

6. For each group of words given below, state what semantic property or properties are shared by the (a) words and the (b) words, and what semantic property or properties distinguish the classes of the (a) words from the (b) words.

   **Example:** a. widow, mother, sister, aunt
   b. widower, father, brother, uncle
   The (a) and (b) words are "human".
   The (a) words are "female" and the (b) words are "male".

   (1) a. bachelor, man, son, paperboy, pope, chief
   b. bull, rooster, drake, ram

   (2) a. table, stone, pencil, cup, house, ship, car
   b. milk, alcohol, rice, soup, mud

   (3) a. book, temple, mountain, road, tractor
   b. idea, love, charity, sincerity, bravery, fear

   (4) a. pine, elm, ash, weeping willow
   b. rose, dandelion, tulip, daisy

   (5) a. ask, tell, say, talk, converse
   b. shout, whisper, mutter, drawl, holler

   (6) a. alive, asleep, dead, married, pregnant
   b. tall, smart, interesting, bad, tired

7. Slips of tongue not only occur in the articulation of sounds, as shown in Unit 2, but also relate to the expression of meaning. Look at the following:

   | Intended Utterance | Actual Utterance (Error) |
   | --- | --- |
   | bridge of the nose | bridge of the neck |
   | when my gums bled | when my tongues bled |
   | he came too late | he came too early |
   | Mary was young | Mary was old |
   | a horse of another color | a horse of another race |

   Discuss what types of semantic slips are represented in the data.

## Task 4  Mini-Project

The expressions used in weather reports form an independent semantic field. Collect such expressions in English and Chinese and attempt a contrastive study to reveal their similarities and differences. You can also resort to componential analysis for discussion.

## Recommended Readings

Reading 1

### Words, Words, Words

Semantics is the study of meaning. In reading history, we may discover that scholars seem always to have been singularly fascinated with the subject of meaning. Hsün Tzu, a Chinese philosopher, said more than 2,000 years ago that even names have no fixed meaning. "It is only by agreement that we apply a name. Once agreed, it becomes customary, and the standard is thus fixed. A name has no fixed actuality; it is only a product of such agreement."

We may thus infer from Hsün Tzu's observation that the only useful definition is the one which all can accept. What happens, though, if we cannot agree on a definition? In the interest of clear understanding, we must agree or disagree. We submit, also, that one definition is not necessarily "better" than any other, and suggest, too, that it can be misleading to accuse someone of "misusing" a word or term. For example, the concept and the various meanings associated with "democracy" have caused much confusion in recent times. A Soviet citizen may ask us, "What do you mean 'democracy'? The people of the United States are not the beneficiaries of a democratic state since they do not own the means of production." But we may counter that "democracy" has little to do with "means of production" or the ownership of such means. "Democracy" consists of government constituted by freely elected representatives who govern with the consent of the governed. The semanticist asks us to accept the fact that we and the Soviet citizen are employing the same word with entirely different meanings. When we cannot agree on a definition we can only cease to employ the word in question and explore alternative words for expressing our message. Although this may at times be awkward, we should, however, note that it may prevent useless arguments. By dropping or clarifying any word we cannot agree on, such as "democracy", we can eliminate a source of misunderstanding—for, as long as we continue to argue about the correct meaning of "democracy", we inhibit understanding and communication.

If there is no such thing as a "correct" definition, what is the purpose of the dictionaries, we may ask ourselves? A dictionary is a history of the meaning of words; it is not a lawbook. If we do not know the meaning of a word, a dictionary can tell us how the word has been employed in the past. *Time* magazine phrased it beautifully in reviewing a newly published dictionary: "When he set out in 1746 to write the first great English dictionary, Samuel Johnson intended his definitions to be laws that would firmly establish meanings. But usage thumbs its nose at laws; the dictionary nowadays is more a Social Register of words than a Supreme Court of language."

*Time* surely states the modern case. Choice of words is a matter of fashion, custom, tradition, learning and environment. "Correct" definitions are like "correct" clothes. They are the ones in favor with the people with whom we associate. Insisting on dictionary definitions is a type of snobbery, no better than insisting that all of our friends must share our values.

(Adapted from Curtis Hayes et al, *The ABC's of Languages and Linguistics: A Practical Primer to Language Science*, p. 94 )

 Food for Thought

(1) To what extent is the naming of people arbitrary?
(2) Is there any alternative to avoiding the use of words like "democracy"?
(3) Does the discussion of the use of dictionaries apply to grammar books?

 Reading 2

## Meaning Properties and Relations

To include semantics in a grammar we have some facts that must be accounted for. Probably the most central meaning property of expressions to be described is "meaningfulness" versus "meaninglessness". An adequate semantic theory of a language must say which expressions are meaningful (and which are not), and for the meaningful ones an adequate theory must specify or represent their meaning. For example,

① a. *procrastinate* means "put things off"
 b. *bachelor* means "unmarried adult male"
 c. *father* means "male parent"

Another important meaning property of expressions is ambiguity. There are three sources of ambiguity in natural language: lexical and surface structural ambiguity and underlying structural ambiguity. A lexical ambiguity can be disambiguated by paraphrasing the relevant expression:

② a. He found a ***bat***. (baseball bat; flying rodent)
　b. She couldn't ***bear*** children. (stand; give birth to)
　c. He ***took her picture***. (removed her picture; photographed her)

As a rule an ambiguity is a surface ambiguity if the expression can be disambiguated by grouping the words appropriately. For example, (a) can be grouped as in (b) and (c) below:

③ a. He visited a little girls' school.
　b. He visited a (little girls') school.
　c. He visited a little (girls' school).

Finally, we will consider an ambiguity to be an underlying ambiguity if it cannot be disambiguated lexically or by surface grouping. Notice that in none of the following are the words relevantly ambiguous:

④ a. The chicken is ready to eat. (to feed; to be eaten)
　b. The whole band didn't show up for the concert. (some did not; none did)
　c. She knows a richer man than Rockefeller. (than Rockefeller is; than Rockefeller knows)

Still another meaning property of expressions is redundancy:

⑤ a. female sister
　b. illegal murder
　c. She killed him dead.

A final meaning property of expressions is anomaly. An expression is anomalous when there is an incompatibility of meaning between constituent expressions:

⑥ a. strawberry truth
　b. colorless green idea
　c. dream diagonally

Of course, it is almost always possible to impose a meaning on such expressions, in part because they are syntactically well-formed. Thus, "to dream diagonally" might be taken to mean "to lie diagonally in a bed while dreaming", but this is not what expression ⑥c means in English.

Not only do expressions have meaning properties like those just surveyed, they also bear various meaning relations to one another. One central meaning relation is synonymy or sameness (in at least one sense) of meaning:

⑦ a. ***Automobile*** is synonymous with ***car***.

　b. ***Sister*** is synonymous with ***female sibling***.

　c. ***Intentionally kill oneself*** is synonymous with ***commit suicide***.

Notice that synonymy is a symmetric relation: if one expression is synonymous with a second expression, then the second is synonymous with the first. However, not all semantic relations are symmetrical.

Another meaning relation is meaning inclusion:

⑧ a. The meaning of ***sister*** includes the meaning of ***female***.

　b. The meaning of ***to chase*** includes the meaning of ***move***.

　c. The meaning of ***is rectangular*** includes the meaning of ***has sides***.

This meaning relation is nonsymmetrical in that, for instance, the meaning of "female" does not include the meaning of "sister".

Even if two expressions are not synonymous and one does not include the other, they still may be related in that they overlap, or share some aspect of meaning:

⑨ a. ***Father***, ***uncle***, ***bull***, and ***stallion*** all express the property "male".

　b. To ***say***, ***speak***, ***whisper***, ***yell***, ***shout***, and ***scream*** all express the property "vocalization".

　c. ***Fortunately***, ***luckily***, ***happily***, and ***fortuitously*** all express the property "good for" something or someone.

This meaning relation is symmetric in that if one expression shares or overlaps in meaning with a second expression, then the second shares or overlaps in meaning with the first.

Finally, expressions can be antonymous, that is, they can share an aspect of meaning but be opposite or incompatible in some other aspect of meaning:

⑩ a. ***Red***, ***blue***, ***green***, ***yellow***, and so on, share the notion "color" but differ in shade (hue).

　b. ***Small***, ***medium-sized***, and ***large*** share the notion "size" but differ in degree.

　c. ***Freezing***, ***cold***, ***cool***, ***tepid***, ***warm***, and ***hot*** share the notion "temperature" but differ in degree.

This completes our initial survey of meaning properties and relations that have been proposed as being within the domain of a semantic theory of natural language. Not all practicing semanticists agree that every one of these properties and relations must be explained, or explained away. There is no doubt, however, that they form the core of a tradition in semantics that has been emphasized in transformational analyses of language.

(Adapted from Adrian Akmajian et al., *Linguistics: An Introduction to Language and Communication*, pp. 232-234)

Food for Thought

(1) How do social conditions bear on the study of meaning?
(2) Can componential analysis be applied to the study of semantic relations?
(3) What else do you think a semantic theory needs to explain?

# Unit 7

## The Meaning of English (II)

* 7.1  Semantic extension
* 7.2  Sentence semantics
* 7.3  Semantic roles

> *Whenever we use the word "dog" to refer to two different animals, or describe two different color sensations by the same word, e.g. "red", we are undertaking acts of categorization. Although different, the two entities are regarded in each case as the same.*
>
> —John Taylor

## Pre-Class Reading

### 7.1 Semantic extension

It is quite noticeable that a high percentage of English words are polysemous. Hypothetically, a polysemous word today might not have acquired all its multiple meanings at birth. Rather, it might have developed new usages and meanings as it was put to use in new contexts. Several processes are likely. One might depend on metaphorical reasoning so that a word like "foot" obtains a symbolic meaning. Or, one turns to metonymic reasoning so that a container term may be used for what it contains (e.g. "He took to <u>the bottle</u>"), a term for the material can be used for the thing from which it is made (e.g. "<u>Silk</u> suits you"), a term for the part can stand for the whole (e.g. "We need a few more hands"), an expression for a representative entity can stand for what is represented (e.g. "Washington is to veto the proposal", "He is going to meet his Waterloo"), or an expression for a unique or conspicuous feature or an act in a temporary context can be taken to refer to someone who has the feature or does the act (e.g. "The cucumber wants another cup of coffee", "The cheeseburger didn't order onions"). The last case may not result in a fixed new meaning.

We will discuss the details of the cognitive processes involved in **semantic extension** of words in Unit 12.

## 7.2 Sentence semantics

Knowing the meaning of a sentence is not so much like knowing the meaning of a word, although the sentence is made up of individual words. Often, to know the meaning of a sentence or, to be more exact, a declarative sentence, is to know what the world would have to be like for the **statement** expressed by the sentence to be true. In other words, if one knows the **truth conditions** for a given statement or **proposition**, one also knows the meaning of the sentence that conveys the expression. Its **truth value**, i.e. whether it is true or false, depends on whether the conditions are met. For instance,

① a. George Washington was the first president of the United States.
   b. It is raining outside.

①a is true provided that the stated message accords with the history of the country. In fact, it does, and therefore it makes a true statement. By getting to know the truth conditions and checking the truth value, we understand the meaning of the sentence.

①b is more complex. Our answer to whether the statement in the sentence is true depends on which window/door the speaker is looking through and when the sentence is uttered. It may be raining outside in one area but not in another. Thus, the truth or falsity of a statement as in ①b presupposes some dynamic state of affairs in the world. It may be, therefore, that we should think of each window/door as relating to a "possible situation" or a "**possible world**", in which a particular state of affairs holds. For further illustration, look at ②:

② There will be a lecture tomorrow.

Once we know the truth conditions of this sentence, we know its meaning. What are the truth conditions, then? Surely, we need to know which day "tomorrow" refers to.

Unless there is a lecture on the day, the statement is false. Since any day after today can be "tomorrow", there may be an infinite number of situations in which the statement may hold true.

## 7.3 Semantic roles

The study of sentence meaning can be undertaken from a different perspective. Specifically, we can examine how it is communicated by checking the roles its elements serve alone and together. These roles are technically termed as "semantic roles", "thematic roles" or "cases" by different scholars. The following table provides the method of analysis made possible by Victoria Fromkin et al:

| Roles | Definitions | Examples |
|---|---|---|
| Agent | The (animate) one who performs an action | Sam opened the door. The door was opened by Sam. |
| Theme | The one or thing that undergoes an action | Sam found the dog. |
| Instrument | The means by which an action is performed | Sam opened the door with a key. The key opened the door. |
| Location | The place where an action happens | The book is put on the table. |
| Source | The place from which an action originates | Sam left Beijing for Nanjing. |
| Goal | The place to which an action is directed | Sam left Beijing for Nanjing. |
| Causative | A natural force that causes a change | The flood killed 25. |
| Experiencer | One who perceives something | Sam was sad. |
| Possessor | One who has something | Sam's uncle is a teacher. |

(Based on Victoria Fromkin et al., *An Introduction to Language*, pp. 192-193)

### Check your understanding

**State whether each of the following statements is True or False.**
(1) Different languages represent the world in completely different ways.
(2) Metaphoric reasoning explains much of the extension of word meanings.
(3) Every sentence has its truth conditions.
(4) "Theme" as a semantic role refers to the topic the sentence is about.

Unit 7   The Meaning of English (Ⅱ)    99

## In-Class Activities

1. Sometimes it is very difficult to draw the demarcation line between one category and another. In other words, the boundary between the two is fuzzy. For instance, one can hardly say one thing is "heavy" and another is "light". There is a continuum of gradual transition. Look at the following picture:

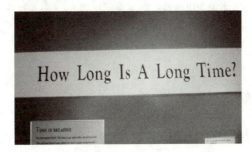

(1) What do you think gives rise to the semantic fuzziness of language?
(2) Can you cite more examples of fuzzy expressions?
(3) What advantages and disadvantages may the fuzzy property of language have as a tool of communication?

2. Different languages dissect the world in both similar and different ways. For example, English-speaking people and Chinese-speaking people are alike as regards how to address many kinds of daily furniture, resulting in sets of exact equivalents for translation. They, however, also differ in other dimensions. For example, they use different systems of terms of address for people, largely because they have their different social background. Similarly, the word "river" in English includes both "江" and "河" in Chinese, whereas "山" in Chinese covers both "mountain" and "hill" in English.

(1) Are you sometimes troubled by the need to choose between "high" and "tall" or "mountain" and "hill"?
(2) Chinese students sometimes confuse "a paper", "an article", "a

thesis" and "a dissertation". Sometimes they confuse "a journal" with "a magazine". Can you explain why?

3. The subject of a sentence is not always interpreted as the "doer" of some action, nor is the object of a main verb always interpreted as the "recipient" of some action. For example, in the sentence "John received a book", the subject is a recipient. Now look at the following sentences:

A. **The garden** is swarming with bees.
B. They loaded **hay** onto the truck.
C. They loaded **the truck** with hay.
D. John gave **Jane** the book.
E. **The dog** died.
F. **Noon** found us waiting at the railroad station.

**ask**

(1) What are the logical roles or meanings of the italicized subject or object?
(2) What effects does the use of different kinds of subjects produce?

4. A sentence may be semantically ill-formed in various ways. For instance, "She is a female student" contains redundant information; "This orphan has no father" is also semantically repetitious; "This program is for the music lovers who dislike music", "My brother is an only child", and "This orphan has a father" all involve contradiction. However, "Boys will be boys" and "NBA is NBA", apparently tautological, are heard in real-life communication.

**ask**

(1) What do the two tautological sentences mean in normal cases?
(2) Can you come up with similar uses of Chinese?

5. One way to identify the semantic structure of sentences is to start with the verb as the central element and define the semantic roles required by that verb. For example, a verb like "kill" requires an agent and a theme, as in "The cat killed the mouse". We can represent this observation as:

KILL [AGENT _____ THEME]

As another example, we can represent the verb "give" in "Mary gave the book to George" as:

GIVE [AGENT _____ THEME, GOAL]

(1) How would you define the set of semantic roles for the following verbs in terms of the pattern just shown?

    cook   break   die   put   happen   offer

(2) What are the Chinese equivalents of these verbs? Do they all share the same semantic structures of the English verbs? If not, give one or two examples to illustrate the differences.

(3) Does it help, in this exercise, to make a distinction between obligatory roles (i.e. you must have these or the sentence will not be grammatical) and optional roles (these are often present, but their absence doesn't make the sentences ungrammatical)?

1. Fuzzy language in weather reports
2. Terms of address in English and Chinese
3. Semantic role analysis of NBA reports

Find in the library or online some information about the following themes:

(1) linguistic fuzziness
(2) hedge
(3) vagueness
(4) Frank Palmer

(5) John Lyons

## Task 2　Term Definition

Study the following definitions and then discuss how they combine to help you understand the terms.

**proposition**: In case grammar, the verb and related nouns in a sentence. [Ronald Wardhaugh]

**proposition**: what is talked about in an utterance; that part of the speech act which has to do with reference [Henry Widdowson]

**truth condition**: the facts that would have to obtain in reality to make a sentence true or false [John Saeed]

**truth value**: a sentence's being true or false [John Saeed]

**modality**: a cover term for devices which allow speakers to express varying degrees of commitment to, or belief in, a proposition [John Saeed]

**evidentiality**: a semantic category which allows a speaker to communicate her attitude to the source of her information [John Saeed]

**tautology**: a meaningless repetition [Ronald Wardhaugh]

**tautology**: an apparently meaningless expression in which one word is defined as itself, e.g. "Business is business" [George Yule]

## Task 3　Study Questions

1. Do Chinese and English dissect the spectrum of color in the same way?

2. How do we differentiate fuzziness from vagueness, generality and approximation?

3. Discuss the following news report in terms of semantic roles.

### Missing Malaysia Airlines Flight

Malaysia Airlines Flight MH370 disappeared on 8 March 2014 carrying 227 passengers and 12 crew. The Boeing 777 had left Kuala Lumpur at 00:41 for Beijing Airport but lost contact with air traffic controllers at around 01:22 am as it crossed the South China Sea. In July 2014 a Malaysia Airlines plane crashed in Ukraine, near the Russian border.

4. Discuss how the meaning of "hot" gets extended in each of the following cases.

(1) hot bowl, said of a surface (sense of touch)

(2) hot food (sense of taste)

(3) hot temper
(4) hot war
(5) hot on the trail of something
(6) hot topic
(7) hot wire
(8) hot news
(9) hot car (stolen)
(10) hot idea (really good idea)

5. Identify the semantic roles of all the noun phrases in this sentence:
   With his new golf club, Fred whacked the ball from the woods to the grassy area near the river and he felt good.

### Task 4  Mini-Project

Randomly select a Chinese newspaper (e. g. *The Yangtse Evening*) and English newspaper (e. g. *The New York Times*) for three consecutive days. Study the headlines carefully. Spot and calculate the metaphors and metonyms used. Check whether there are quantitative differences between English and Chinese newspapers in terms of the use of the rhetorical devices and whether there are differences across different columns.

Reading 1

## Case Grammar

Charles Fillmore argues in his article, "The Case for Case", that semantic features and syntactic features may be combined; he uses the term "case" to identify the underlying syntactic-semantic relationships. Fillmore hypothesizes that "The case notions comprise a set of universal, presumably innate concepts which identify certain types of judgments human beings are capable of making about the events that are going on around them, judgments about such matters as who did it, who it happened to, and what got changed".

Case relationships in some older stages of Indo-European (the parent language of English) such as Indo-European itself, Sanskrit, Greek, and Latin were signaled by suffixes (inflections) placed on nouns. What was signaled by placing suffixes on nouns in the above languages is signaled by word order and prepositions in English. The case relationships for English, and presumably for other languages as well, include:

| Name of case | Definition | Example (case is italicized) |
| --- | --- | --- |
| Agent (A) | Instigator of action. Must be +animate. | *Sam* opened the door. The door was opened by *Sam*. |
| Instrumental (I) | The animate force involved in the event as stated or named by the verb. | *The key* opened the door. Sam opened the door with a *key*. |
| Dative (D) | Indicates animate being affected by events named by the verb. | Sam sees *Bill*. Sam gave the book to *Bill*. |
| Factive (F) | The object or being resulting from the state or action indicated by the verb. | Sam built a *chair*. God created the *universe*. |
| Locative (L) | Location as specified by the verb. | The book is on the *chair*. *San Antonio* is warm. Sam ran to the *store*. |
| Objective (O) | The most neutral semantic case. The case of anything represented by a noun whose role in the action or state identified by the verb depends on the meaning of the verb itself. | Sam sees *Mary*. Sam opened the *door*. |

Fillmore uses the cases to classify verbs. The verb "open" may appear with objective, instrumental, and agent cases. "Open" would appear in Fillmore's theory within a "case frame".

[open O (I) (A)]

Parentheses point to the fact that the (I) and (A) do not have to be specified in a sentence containing "open". The objective case, with no parentheses, has to appear, however. This is a constraint on the use of "open". Let us examine the following sentences containing "open" as the verb.

**The door opened. [open O]**

Here we have the objective case occurring in the first position in the sentence. We "know" that "someone" or "something" had to open the door, and we "know" this without having agent specified.

**John opened the door. [open O (A)]**

We have the obligatory O, which appeared in the first position in the previous sentence, appearing here after the verb, with the agent "John" (the "someone" [A] appearing in the first position).

**The key opened the door. [open O (I)]**

In this sentence, the objective case appears along with the instrumental (I), with the (I) occurring in the first position.

**John opened the door with the key. [open O (A) (I)]**

All three case relationships are explicit.

We can see from these examples that syntax and semantics are closely related. Syntax can express semantic relationships and semantic relationships can be expressed by positions in sentence or by a preposition. Fillmore believes that the above cases [A, O, D, I, L, F] are the absolute minimum for any language, but he also says that there may be other case relationships. Case relationships, to sum up, express the experience of the speaker as to:

(1) who did what,

(2) who it happened to, and

(3) what got changed.

(Adapted from Curtis Hayes et al, *The ABC's of Languages and Linguistics: A Practical Primer to Language Science*, pp. 105-106)

 Food for Thought

(1) Can you find more cases aside from the ones mentioned in the passage?

(2) Are there any case markers in Chinese?

(3) Do you think it surprising that syntax and semantics are intrinsically related?

 Reading 2

## Truth Conditions

The most successful theory of sentence meaning relies on the notion of truth. Sentences are about the world. Declarative sentences describe situations in the world correctly or incorrectly, that is, they can be true or false. Truth means correspondence with facts, correct descriptions of states and events in the world. There are also other definitions of truth but in the theory described here we accept the traditional correspondence theory of truth. "True" and "false", when predicated of sentences (or propositions expressed by them), are called the truth values of the *sentence* (or proposition). This notion of truth is used in semantics in the following way. The meaning of the sentence is revealed in the relation between the sentence and the world. We know the meaning of the sentence when we know what the world would have to be like for this sentence to be true. These facts that would have to be the case for the sentence to be true are the truth conditions of the sentence.

If I utter ①, the conditions for making this sentence true would be that there is one person who is the Pope and that this person lives in the Vatican.

① The Pope lives in the Vatican.

So, to know the meaning of the sentence is to know under what conditions this sentence would be true. A Polish logician, Alfred Tarski (1933, 1944), proposed a theory of meaning that relies on a matching procedure between sentences and sets of conditions. This procedure can be briefly stated as in ②, where *p* is a set of conditions applicable to all sentences of the language and "iff" stands for "if and only if".

② S is true iff *p*

The best-known formulation of the idea is the one in ③, where "…" contains a "name" of the sentence, or, in other words, an uninterpreted string.

③ "Snow is white" is true iff snow is white.

There has to be a set of rules that pairs each sentence with a set of conditions. Otherwise, we could not account for the infinite number of sentences allowed by languages.

In the previous chapters we looked at the denotational approaches to word meaning, according to which meaning is reference, and at representational approaches to word meaning, according to which meaning is given by mental models. Truth-conditional semantics subscribes to the first option: meaning is reference, correspondence with the facts in the world. Naturally, this is only an idealization; there are many sentences for which the denotational approach will not work and we shall have to resort to mental representations. In this respect, the semantic theory described here allows for a considerable degree of eclecticism; if the simple route to the referent is not available, mental representations are invoked. Secondly, the theory is an idealization for the following reason. The truth conditions of the sentence may prove rather useless when speaker meaning differs from sentence meaning. The aim of semantic theory is to identify sentence meaning to the extent to which it is relevant for the recognition of "what is said by the speaker", that is utterance meaning. Thirdly, some sentences may not be sufficiently informative to allow for the identification of their truth conditions and we have to resort to contextual clues, including the speakers' intentions, after all. So, semantics is eclectic in that it allows for pragmatic information, including assumptions about the speaker's intentions, to enter into the truth-conditional analysis of the sentence. In other words, the unit of analysis is the proposition understood "as what is said" by the speaker rather than as semantic mirror image of the sentence where the latter is the unit of syntax. As a consequence, sentences can be true or false, but also "what is said" can be true or false. They inherit truth conditions from propositions where the latter are conceptual representations, the proper bearers of meaning.

(Kasia Jaszczolt, *Semantics and Pragmatics: Meaning in Language and Discourse*, pp. 53-54)

 Food for Thought

(1) What are the denotational approaches and representational approaches to word meaning respectively?
(2) What problems may truth-conditional semantics suffer?

# Unit 8

# The Use of English (Ⅰ)

*8.1 Study of English in context
*8.2 Anchoring the use of English in context
*8.3 Using English as a speech act
*8.4 Using English as a social act
*8.5 Presuppositions in the use of English

> *Language is at the center of human life. It is one of the most important ways of expressing our love or our hatred for people; it is a source of artistic satisfaction or simple pleasure.*
> —Vivian Cook

**Pre-Class Reading**

## 8.1 Study of English in context

In previous units, we have been dealing with aspects of English at various linguistic levels. We found that the language, perhaps like any other one, is creative in that it allows its users to produce and understand novel utterances. Part of the explanation is that it has **recursive syntax**, so words, phrases, and even sentences can be combined in accordance with all sorts of rules. Another part of the explanation, though not explored in any detail, is the possibility of **semantic compositionality**, which states that the meaning of complex expressions is determined by their constituents. But recursive syntax and **compositional semantics** alone do not guarantee the appropriateness of use, nor do they explain how people make sense of some seemingly difficult utterances. For instance, when hearing the following sentences,

① a. Your wallet or your life.
   b. Move and I'll shoot.

one would realize that the speaker of ①a is threatening the hearer and demanding that he hand over his wallet while the speaker of ①b is warning the hearer not to move. How can this happen? One explanation is that language use, like language structuring, is also rule-governed.

The study of the use of English in **context** falls under the category of **pragmatics**. It is concerned with both the production and comprehension of language for communicative purposes. There are two ends under focus: a linguistic end (i.e. how linguistic forms are used to perform certain social functions) and a social end (i.e. how social cultural factors bear on the use of language). A relatively systematic study will attempt to shed light on how English is put to actual use along some principled lines, and also show what factors, human and non-human, contribute to the use of English, what principles govern the process of English production and comprehension, how English communication converges and diverges from that in other languages and cultures, and what strategies one may have available in order to achieve desired communicative effects.

## 8.2 Anchoring the use of English in context

The notion of context is central to the study of English or any language in use. Despite its significance, no consensus has been reached regarding its definition. A narrow—and also very traditional—one, is that of **co-text**, that is, the preceding and following linguistic items for a given word or sentence. A broader definition covers not only the co-text but also the **situational context**, concerning when and where the communication takes place and also the number and identity of the participants involved. A still more inclusive definition incorporates the **background knowledge** and assumptions of the communicators as well as social-cultural customs and conventions. An extreme version, perhaps too broad to be feasible, involves everything other than the utterance in question.

Normally, when we talk, we assume a variety of centers in the communicative context:

—the central person is the current speaker;
—the central time is the time at which the speaker produces the utterance (though

"now" is often omitted);

—the central place is the speaker's location at the utterance time (though "here" is often omitted);

—the discourse center is the point which the speaker is currently at in the production of his utterance;

—the social center is the speaker's social status and rank, to which the status or rank of addressees or referents is relative.

**Deictic** or **indexical expressions** are linguistic items used to anchor these specific points in the communicative event. Without knowing the points one would fail to understand utterances like "I'll bring this to your father here tomorrow".

In line with the five **deictic centers**, five categories of deictic expressions are classified, namely **person deixis** (like "I"), **time deixis** (like "tomorrow"), **place deixis** (like "here"), **discourse deixis** (like "this chapter"), and **social deixis** (like "您" in Chinese).

Some motion verbs in English, such as "come" and "go", have built-in deictic components. Look at the following utterances:

② He is coming.
③ When I'm in the office, you can come to see me.
④ I came over several times to visit you, but you were never there.

Clearly, "come" assumes the speaker as the deictic center.

Compared with non-deictic equivalents, deictic expressions are generally characterized by their **pre-emtive usage**. Suppose it is 26 July, Monday, today. When we want to mention July 27, Tuesday, we normally will say "tomorrow" instead of "on July 27" or "on Tuesday".

## 8.3 Using English as a speech act

In English, we may hear people say "Actions speak louder than words" and "Easier said than done". However, there seems to be no clear-cut boundary between speaking and acting. Rather, saying is sometimes acting. For example, when we congratulate someone by saying "Congratulations!" it means as much as giving him or her a pat on the back or the thumbs up sign. Apparently, some utterances are **constative**, i.e. descriptions of facts or states of affairs (like "China has the biggest population in the world"), whereas some others are **performative**, i.e. the saying itself accomplishing a certain action (like "I promise I'll come here tomorrow on time"). A performative utterance is characterized by the use of first person subject, simple present tense, indicative mood, active voice and a performative verb (like "promise" and "apologize"), and can be tested by the insertion of "hereby". Yet, later research shows that all utterances in communication are direct or indirect performances of certain acts, whether or not they contain **performative verbs**. In effect, the presence of a performative verb does not necessarily make the utterance itself performative, as in "She thanks you".

To portray the actions performed via utterances, we use the term "**speech acts**", which are considered to be the basic or minimal units of linguistic communication.

A speech act itself can be performing three component acts at the same time: **locutionary act** (the act of verbally saying something), **illocutionary act** (the intended act behind saying something) and **perlocutionary act** (the intended effect/happening of an illocutionary act). For example, when Jane says to John, "I'm hungry" and John, hearing that, leaves and comes back with some food for Jane, the locutionary act Jane performed is the saying of the English sentence; the illocutionary act Jane performed is an implicit request for John to bring some food to her; and the perlocutionary act performed via the uttering of the sentence is the effect or outcome brought about, i.e. John gets some food for Jane. Illocutionary acts that utterances are intended to perform, or speech acts in a loose sense, are the focus of pragmatic study. They are categorized into five major types: **representatives** or **assertives** (covering such acts as stating, asserting, explaining, predicting, and classifying), **directives** (covering such acts as ordering, commanding, requesting, instructing, and pleading), **commisives** (covering such acts as promising, vowing, pledging, offering, and betting), **expressives** (covering such acts as thanking, apologizing, congratulating, and condoling), and **declarations** (covering such acts as appointing, naming, christening, vetoing, dismissing, and declaring).

In daily life, people often perform one act via performing another linguistically as well as non-linguistically. This results in what we call **indirect speech acts**. For instance, if a robber says to his victim "I advise you to give me all in your pocket", he is not really advising, but threatening. Therefore, an utterance with a performative verb may not be executing the type of act suggested by the verb.

A speech act has to satisfy a few conditions in order to count as an appropriate or felicitous one. Such conditions are thus termed **felicity conditions** or **appropriateness conditions**. These conditions include some general conditions. For instance, it is necessary that interlocutors understand the language being used and they are not play-acting or being nonsensical. There are specific conditions, as listed below:

- propositional content condition
- preparatory condition
- sincerity condition
- essential condition

Take the utterance "I promise to give you an A⁺ if you work hard" for example. The felicity conditions are analyzed as follows:

a. I have said something about a future act of my giving you an A⁺. [propositional content condition]

b. You'd prefer getting an A⁺ to not getting an A⁺. I wouldn't have given you an A⁺ in the normal course of events unless you would work hard. There will be another test or exam. [preparatory condition]

c. I actually intend to fulfill my promise to give you an A⁺. [sincerity condition]

d. We both understand that my saying that I'll give you an A⁺ is an obligation on my part to do so, provided you work hard. [essential condition]

## 8.4 Using English as a social act

Using English to perform speech acts is constrained by social factors. People of superior status are entitled to issue commands and orders. Holders of certain rights can be direct in getting people under corresponding obligations to act in their interests. A telling example is that a passenger can say to the bus driver "Put me down at the next stop" but has to convey more politeness if he or she intends to depart at a non-stop point, if possible.

Moreover, people of different social milieus may enact the same thing differently. For instance, naming a princess in a royal family may involve a lot of ceremonies and formality whereas naming a child in a needy family can be very simple. Similarly, taking an oath in court is much more formal than swearing in daily encounters.

## 8.5 Presuppositions in the use of English

Communication often hinges on some information or beliefs assumably shared by the interlocutors. Thus, when a speaker utters "Jane had another date with John" he **presupposes** the assumption or fact that Jane has had (at least) one date with John before. Even if we negate the original sentence, i.e. "Jane did not have another date with John", the same **presupposition** remains intact.

Presupposition has been defined in numerous ways. One definition treats it as a speaker's assumptions (or beliefs) about the speech context. Another more restrictive notion says that the (pragmatic) presupposition of a sentence is the set of conditions that have to be satisfied in order for the intended speech act to be appropriate in the circumstances, or to be felicitous. A final notion about (pragmatic) presupposition is that of shared background information. In essence, presupposition is a pragmatic notion, because it is the speaker who presupposes by means of an utterance, rather than the sentence or the utterance itself. It differs from the notion of entailment, which is based on the relation of semantic inclusion, as shown by "John has a boy" entailing "John has a child".

We often depend on some lexical or syntactic items to derive what is presupposed by the speaker or writer. The linguistic items are called **presupposition triggers**. A lot of presupposition triggers in English are verbs of various types. The first type are called **factive verbs**, those whose objects or objective clauses reflect what has really happened, e.g. "regret", "realize", and "know". The second type are **implicative verbs**, such as "manage", "forget", "happen", and "avoid". The third type are **change of state verbs**, including "stop", "finish", "begin", "start", "carry on", "continue", "cease", "leave", "arrive", "enter", "come", "go", "turn", and "transform". The last major type are **verbs of judging**, conveying the agent's evaluation of what is concerned, e.g. "accuse", "charge", "criticize", and "repudiate". Besides the verbs, we may have other types of triggers such as **definite descriptions** (like "Jack's girlfriend" in "Jack's girlfriend is a lawyer"), and **iterative adverbs or verbs** (like "again", "rewrite").

One of the peculiar things about presuppositions is that they are **defeasible** or **cancellable**: that is, they are liable to evaporate in certain contexts, either immediate linguistic context or the less immediate discourse context, or in circumstances where there are contrary assumptions. Look at the following examples:

⑤ a. John managed to pass his exams.
   b. John didn't manage to pass his exams.
   c. John didn't manage to pass his exam; in fact he didn't even try.
   d. John didn't manage to pass his exams, if indeed he ever tried.

The presupposed information that John tried to pass his exams in ⑤c and ⑤d, but not in ⑤a and ⑤b, is canceled. Also compare:

   e. John married Jane before he finished his new book.

>> John finished his new book.

f. John died before he finished his new book.

? >> John finished his new book.

## Check your understanding

State whether each of the following statements is True or False.

(1) In pragmatics, context refers to the sentences preceding and following the current word or sentence.

(2) Not all sentences we produce are meant to do things.

(3) A perlocutionary act is performed by the hearer.

(4) "I", "now", "here", and "yesterday" are all deictic expressions.

(5) "John cooked Jane a cake" presupposes "John cooked something for Jane".

## In-Class Activities

**1.** Context plays a key role in the production and comprehension of an utterance or a whole text. Look at the pictures below.

ask—

(1) What is the intended meaning in each case?

(2) Where do you expect to find them?

(3) Do the non-linguistic illustrations help you understand the language used?

Unit 8　The Use of English (I) 　115

**2.** Deictic expressions are not just used in face-to-face interaction. They appear on many other occasions. Now, look at the following utterances, all of which have deictic elements in them.

A. **Notice on office door**: Back in one hour.
B. **Telephone answering machine**: I'm not here now.
C. **Watching a horse race**: Oh, no, I'm in last place.
D. **On a map/directory**: YOU ARE HERE.
E. **In a car that won't start**: Maybe I'm out of gas.

**ask—**

(1) How do you interpret the expressions above?
(2) Are there any problems with understanding the utterances?
(3) How can the follow statements be exploited to cheat people?
　　1) 本饮料自购买之日起3个月内可饮用。
　　2) 大甩卖最后3天。

**3.** Person deictic expressions are often taken advantage of in interpersonal communication. For example, the English pronoun "we" may be understood as inclusive-of-addresser, exclusive-of-addresser, inclusive-of-addressee, and exclusive-of-addressee, as in part grammaticalized in "Let us; will you?" and "Let's; shall we?"

**ask—**

(1) Can you give an example for each of the cases to demonstrate the varied usages of "we"?
(2) Does the Chinese "我们" share the deictic properties of "we"?
(3) Discuss the use of "me" in the following pictures.

4. Daily conversations abound in indirect speech. For example, when we perform a request, we might use the following:
   A. Could you give me the keys of the library?
   B. Would you give me the keys of the library?
   C. Do you mind giving me the keys of the library?
   D. The library is closed.

   **ask**

   (1) How are the expressions different in realizing the request?
   (2) Why are people indirect in communication? Meanwhile, take the following into consideration:
       Customer: Waiter! There's a fly in my soup.
       Waiter: Don't worry. There's no extra charge.
   (3) Are Chinese people equally indirect when performing requests? How about you?

5. Some utterances involve ellipsis of various kinds. Compare the following:
   A. Thank you.
   B. I see your point.
   C. He's dishonest.
   D. Will you go or not?

   **ask**

   (1) For (A), we can also say "I thank you". What would be the difference?
   (2) We can say "Sorry" in English as a way of apologizing but we don't say "Apologize" for the same purpose. What might be your explanation for this difference?
   (3) For (B), we can also say "I see your point now". What would be the difference? Also consider the use of "now" in the following pictures.

Unit 8  The Use of English (I)    117

(4) For (C), we can also say "I'm telling you that he is dishonest", and for (D) we might have said "I'm asking you if you will go or not". What would be the difference?

6. Presupposition is widely used in advertising language. Look at the following:

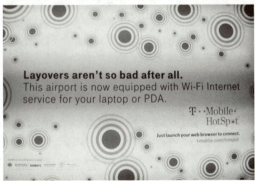

(1) What is the presupposed information in each of the ads?
(2) What is the linguistic device that makes the presupposition inferable? Presupposition is also extensively employed in newspaper headlines. The following are cited from *The New York Times*.

1) Proposal to Ban Same-Sex Marriage Renews Old Battles
2) New Scrutiny for Every Speck on the Shuttle
3) Federer Defends Turf for Fourth Wimbledon Title
4) Missile Tests Divide Seoul from Tokyo

(3) What is the presupposed information in each of the above headlines?

(4) What is the linguistic device that makes the presupposition inferable? Can you think of some other presupposition triggers?

(5) Presupposition may also be taken advantage of by judges at court. Here are some questions they might raise. What presupposition(s) might have been objected to in each case?
1) How did you know that the defendant had bought a knife?
2) How long have you been selling cocaine?
3) Did you see the murdered woman before she left the office?
4) How far was the car going when the driver ran the red light?
5) Why did you leave the scene of the crime?

## Presentation Topics

1. Complimenting in English
2. Presupposition triggers in English newspaper headlines
3. Social deixis in English

## Exercises

 **Task 1　Reference Search**

Find in the library or online some information about the following themes:
(1) context
(2) performative
(3) felicity conditions
(4) John Austin
(5) John Searle

Unit 8  The Use of English (I)

## Task 2  Term Definition

Study the following definitions and then discuss how they combine to help you understand the terms.

**deixis**: "pointing" via language, using a deictic expression, e. g. "this", "here" [George Yule]

**deixis**: The property of a restricted set of demonstratives such that their reference is determined in relation to the point of origin of the utterance in which they occur. Examples include I, here, and now. [Peter Grundy]

**indexical expressions**: A particular kind of referential expression which, in addition to the semantics of their "naming", their sense, include a reference to the particular context in which that sense is put to work. [Jacob Mey]

**indexical expressions**: expressions whose reference is a function of the context of their utterance [Georgia Green]

**presupposition**: a meaning taken as given which does not therefore need to be asserted; variously defined as "semantic presupposition" (non-defeasible, contributes to the truth-conditional-meaning of the sentence), "conventional implicature" (non-feasible, non-truth-conditional), and "pragmatic presupposition" (cancellable where inconsistent with speaker/hearer knowledge about the world [Peter Grundy]

**presupposition**: something that the speaker assumes to be the case [George Yule]

## Task 3  Study Questions

1. Do the following count as promises? If not, why?
   (1) I promise I'll fail you in the exam.
   (2) I promise that next Friday will be his birthday.
   (3) I promise that I saw him yesterday.
   (4) I promise that you'll help me out of trouble.
   (5) John promises that he'll help Jane.
   (6) I promised that I would help him.

2. What are the specific felicity conditions for thanking? Do the following count as thanking acts in the strict sense?

3. How are the deictic expressions in the following utterances projected for special effects?

   (1) (*Boss to clerk*) We complimented ourselves too soon, John.
   (2) (*Doctor to patient*) How are we feeling today?
   (3) (*Mum to Dad*) We're in a bad mood today.

   Can you add more examples of a similar kind either from English or Chinese?

4. All of the following expressions have deictic elements in them. What aspects of context have to be considered in order to interpret such expressions? Perhaps there are others of a similar type that you could add to this list.

   (1) **NBA slogan**: I love this game!
   (2) **McDonald's slogan**: I'm lovin' it.
   (3) **Advertisement for Nike sports shoes**: Just do it.
   (4) **Answering a telephone**: Oh, it's you.
   (5) **Pointing to an empty chair**: Where is she today?

5. Writers do not assume their readers have blank minds. Rather, they depend on the readers' background knowledge to develop their ideas and interact with them. One way of doing so is the use of presupposition. The following excerpt is the opening of Emily Brontë's *Wuthering Heights*. Read it carefully and detect the presupposed information as much as you can.

   I have just returned from a visit to my landlord—the solitary neighbor that I shall be troubled with. This is certainly a beautiful country! In all England, I do not believe that I could have fixed on a situation so completely removed from the stir of society. A perfect misanthropist's heaven; and Mr. Heathcliff and I are such a suitable pair to divide the desolation between us. A capital fellow! He little imagined how my heart warmed towards him when I beheld his black eyes withdraw so suspiciously under their brows, as I rode up, and when his fingers sheltered themselves, with a jealous resolution, still farther in his waistcoat, as I announced my name.

"Mr. Heathcliff!" I said.

A nod was the answer.

6. Discuss the following utterances in terms of locutionary act, illocutionary act, and perlocutionary act.

7. Compare the following utterances. How are they different, pragmatically speaking?

   (1) If I were you, I'd leave the room.
   (2) If you know what's good for you, you'll leave the room.
   (3) I'd better not see you in this room the next time I turn around.

## Task 4   Mini-Project

Collect some classroom data involving how foreign English teachers and Chinese English teachers ask students to respond in class. Study carefully how the two kinds of teachers get their students to give responses and compare how indirect their speech is respectively.

## Is Pragmatics part of a grammar?

Probably the most pervasive characteristic of human social interaction, so pervasive that we hardly find it remarkable, is that we talk. Sometimes we talk to particular persons, sometimes to anyone who will listen; and when we cannot find anyone to listen, we even talk to ourselves. Although human language fulfills a large variety of functions, from waking someone up in the morning with a cheery "Wake up!" to christening a ship with a solemn "I hereby christen this ship 'H.M.S. Britannia'", we will be focusing here on those uses of language that are instrumental for human communication. But, one might ask, why should a linguist be concerned with language use when describing a language? And what are these various uses of language, especially those central to communication?

One way of motivating the inclusion of pragmatic information in a grammar is by way of semantics ... a promising conception of meaning was one in which meaning is determined by use. If use does determine meaning, then the theory of language use will provide the foundations for semantics, so at least that part of pragmatics that concerns itself with meaning and reference will be a part of a grammar.

A second way to motivate the inclusion of pragmatic information in a grammar is by considering the linguistic competence of a fluent speaker. Would we want to say of speakers who did not know any of the kinds of information in ① that they spoke the English language fluently? We think not.

①  a. "Hello" is used to greet.
    b. "Goodbye" is used to bid farewell.
    c. The phrase "that desk" can be correctly used by a speaker to refer to some particular desk.
    d. The phrase "is a desk" can be correctly used to characterize any number of desks.
    e. "Pass the salt, please" is used to request some salt.
    f. "How old are you?" is used to ask for someone's age.

Unit 8　The Use of English (I) 　123

g. "It's raining" is used to state that it is raining.
h. "I promise I will be there" is used to promise.
...

From the above list we get a glimpse of the wide variety of possible uses of language, but before we survey these various uses, we must first distinguish between using language to do something and using language in doing something. It is certainly a very important fact about human beings that they use language in much of their thought. It is likely that people could not think some of the thoughts they think, especially abstract thoughts, if they did not have language at their disposal. Central as this fact may be to our cognitive life, it is not central to the pragmatic notion of language use, the use of language to do things. When we focus on what people use language to do, we focus on what a person is doing with words in particular situations; we focus on the intentions, purposes, beliefs, and wants that a speaker has in speaking—in performing speech acts.

(Adrian Akmajian et al., *Linguistics: An Introduction to Language and Communication*, pp. 267-268)

 Food for Thought

(1) How do pragmatic studies of conversation relate to conversation analysis dealt with in Unit 5?
(2) How would you define the notion of pragmatic competence?

## Pragmatic Development

Context is needed to determine the reference of pronouns. A sentence like "Amazingly, he loves her" is uninterpretable unless both the speaker and the hearer understand who the pronouns "he" and "her" refer to. If the sentence were preceded by "I saw John and Mary kissing in the park", then it would be clear to the listener who the pronouns refer to. Children are not always sensitive to the needs of their interlocutors and they may fail to establish the referents for pronouns. It is not unusual for a three- or four-year-old (or even older children) to use pronouns "out of the blue", like the child who cries to his mother "he hit me" when Mom has no idea who did the deed.

The speaker and the listener form part of the context of an utterance. The meaning of "I" and "you" depends on who is talking and who is listening, and this changes from situation to situation. Younger children (around age two) have difficulty with the "shifting reference" of these pronouns. A typical error that children make at this age is to refer to themselves and "you", for example, saying "You want to take a walk" when he means "I want to take a walk".

Children also show a lack of pragmatic awareness by the way they sometimes use articles. Like pronouns, the interpretation of articles depends on context. The definite article "the" as in "the boy" can be used felicitously only when it is clear to the speaker and the hearer which boy is being discussed. In a discourse the indefinite article (a/an) must be used for the first mention of a new referent; the definite article (or pronoun) may be used in subsequent mentions, as illustrated below:

A boy walked into the class.
He was in the wrong room.
The teacher directed the boy to the right classroom.

Children do not always respect the pragmatic rules for articles. In experimental studies, three-year-olds are just as likely to use the definite article as the indefinite article for introducing a new referent. In other words, the child tends to assume that his listener knows who he is talking about without having established this in a linguistically appropriate way.

It may take a child several months or years to master those aspects of pragmatics that involve establishing the reference for function morphemes such as determiners and pronouns. Other aspects of pragmatics are acquired very early. Children in the holophrastic stage use their one-word utterances with different illocutionary force. The utterance "up" spoken by J.P. at sixteen months might be a simple statement such as "The teddy is up on the shelf", or a request "Pick me up".

(Adapted from Victoria Fromkin et al., *An Introduction to Language*, pp. 367-368)

 **Food for Thought**

(1) How do children gradually develop the notion of context?
(2) Do some adults suffer a lack of adequate pragmatic awareness? Justify your answer with evidence, if any.

# Unit 9

# The Use of English (II)

* 9.1  Cooperation in using English
* 9.2  Politeness in using English
* 9.3  Face considerations in using English
* 9.4  Using English as a strategic act
* 9.5  Using English as a cultural act

> *Language is the cement of society, allowing people to live, work, and play together, to tell the truth but also to tell a lie, or lies.*
>
> —Ronald Wardhaugh

## Pre-Class Reading

## 9.1 Cooperation in using English

English conversation is not a mess. People take turns talking. A less obvious, yet equally ubiquitous, pattern is that people cooperate with each other, in terms of the quality, quantity, relevance, and manner of their conversational contribution. These dimensions form the basis of a general principle named the **Cooperative Principle**: Make your conversational contribution as required, at the stage where it occurs, by the accepted purpose or direction of the talk exchange in which you are engaged (Grice, 1989).

The first maxim, **maxim of quality**, requires the speaker to be truthful: Do not say what you believe to be false; do not say that for which you lack adequate evidence. For example,

① "Oh, have you hurt yourself?"

To say this to someone who is clearly badly injured is to flout the maxim of quality. The second maxim, **maxim of quantity**, requires the speaker to be informative: Make your contribution as informative as required (for the current purposes of the exchange); do not make your contribution more informative than is required. For example,

② Jane: Where were you last night?
John: I was out.

Clearly, John is being underinformative since he must know his specific whereabouts last night.

The third maxim, **maxim of relation**, requires the speaker to be relevant: Make sure that whatever you say is relevant to the conversation at hand. For example,

③ John: Let's play tennis.
Jane: I have a stomachache.

Jane's response obviously has no connection with John's request. The lack of relevance is at the literal level, of course, because at an interactional level, Jane does give John a sufficient reply.

The final maxim, **maxim of manner**, requires the speaker to be clear and lucid: Avoid obscurity of expression; avoid ambiguity; be brief, and be orderly. For example,

④ a. Open the door.
b. Walk up to the door, put the key into the lock, turn the key clockwise twice and push.

Compared with ④a, ④b is surely a lengthy, unusual way of giving the command, used only in some special contexts.

There are various ways in which a participant in a talk exchange may not fulfill a maxim:

△ by violation (which is likely to mislead), e.g. to tell lies;
△ by opting out (saying, for example, "I don't want to talk about it");
△ by fulfilling one at the expense of another owing to a conflict of maxims (you cannot be as informative as is required if you do not have enough evidence); for example,

⑤ A: Where does Tom live?
B: Somewhere in the suburbs of the city.

△ by blatantly flouting a maxim; for example,
⑥ A: Let's get the kids something.
B: Okay, but I veto I-C-E-C-R-E-A-M.

In the last two cases, the speaker generally communicates a **conversational implicature** or implied meaning. The term "**implicature**", not found in any general dictionary, is derived from the verb "to imply" (from the Latin verb *plicare* "to fold") meaning "to fold something into something else"; hence, that which is implied is "folded in", and has to be "unfolded" in order to be understood. A conversational implicature is, therefore, something that is implied or left implicit in a conversation or beyond. Implicature is different from the familiar term "**implication**" because the latter technically defines a logical relationship between two propositions: If the two propositions are symbolized as $p$ and $q$, then the logical implication is the relation "if $p$, then $q$", or: $p \rightarrow q$. For instance, if all men are mortal, then an individual person is mortal. However, we cannot run such an operation in the case of a conversational implicature. Take ③ for example. B's words may not necessarily mean Jane will not play tennis with John, even if this is the conversational implicature of her utterance in the context.

According to Paul Grice, conversational implicatures are of two types: **generalized conversational implicatures**, which need no special contextual information to make the inference; **particularized conversational implicatures**, which require the hearer(s) to have special knowledge of context in order to derive them. Compare the following:

⑦ a. John: Let's go out drinking tonight.
   Jane: My grandmother is here.
   b. Jane likes some of the pictures.

In the former case, Jane implies that she is not going out drinking today, which is a particularized conversational implicature because we need to consider the background information Jane provided to derive it. In the latter case, the speaker conveys the implicature that "Jane does not like all of the pictures", which is a generalized conversational implicature because no specific background information is necessary for its inference.

In everyday talk, we often convey propositions that are not explicit in our utterances but are merely implied by them. Sometimes we are able to draw such inferences only by referring what has been explicitly said to some conversational principle. This explains why pragmatics is interested in the study of (conversational) implicature. Basically we seem to be dealing here with a regularity that cannot be captured in any straightforward syntactic or semantic analysis, but has to be accounted for in other ways.

## 9.2 Politeness in using English

Sometimes people intentionally opt not to comply with some maxim(s) of cooperation because they want to be polite. Interpersonal communication is, after all, not simply a matter of information exchange. There is a general principle of **politeness**: to be polite, one needs to minimize (other things being equal) the expression of impolite beliefs and maximize (other things being equal) the expression of polite beliefs. Analogous to the Cooperative Principle, the **Politeness Principle** proposed by Leech (1983b) is also defined in terms of some maxims:

1. **Tact Maxim**: minimize cost to others; maximize benefit to others (other-perspective); for example,

⑧ a. You can travel by train. It's safer.
   b. You can take the morning flight. It's more expensive.

2. **Generosity Maxim**: minimize benefit to self; maximize cost to self (self-perspective); for example,

⑨ a. I can offer you my car if you need it.
   b. You can offer me your car because I need it.

3. **Approbation Maxim**: minimize dispraise of others; maximize praise of others (other-perspective); for example,

⑩ a. What a marvelous meal you cooked!
   b. What an awful meal you cooked!

4. **Modesty Maxim**: minimize praise of self; maximize dispraise of self (self-perspective); for example,

⑪ a. John, you know I'm rather inexperienced.
   b. John, you know I'm perfectly good at it.

5. **Agreement Maxim**: minimize disagreement between self and others; maximize agreement between self and others; for example,

⑫ A: This is one of the best articles I've ever read.
   $B_1$: Yes, it's brilliant, isn't it?
   $B_2$: I don't think so.

6. **Sympathy Maxim**: minimize antipathy between self and others; maximize sympathy between self and others. For example,

⑬ A: My cat died last night.
B₁: I'm sorry to hear that.
B₂: Glad to hear that. It's been such a nuisance!

For an update of the maxims in particular and the Politeness Principle, refer to Leech (2014).

## 9.3 Face considerations in using English

In our daily lives, face as a socio-psychological concept is often tied up with notions of being embarrassed or humiliated. Thus face is something that is emotionally invested, and that can be lost, maintained, or enhanced, and must be constantly attended to in interaction.

Chinese are not alone in attending to face; native speakers of English are also sensitive to the issue of face. Somewhat differently defined in English, the concept of face is the public self-image that every member wants to claim for himself or herself. According to Brown and Levison (1987), it consists of two related aspects:

1. **negative face**: the basic claim to territories, personal preserves, rights to non-distraction, i.e. to freedom of action and freedom from imposition;

2. **positive face**: the positive consistent self-image or "personality" (crucially including the desire that this self-image be appreciated and approved of) claimed by interactants.

Some speech acts like requesting and apologizing are intrinsically **face threatening acts** (FTAs). Even thanking, which signifies one's "debt" to the addressee and thus obligation to acknowledge it, is considered to involve threat to one's own negative face.

## 9.4 Using English as a strategic act

In order to succeed in interpersonal communication, one needs to take good care of one's interlocutor's positive and negative face. To do so, one needs to attend to his or her interest, feelings, physical state, material benefit, opinions, and so forth. On the one hand, one can try to enhance his or her positive face, when possible. Or, one can try to minimize the threat to his or her negative face, if the threat is inevitable. English provides a lot of devices for performing face-enhancing and face-threatening acts strategically.

One device is the use of **impersonalization**, either to avoid mentioning oneself or the interlocutor, or to appeal to a public rule or institutional regulation.

⑭ a. Could you sharpen these pencils, please? (less polite than b)
　b. Could these pencils be sharpened, please? (more polite than a)
　c. Could I have some more soup? (less polite than d)
　d. Is there some more soup? (more polite than c)
　e. I don't think you can smoke in the waiting room, sir. (less polite than f)
　f. Smoking is not allowed in the waiting room, sir. (more polite than e)

Another device characteristic of English is reducing the degree of directness as much as necessary. For instance, the following options form a politeness scale: other things being equal, the more direct, the less polite; the less direct, the more polite:

⑮ a. Could you possibly lend me your car, John?
　b. Would you mind lending me your car, John?
　c. Can you lend me your car, John?
　d. Will you lend me your car, John?
　e. I want you to lend me your car, John.
　f. Lend me your car, John.

Politeness decreases from ⑮a to ⑮f if the current speaker is on regular terms with John.

## 9.5　Using English as a cultural act

Using language to communicate is often culturally-specific. Some norms in English, for example, are not shared by native speakers of Chinese, and vice versa. For instance, parents in English-speaking countries thank their kids for a little help, whereas their Chinese counterparts do not often do likewise. Moreover, despite the universality of the maxims of politeness, different cultures assign different weight to the maxims when conflicts between maxims arise under certain circumstances. For example, native speakers of English seem to pay more heed to tact and agreement maxims but less to the modesty maxim than Chinese do. Thus, in the face of a compliment, the former generally accept it by acknowledging their thanks or even returning a compliment, whereas the latter generally decline it, at least superficially, as a token of modesty. Thus, pragmatic divergences between English and Chinese cultures will be potential trouble areas for Chinese learners.

## Check your understanding

*State whether each of the following statements is True or False.*

(1) Maxim of quantity requires one to provide as much information as possible.

(2) In order to be polite, one needs to cooperate in all possible ways.

(3) Every normal speaker needs to mind his own and others' face.

(4) Politeness is a matter of degree.

(5) Cultures vary as far as politeness issues are concerned.

1. Being underinformative or overinformative in daily conversation is not rare. When either happens, some implicature is intended. Look at the following fragment of talk:

   Jane: What's your stepmother like?

   John: She's a woman and she married my father.

(1) What does John want to say in actuality?

(2) Why does John answer that way, you suppose?

Now consider the following:

Jane: When did you come back last night?

John: Two o'clock in the morning. The meeting was just too long.

(3) What does John imply in the second part of his reply?

(4) Why does John give that additional information?

Public signs and ads also employ additional information sometimes. Look at the following pictures:

(5) What is the extra information in each of the cases?

(6) What is the effect, if any, of providing the additional information?

2. Conversational implicatures have the property of **calculability**, which means that it can be inferred or calculated on the basis of what is said, the presumption of the Cooperative Principle, plus related background information. Take the following for example:

John: Are you coming with us tomorrow?

Jane: My boyfriend is sick.

(1) What implicature does Jane want to communicate with John?

(2) What steps does one need to take before arriving at the implicature?

(3) Are there any steps one has to take for granted?

3. Another property of conversational implicatures is their **indeterminacy**: in many cases, the list of possible implicatures of an utterance is open. Take the following for example:

John: Tom broke my glasses this morning.

Jane: Boys will be boys.

(1) What implicature(s) can Jane communicate with John?

(2) Can you find other contexts in which "Boys will be boys" may be heard but used for different meanings?

(3) Look at the following picture. How would you make sense of the announcement?

4. Some English words seem to be associated with generalized conventional implicatures. Look at the following utterances:

A. John cut a finger.
B. Jane went into a house.
C. Mom, I found out that my brother dined with a woman in a downtown restaurant last night.
D. He's Chinese, but doesn't play table tennis.

(1) Did John cut his own finger or that of somebody else? Why?
(2) Did Jane go into her own house or that of somebody else? Why?
(3) Was the woman John dined with his wife?
(4) Do you find the use of "but" in the last example interesting?

5. Performing a face-threatening act (FTA) is constrained by some important factors. Compare the following:
   A. Excuse me, would you by any chance have the time?
   B. Got the time, mate?

(1) What factor gives rise to the difference in the way the requests above are performed?
(2) What other factors might influence how one performs a request? Use examples for illustration.

6. Look at the following picture. The commonest way of informing found in this context is to use "OPEN".

(1) How is the way of informing shown in the picture different from the usu-

al way?

(2) Why is "yes" used now that one might also use "WE'RE OPEN"? Do you agree that public signs and advertisements are essentially dialogic rather than monologic?

7. Speakers often show they are aware of the Cooperative Principle when they use "hedges" which indicate that they may be violating a maxim.
   A. I don't mean to change the subject, but there's an enormous wasp in here.
   B. Wait, let me simplify that.
   C. That reminds me of something that ...
   D. You probably already know this but ...
   E. I don't know how exactly it happened, but ...
   F. I know this is long and involved, but it is really important.

**ask**

(1) What maxim is being alluded to in each case?
(2) Does the hedging effort suggest the plausibility of the Cooperative Principle?

8. The acquisition of one's mother tongue has a pragmatic aspect to it. Children, after all, are not born to speak a language appropriately as well as grammatically. The study of how children grow to become competent language users, sensitive to the influence of context and interlocutors' intentions, falls under the category of **developmental pragmatics**. Look at the following conversation.
   Child: Mommy, I want more milk.
   Mom: Is that the way to ask?
   Child: Please.
   Parent: Please what?
   Child: Please give me milk.

**ask**

(1) Which aspect of **pragmatic competence** is being called into question here?
(2) Do parents often give explicit pragmatic instructions to their children while the latter are growing up? Do you think such instructions are helpful or not? Effective or not?

(3) Are there any other aspects of pragmatic competence likely to be reinforced by adults? Consider the following fragment of conversation:
Parent: Where are your shoes, young man?
Child: Under my bed.
Parent: When I asked where your shoes were, I wanted you to put them on!

## Presentation Topics

1. Politeness at the Chinese dinner table
2. (Non)cooperation in doctor-patient talk
3. Strategies for making face-threatening refusals in English

## Exercises

### Task 1  Reference Search

Find in the library or online some information about the following themes:
(1) politeness
(2) face
(3) pragmatic competence
(4) Paul Grice
(5) Geoffrey Leech

### Task 2  Term Definition

Study the following definitions and then discuss how they combine to help you understand the terms.

**hedge**: cautious notes expressed about how an utterance is to be taken, e.g. "as far as I know" used when giving some information [George Yule]

**hedge**: a way of declining responsibility for the truth value of the proposition embedded [Richard Watts]

**conventional implicature**: An additional unstated meaning associated with the use of a specific word, e.g. "A but B" implies a contrast between A and

B, so "contrast" is a conventional implicature of "but". [George Yule]

**conventional implicature:** Non-truth-conditional inferences that are not derived from superordinate pragmatic principles like the maxims, but are simply attached by convention to particular lexical items or expressions. [Stephen Levinson]

**scalar implicature:** An additional meaning of the negative of any value higher on a scale than the one uttered, e.g. in saying "some children", I create an implicature that what I say does not apply to "all children". [George Yule]

**scalar implicature:** We normally assume (following the cooperative principle) that, where speakers have a scale of values at their disposal, they will choose the one that is truthful (maxim of quality) and optimally informative (maxim of quantity). So we normally draw the implicature "not any of the higher values on the scale". In other words, if Steve has chosen the word "sometimes", it created the implicatures "not always" and "not often". [Jean Peccei]

## Task 3  Study Questions

1. The following fragments of conversation are cited from Oscar Wilde's *The Importance of Being Earnest*. What maxim(s) may have been deliberately flouted by the characters in each fragment?

    (1) **Algernon:** Did you hear what I was playing, Lane?
    **Lane:** I didn't think it polite to listen, sir.

    (2) **Algernon:** And who are the people you amuse?
    **Jack:** [*Airily.*] Oh, neighbors, neighbors.

    (3) **Algernon:** Where is that place in the country, by the way?
    **Jack:** That is nothing to you, dear boy. You are not going to be invited … I may tell you candidly that the place is not in Shropshire.

    (4) **Jack:** Well … may I propose to you now?
    **Gwendolen:** I think it would be an admirable opportunity. And to spare you any possible disappointment, Mr. Worthing, I think it only fair to tell you quite frankly before-hand that I am fully determined to accept you.

    (5) **Algernon:** By the way, did you tell Gwendolen the truth about your being Ernest in town, and Jack in the country?
    **Jack:** [*In a very patronizing manner.*] My dear fellow, the truth isn't quite the sort

Unit 9　The Use of English (II)

of thing one tells to a nice, sweet, refined girl. What extraordinary ideas you have about the way to behave to a woman!

(6)　Algernon: What shall we do after dinner? Go to a theatre?
　　Jack: Oh no! I loathe listening.
　　Algernon: Well, let us go to the Club?
　　Jack: Oh, no! I hate talking.
　　Algernon: Well, we might trot round to the Empire at ten?
　　Jack: Oh, no! I can't bear looking at things. It is so silly.
　　Algernon: Well, what shall we do?
　　Jack: Nothing!

2. Read the following extract by Jerry Seinfeld (1993):

　　There're two types of favors, the big favor and the small favor. You can measure the size of the favor by the pause that a person takes after they ask you to "Do me a favor". Small favor—small pause. "Can you do me a favor, hand me that pencil." No pause at all. Big favors are, "Could you do me a favor ... " Eight seconds go by. "Yeah? What?"

　　"... well." The longer it takes them to get to it, the bigger the pain it's going to be.

　　Humans are the only species that do favors. Animals don't do favors. A lizard doesn't go up to a cockroach and say, "Could you do me a favor and hold still, I'd like to eat you alive." That's a big favor even with no pause.

　　Do you agree with what Jerry Seinfeld says? How is such a remark related to the doing of FTAs?

3. Analyze the following extract from Oscar Wilde's *The Importance of Being Earnest* in terms of the Politeness Principle. Which maxim is at issue?
　Algernon: I hope tomorrow will be a fine day, Lane.
　Lane: It never is, sir.
　Algernon: Lane, you're a perfect pessimist.

4. Read the following excerpt from Chapter XIX of Jane Austin's *Pride and Prejudice*. How is politeness or impoliteness reflected by the way the characters talk? You may just focus on the parts in bold face.

　　THE next day opened a new scene at Longbourn. Mr. Collins made his declaration in form. Having resolved to do it without loss of time, as his leave of absence extended only to the following Saturday, and having no feelings of diffidence to make it distressing to himself even at the moment, he set about it in a very orderly manner, with all the observances which he supposed a regular part of the business. On finding Mrs. Bennet, Elizabeth, and one of the younger girls together soon after breakfast, he addressed the mother in these words,

"May I hope, Madam, for your interest with your fair daughter Elizabeth, when I solicit for the honor of a private audience with her in the course of this morning?"

Before Elizabeth had time for any thing but a blush of surprise, Mrs. Bennet instantly answered,

"Oh dear!—Yes—certainly.—I am sure Lizzy will be very happy—I am sure she can have no objection.—Come, Kitty, I want you up stairs." And gathering her work together, she was hastening away, when Elizabeth called out,

"Dear Ma'am, do not go.—I beg you will not go.—Mr. Collins must excuse me. —He can have nothing to say to me that any body need not hear. I am going away myself."

"No, no, nonsense, Lizzy.—I desire you will stay where you are."—And upon Elizabeth's seeming really, with vexed and embarrassed looks, about to escape, she added, "Lizzy, I insist upon your staying and hearing Mr. Collins."

Elizabeth would not oppose such an injunction—and a moment's consideration making her also sensible that it would be wisest to get it over as soon and as quietly as possible, she sat down again, and tried to conceal by incessant employment the feelings which were divided between distress and diversion. Mrs. Bennet and Kitty walked off, and as soon as they were gone Mr. Collins began.

"Believe me, my dear Miss Elizabeth, that your modesty, so far from doing you any disservice, rather adds to your other perfections. You would have been less amiable in my eyes had there not been this little unwillingness; but allow me to assure you that I have your respected mother's permission for this address. You can hardly doubt the purport of my discourse, however your natural delicacy may lead you to dissemble; my attentions have been too marked to be mistaken. Almost as soon as I entered the house I singled you out as the companion of my future life. But before I am run away with by my feelings on this subject, perhaps it will be advisable for me to state my reasons for marrying—and moreover for coming into Hertfordshire with the design of selecting a wife, as I certainly did."

The idea of Mr. Collins, with all his solemn composure, being run away with by his feelings, made Elizabeth so near laughing that she could not use the short pause he allowed in any attempt to stop his farther, and he continued:

"My reasons for marrying are, first, that I think it a right thing for every clergyman in easy circumstances (like myself) to set the example of matrimony in his parish. Secondly, that I am convinced it will add very greatly to my happiness; and thirdly—which perhaps I ought to have mentioned earlier, that it is the particular advice and recommendation of the very noble lady whom I have the honor of calling patroness. Twice has she condescended to give me her opinion (unasked too!) on this subject; and it was but the very Saturday night before I left Hunsford—between our pools at quadrille, while Mrs. Jenkinson was arranging Miss de Bourgh's foot-stool, that she said, 'Mr. Collins, you must marry. A clergyman like you must marry. —Chuse properly, chuse a gentlewoman for my sake; and for your own, let her be an active, useful sort of person, not brought up high, but able to make a small income go a good way. This is my advice. Find such a woman as soon as you can, bring her to Hunsford, and I will visit her.' Allow me, by the way, to observe, my fair cousin, that I do not reckon the notice and kindness of Lady Catherine de Bourgh as among the least of the advantages in my power to offer. You will find her manners beyond any thing I can describe; and your wit and vivacity I think must be acceptable to her, especially when tempered with the silence and respect which her rank will inevitably excite. Thus much for my general intention in favor of matrimony; it remains to be told why my views were directed to Longbourn instead of my own neighborhood, where I assure you there are many amiable young women. But the fact is, that being, as I am, to inherit this estate after the death of your honoured father (who, however, may live many years longer), I could not satisfy myself without resolving to chuse a wife from among his daughters, that the loss to them might be as little as possible, when the melancholy event takes place—which, however, as I have already said, may not be for several years. This has been my motive, my fair cousin, and I flatter myself it will not sink me in your esteem. And now nothing remains for me but to assure you in the most animated language of the violence of my affection. To fortune I am perfectly indifferent, and shall make no demand of that nature on your father, since I am well aware that it could not be complied with; and that one thousand pounds in the 4 per cents, which will not be yours till after your mother's decease, is all that you may ever be entitled to. On that head, therefore, I shall be uniformly silent; and you may assure yourself that no ungenerous reproach shall ever pass my lips when we are married."

It was absolutely necessary to interrupt him now.

"You are too hasty, Sir," she cried. "You forget that I have made no answer. Let me do it without farther loss of time. Accept my thanks for the compliment you are paying me, I am very sensible of the honour of your proposals, but it is impossible for me to do otherwise than decline them."

5. What counts as polite behavior can differ substantially from one culture to the next. Lakoff (1990) describes three different types as distance, deference and camaraderie. Read the following citation:

Distance politeness is the civilized human analogue to the territorial strategies of other animals. An animal sets up physical boundary markers (the dog and the hydrant) to signal its fellows: My turf, stay out. We, being symbol-using creatures, create symbolic fences.

Distancing cultures weave remoteness into their language.

Where distance politeness more or less assumes equality between participants, deference works by debasing one or both.

While distance politeness has been characteristic of the middle and upper classes in most of Europe for a very longtime, deference has been typical in many Asian societies. But it is also the preferred mode of interaction for women in the majority of societies, either always or only when talking to men.

A third strategy (camaraderie) that has recently emerged in this culture makes a different assumption: that interaction and connection are good in themselves, that openness is the greatest sign of courtesy.

In a camaraderie system, the appearance of openness and niceness is to be sought above all else. There is no holding back, nothing is too terrible to say.

Which type of politeness are you most familiar with? Have you encountered the others on any occasion? What kind of language do you think characterizes each?

6. Suppose you were Li Min in the following dialogue. You brought your wife, Gao Yun, to attend a family party hosted by your American friend, Jack.
Li Min: Jack, this is my wife, Gao Yun.
Gao Yun: Nice to meet you.
Jack: How pretty! Nice to meet you. (*turning to Li Min*) Li Min, I like your new necktie.

Does Jack's compliment to Li Min and his wife sound natural to you? Why or why not? How do Chinese compliment each other on such occasions? How would Li Min and his wife respond to Jack's compliment in an English way?

7. It is customary for native speakers of English to rely on their own pragmatic conventions even when they are engaged in a conversation with a non-native speaker. Look at the following episode:
A Chinese student, Wang Ping, has borrowed a book from her American teacher, John. She has promised to return it today. Now she is at the professor's office. Yet she has forgotten to bring the book along.
John: Wang Ping, I hoped you brought the book I lent you.
Wang Ping: [*silence*]
John: OK, but please remember it next week.

How are John's two utterances different from each other? Do you expect John, as Wang Ping's teacher, to produce the first utterance that way? Why or why not?

### Task 4  Mini-Project

Collect an assortment of advertisements from magazines, newspapers, public places, etc. and analyze the data in pragmatic terms.

## Recommended Readings

### Reading 1

### Politeness Rules

A central concept in linguistic pragmatics is politeness. It has been suggested (for example, R. Lakoff, 1972, 1973b; Brown and Levinson, 1978; Leech, 1980, 1983) that politeness is another level to conversational interaction besides the rules of the cooperative principle. Robin Lakoff, (1977b) sees Grice's rules as essentially rules of clarity, and proposes that there are two prior rules of "pragmatic competence". These are: "Make yourself clear" and "Be polite". She takes Grice's maxims as an approximation, at least, of how you conform to the rule "Make yourself clear", and proposes her own three rules of politeness (R. Lakoff, 1977b:88):

1. **formality:** don't impose/remain aloof;
2. **hesitancy:** give the addressee his options;
3. **equality or camaraderie:** act as though you and the addressee were equal/make him feel good.

Lakoff (1977b:89) elaborates the second rule as "Permit addressee to decide his own options". It is not difficult to see how the operation of this rule could lead directly to the troublesome inference in "Henry likes apples or bananas". If we imagine, for example, that Henry's wife knows her host is about to serve fruit, she might well make this utterance, conveying and intending to convey that Henry is fond of both fruits; the host may select either option without fear of making a mistake. In such a case, Henry's wife can felicitously give the host the option only if either option will be successful, and that can only be true if Henry likes both fruits.

Leech's view of politeness involves a set of politeness maxims analogous to Grice's maxims. Among these are (Leech, 1983:132):

TACT MAXIM: Minimize cost to **other**. Maximize benefit to **other**.
GENEROSITY MAXIM: Minimize benefit to **self**. Maximize cost to **self**.
APPROBATION MAXIM: Minimize dispraise of **other**. Maximize praise of **other**.
MODESTY MAXIM: Minimize praise of **self**. Maximize dispraise of **self**.

These add up to "an essential asymmetry in polite behaviour, in that whatever is a polite belief for the speaker tends to be an impolite belief for the hearer, and vice versa" (Leech, 1983:169).

Frequently-cited examples first discussed by R. Lakoff (1972) are amenable to this general kind of analysis. Lakoff pointed out that a hostess would be seen as polite if she said, "You must have some of this cake." On the face of it this is strange, since ordinarily you would think telling someone what they must do removes all other options, imposes on them, and is therefore impolite. On the other hand, granting permission, if one is in a position to do it, makes it possible for the hearer to do what he or she wants to do, and would seem polite, or at least considerate. The answer hinges on the fact that the hostess is responsible for the quality of the cake. Offering the cake by placing an obligation on the hearer conforms nicely to the modesty maxim. By implying that she cannot assume that the guest will want the cake is a way in minimizing praise to herself. If the hostess had offered the cake by saying "You may have some of this cake", she would have violated modesty by appearing to assume that the cake is so good that the guest naturally wants a piece of it, and is only waiting to get permission.

Leech's politeness principle also seems to be applicable to the disjunction example in a natural way. One way that Henry's wife can conform to the maxim of tact, minimizing the cost to the host, is by making sure no one has to go to any special trouble to supply just the fruit Henry likes. Whichever of the two fruits can be supplied with minimum difficulty will be satisfactory. As I have said, this can only be really true if Henry likes both apples and bananas.

(Adapted from Ralph Fasold, *The Sociolinguistics of Language*, pp. 159-160)

## Food for Thought

(1) Do you think Robin Lakoff's two rules can explain all conversational behavior?
(2) Do you agree with the rule of equality?
(3) Is there any other area of potential conflicts between the maxims of politeness?

## Reading 2

### Pragmatics and Written Discourse

One of the reasons people have often tended to view literary works as objects rather than communicative acts is that most literary works have the form of written texts, at least in our time. In this sense, they are objects in a way spoken discourses are not. They are visible and tangible, and can be looked at and owned. One of the challenges facing pragmatics is that of developing an approach to written discourse that takes account of its differences from spoken discourse, and that characterizes the varieties of written discourse and the kind of linguistic context writing constitutes. This is another area in which there is no coherent body of research.

Equally important for many written messages is the fact of their being addressed to a public audience. The speaker who constructs a public discourse does not know or control who will receive it, though the speaker may have a particular group or kind of people in mind as addressees. With public discourse, of which literature and the news media are salient examples, we have the curious situation that the speaker (writer) is unknown or known only by name to the hearers (readers), and hearers are unknown to the speaker. Speaker/hearer relations are thus extremely depersonalized and abstract in comparison with face-to-face spoken discourse. The publicness of public discourse is doubtless responsible for the formality of the norms in writing and tendency of written discourse towards standardization.

Also important for literature is the difference between oral and written composition. Oral composition is, as we call it, spontaneous; one composes what one says on the spot, making corrections as one goes, and revising or clearing up misunderstandings as the exchange proceeds. A written utterance, on the other hand, is produced over a much greater and more flexible timespan and is subject to reflection, correction, and revision by the speaker; once it is delivered to the addressee, however, it is fixed, and there is little possibility for clearing up misunderstandings or revising further. These differences in manner of composition and delivery have a great many consequences, one being that the writer regards the written text as more "authoritative" and definitive than spontaneous speech. It is partly because of the possibilities afforded by written composition that, in literary works, weight is given to the smallest particulars of language, and choice is thought of as particularly reflective, careful, and conscious. By the same token, speakers are held very much responsible for what they say in writing. They cannot excuse something by saying they were speaking off the top of their head or in the heat of the moment.

Another factor influencing speaker/hearer relations in written discourse, especially literature, is the selection process that publishing involves. Writers submit manuscripts to publishers, who hire specialists to read them and make recommendations on whether they should be published or not. On the one hand, this selection process increases our trust in the value and communicativeness of the utterance, since it has come to us through winning a kind of competition. On the other hand, we must be skeptical, because the selection procedure is shaped by such factors as the biases of readers, the policies of particular publishers, and above all, economics.

It would be difficult to assess the overall impact of the composition and selection process on reader/author relations in literature. But it does seem that our awareness of these processes plays a role in how we treat deviance in literature. There are a great many literary texts which, in any other context, would be taken as pure gibberish or incompetent communication. But partly because of what we know of the composition and selection processes, when we encounter such deviance in literature, we assume that it is intentional and connected with some serious communicative intent, and that at least some people other than the author have found the text accessible, meaningful, and generally worthwhile. It is fruitful to think about this situation in terms of the Cooperative Principle. In the literary speech situation, we are prepared to cooperate as hearers to a greater extent than we would in conversation; we are prepared to make more of an effort to "decipher" deviance, to work at understanding beyond the point at which in other contexts the Cooperative Principle would have broken down. Knowing this to be the case, authors are more free to exploit and explore communicative deviance in literature. Thus we could say that the composition and selection processes in literature work to "insulate" the Cooperative Principle. This is surely one of the reasons why literature is so often used to portray and explore the vulnerability of language.

(Adapted from Elizabeth Traugott and Marry Pratt, *Linguistics for Students of Literature*, pp. 260-262)

## Food for Thought

(1) Can you find any other differences between spoken and written discourses?
(2) Do you agree that the principles of conversation are also applicable to the study of literature?
(3) What should we pay attention to when we study literary communication from the pragmatic perspective?

# Unit 10

# The Use of English (Ⅲ)

10.1 Turn-taking in English conversation
10.2 Adjacency pairs in English conversation
10.3 Pre-sequences in English conversation
10.4 Repairs and interruptions in English conversation
10.5 Backchannel signals in English conversation

> *People spend a lot of their time talking... Indeed, if an extra-terrestrial anthropologist were to visit Earth, talking would stand out as a frequent and universal activity of human kind.*
> —William Turnbull

## Pre-Class Reading

## 10.1 Turn-taking in English conversation

In **conversation**, dialogue rather than monologue dominates. Conversationalists **take turns** speaking. The chance or right to speak is technically termed **floor**. Having control of this right at any time is called a **turn**. In any situation where control is not fixed in advance, anyone can attempt to get control. This is called **turn-taking**. The current speaker may try to maintain the floor, or give up the floor. While the next speaker may opt to interrupt in order to seize the floor, he or she can wait to be nominated by the current speaker, or take the hints from him such as a long pause, a gesture, or a gaze.

There are some turn-taking rules that regulate our talking in group conversation such as when one person's turn ends, when the next person can start, who that person will be, what they can talk about, and so on. One basic rule of turn-taking is about timing and can be generalized as "no gap, no overlap". The current speaker generally has the priority to pick out the next speaker, if he or she prefers to do so. The speaker may do this by saying the other person's name (e.g. "Excuse me for being late, Mr. Baker. I was held up by the traffic."), or by simply gazing, nodding or making some gestures to a particular person. Or, the current speaker may proceed more indirectly, by throwing the floor wide open to whoever feels like getting into the fray (e.g. "Can anyone of you describe the picture?"). If the current speaker does not give any indication to select the next speaker, then there will generally be a brief pause and another person in the group may start speaking by "self-selecting" (e.g. "OK. Let me put in a few words."). However, those who want to hold the floor should avoid an open pause at the end of a syntactic unit. The speaker may fill each of his pauses with "um" or "uh". Or, you can indicate that there is a larger structure to your turn by beginning with expressions of "There are three points I'd like to make—first", "There's more than one way to do this—one example would be", "Didn't you know about Melvin? —Oh it was last October", "Did you hear about Cindy's new car? —She got it in", etc.

Turn-taking usually takes place at what is called **Transition Relevance Places** (TRPs), often identifiable with pauses at the end of a syntactic unit in an utterance or questions with a rising tone, as shown below:

① Mr. Strait: What's your major, Dave?
   Dave: English—well I haven't really decided yet.
      (3 seconds)
   Mr. Strait: So—you want to be a teacher?
   Dave: No—not really—well not if I can help it.
      (2.5 seconds)
   Mr. Strait: Wha- // Where do you—go ahead
   Dave: I mean it's a—oh sorry // I em—

In fact, the turn-taking system is not unique to daily conversation. There are "floor" rules governing all kinds of speech genres and speech events regarding which participants get to talk, and at what points. In a formal meeting, for example, a moderator (very often the chairperson) designates who gets the floor.

## 10.2 Adjacency pairs in English conversation

There are many automatic patterns in the structure of conversation, in spite of differ-

Unit 10    The Use of English (Ⅲ)    147

ences in style. The typical examples are the greetings and goodbyes as shown below:

② A: Good morning.
B: Good morning.
③ A: How are you?
B: Fine. Thank you.
④ A: Bye!
B: See you!

These automatic sequences are termed **adjacency pairs**. They always comprise a first part called **initiation** (e.g. a question or a request), and a second part called **response** (e.g. an answer or a refusal), produced by different speakers. The utterance of a first part immediately creates an expectation of the utterance of a second part of the same pair. If the second part of the adjacency pair is positive, it is preferred; if the second part of the adjacency pair is negative, it is dispreferred. The latter is characterized by the use of such signals as "well", **hesitation markers** like "em", **pauses**, explanations or **accounts**. Compare:

⑤ A: Can you help me carry this heavy box?
$B_1$: Sure.
$B_2$: Em—well—I'm afraid I'm not strong enough.

Conversation is characterized by the efficient mode of organization in terms of adjacency pairs. However, in daily life, it is not always composed of such pairs. It is often more complex. Read the following conversation:

⑥ Lady: Do you have any shoes like these?
Shop Assistant: What size?
Lady: Size five.
Shop Assistant: What color?
Lady: Black.
Shop Assistant: I'm sorry. We don't have any.

When responding to the lady's question, the shop assistant does not provide an answer but asks two questions. Until she gets answers to her questions, she reverts to answer the lady's question. Here, we have an **insertion sequence** formed by the shop assistant's questions and the lady's answers.

## 10.3    Pre-sequences in English conversation

In some contexts, a speaker may exchange with the hearer something, very often in the form of a question, that does not seem relevant to his or her goal when performing a request, an invitation, an announcement, and the like. After this initial exchange has been concluded, he or she will decide whether to come up with the request, invitation or announcement. Utterances that serve as "precursors" to others are often called **pre-sequences**. Here are some examples:

### Pre-invitation(前置邀请)

⑦ A: Say, what are you doing?
 B: Well, we're going out. Why?
 A: Oh, I was going to say come out and come over here and talk to the people.

### Pre-announcement(前置宣告)

⑧ A: Oh, guess what?
 B: What?
 A: Professor Smith came in and he put another book on his order.

Pre-sequences have two features:
- They are independent in structure and are often composed of a pair of question and answer.
- Their function is to make sure that the request, invitation or announcement about to be made is indeed, from the point of the hearer, within the limits of the possible.

## 10.4 Repairs and interruptions in English conversation

Conversation may run into "trouble" from time to time. When this occurs, a **repair** will often follow. By repair, we refer to an alteration that is suggested by a speaker, the addressee, or audience in order to correct or clarify a previous conversational contribution.

Four types of conversational repairs are identified:
- **Self-initiated and self-repaired**
 ⑨ A: I'm going to Jane's— I mean *Jerry's* house tonight.
- **Other-initiated and self-repaired**
 ⑩ A: I'm heading off to vacation next week.
 B: What?
 A: *I said I am going on vacation next week.*
- **Self-initiated and other-repaired**
 ⑪ A: May I help you?
 B: Yes. Do you have the small machine that you push with your hand to bind pa-

per together, I mean a umm ...

A: Oh, you mean *a stapler*?

B: Yes, that's right, a stapler.

- **Other-initiated and other-repaired**

    ⑫ A: Aren't you glad that today is your birthday?

    B: *My birthday is actually tomorrow.*

**Interruption** is another situation where we experience conversational "trouble". Interruption is a familiar case that we all have experienced in daily conversation. It is normally considered impolite and inappropriate to cut off others' speaking, especially in formal occasions. It may happen before and in the middle of the speaker's speech or during the pause.

Interruption is deemed as a violation of speaker rights. Therefore, except on special occasions, we should try not to interrupt others' speaking. In fact, people are well aware of this social convention that whenever we interrupt others we tend to start with an apology such as "I'm sorry that I have to interrupt you ..."

## 10.5 Backchannel signals in English conversation

In conversation, speakers normally expect that their conversational partners are listening attentively. Being aware of this expectation, the listeners would make some signs to indicate that they are listening. There are many different ways of doing this, including nodding heads, smiling, and employing other facial expressions and gestures, but the most common vocal indications are **backchannel signals**, or simply **backchannels**. For example:

⑬ John: If you have also watched this movie, I would

Mary: uh-uh

John: like to talk a bit about my opinions on it because

Mary: mmm

John: it is really controversial and impressive.

Mary: yeah

During face-to-face conversation, the lack of backchannels may be considered as an indication of absence of mind or a way of showing disagreement.

## Check your understanding

State whether each of the following statements is True or False.

(1) Conversation is chaotic and messy.
(2) Superior people do not take turns talking with their inferiors.
(3) Invitation and declination can make an adjacency pair.
(4) Presequences only occur in the performance of requests and invitations.
(5) In conversation, we must avoid silence.

## In-Class Activities

1. Conversation is characterized by efficient mode of organization in terms of adjacency pairs. However, in daily life, it is often more complex. Read the following conversation:

   Lady: Do you have any shoes like these?
   Shop Assistant: What size?
   Lady: Size five.
   Shop Assistant: What color?
   Lady: Black.
   Shop Assistant: I'm sorry. We don't have any.

   (1) Is the conversation composed of adjacency pairs?
   (2) If not, how would you characterize the conversation?

2. Conversation is generally a process of impromptu speech. Error making and correcting are by no means rare. Read the following stretch of conversation. Pay special attention to the bold-faced parts, which involves what is technically termed as **a repair**.
   (Zhang Wei and Mr. Li, a new teacher, are waiting for Professor Liu, the dean, in his office.)
   Li: I don't think we've met. My name is Li Guang.
   Zhang: Hello, I'm Zhang Wei. Delighted to meet you.
   Li: Pleased to meet you, too. Where are you from?
   Zhang: **Nanning.**

Li: **Nanjing**?
Zhang: **No, Nanning.**
Li: **Well, it's certainly a small world. I'm from Nanning, too.**
Zhang: By the way, are you one of the new students?
Li: No, I'm a new teacher.
Zhang: Oh, I'm sorry, Mr. Li.
Li: That's all right. Zhang Wei, call your monitor. I've something to tell him.
Zhang: May I use the office telephone?
Li: Yes.
Zhang: OK.

**ask**

(1) How would you describe a conversational repair?

(2) Are there other types of repair in daily conversation?

3. Conversation is culturally bound to a certain degree. A case in point is that speakers from different cultural backgrounds may start and end a conversation in different ways. The following excerpt is a telephone conversation.

(*A picks up the phone and dials a number.*)
A: Hello, may I speak to Mary?
B: This is Mary.
A: Oh, I just called to tell you something about the birthday party for Jack.
...
B: Then where shall I go?
A: Jack's home.
B: OK, anything else?
A: No. Goodbye.
B: Goodbye.

**ask**

(1) What is the pattern for opening a telephone conversation in English?

(2) How is the pattern different from that of a Chinese telephone conversation?

(3) Are there any differences between English and Chinese in terms of closing a telephone conversation?

4. The following conversation is taken from Harold Pinter's *The Birthday Party*. What aspects of this fragment of conversational speech would you point to as characteristic features of this type of language-in-use?

   Meg: You got your paper?
   Petey: Yes.
   Meg: Is it good?
   Petey: Not bad.
   Meg: What does it say?
   Petey: Nothing much.
   Meg: You read me out some nice bits yesterday.
   Petey: Yes, well, I haven't finished this one yet.
   Meg: Will you tell me when you come to something good?
   Petey: Yes.
   (*Pause*)
   Meg: Have you been working hard this morning?
   Petey: No. Just stacked a few of the old chairs. Cleaned up a bit.
   Meg: Is it nice out?
   Petey: Very nice.

5. Read the following talk between Tom Cruise, the famous movie star, and a well-known TV host named David.

   David: How long have you known the woman (note: Katie Holmes, Tom's third wife)?
   Tom: Uhh, like, "known her" known her? Like both of us, like known, I mean I've known of her for many years.
   David: Alright, the first time you actually, uhh,…
   Tom: I've known, I met her, uh,…
   David: Yeah, there you go.
   Tom: Yeah. You know, I met her, I think about ten weeks ago.
   David: Ten weeks ago, and, uh,…
   Tom: Yeah.
   David: …and then you started dating more or less?
   Tom: I knew, yeah, I gotta tell you, I knew the moment that I met her that I wanted to marry her.
   David: … and then … and then after you met her, and had your first date, uhh, and as the relationship progressed,
   Tom: Uhm hm.

David: ... you know what I'm saying?
Tom: Then I ... ask her to marry me.

(1) What are the backchannel signals used in this conversation?

(2) What attitudes do they seem to convey?

6. Read the following conversation selected from *Pride and Prejudice* by Jane Austen and answer the questions that follow.

After sitting for a moment in silence, she (note: Lady Catherine de Bourgh) said, very stiffly, to Elizabeth:

"I hope you are well, Miss Bennet. That lady, I suppose, is your mother?"

Elizabeth replied shortly that she was.

"And that, I suppose, is one of your sisters?"

"Yes, madam," replied Mrs. Bennet, to whom Elizabeth had mentioned the visitor's name, and who was feeling highly honored by her coming.

"You have a very small park here," observed Lady Catherine, after a short silence, "and this must be a most inconvenient sitting room for the evening in summer. The windows are full west."

Mrs. Bennet informed her that they never sat there after dinner, and then added:

"May I be so bold as to ask your ladyship whether you left Mr. and Mrs. Collins well?"

"Yes, very well."

(1) How do Elizabeth, Lady Catherine and Mrs. Bennet take turns talking in this episode?

(2) Who dominates the floor? What is the evidence on the basis of which you can detect this domination?

(1) Teacher repairs in classroom lectures

(2) Overlaps in friends' small talk

(3) Silence in TV interviews

# Exercises

 **Task 1 Reference Search**

Find in the library or online some information about the following themes:
(1) conversational repair
(2) presequences
(3) backchanneling
(4) Emanuel Schegloff
(5) Havey Sacks

 **Task 2 Term Definition**

Study the following definitions and then discuss how they combine to help you understand the terms.

**turn-taking:** the change of speakers during conversation [George Yule]

**adjacency pair:** a sequence of two utterances by different speakers in conversation. The second is a response to the first, e.g. question-answer. [George Yule]

**preference structure:** a pattern in which one type of utterance will be more typically found in response to another in a conversational sequence, e.g. an acceptance will more typically following an invitation than a refusal. [George Yule]

**overlap:** more than one speaker talking at the same time in conversation [George Yule]

 **Task 3 Study Questions**

1. Explore some turn-taking methods teachers use in discussion class.

2. Apart from the types of adjacency pairs, can you suggest some more types? Use conversational data to illustrate them.

3. Read the following conversation. Describe how the mother is making a conversational repair.
   (1) **Child:** But you know single beds are awfully thin to sleep on.

(2) Mother: What?
(3) Child: Single beds. They are ...
(4) Mother: You mean narrow?
(5) Child: They're awfully narrow, yeah.

4. Now look at the following conversation and discuss the various ways in which B's repair is different from the mother's above.
    A: So I was trying to pick up this chick when ...
    B: Excuse me. Did I hear that right?
    A: Awfully sorry, I mean, woman ...
    B: Pick up?
    A: Awfully sorry, I mean, meet ...
    B: So you're trying to imply that there actually are women around who would go out with a male chauvinist pig like you.

5. Read the following conversation. There are several overlaps. Discuss why they occur.
    John: Do you know Jack failed in the final math exam?
    Jane: Mary told me that. // He was* =
    John: // I'm very* sorry for him.
    Jane: = Yeah, he was very sad.
    John: Why not ask him // to come out* =
    Jane: // I don't think*
    John: = for a walk?
    Jane: Good idea.

## Task 4   Mini-Project

Record an episode of a TV interview. Focus on the backchannels used by the two sides and check whether their use of backchannels differs. If so, discuss the possible reasons.

## Conversation

Conversations almost always open with an exchange of greetings involving an initiator and a responder. As elsewhere in the linguistic system, styles must be used consistently. Selection of the greeting form by the initiator A immediately establishes degree of formality. Often the responder B will simply repeat A's formula, as in "A: Hi—B: Hi", or "A: Good Morning—B: Good Morning". Or there may be variation, within limits: "A: Hi—B: Oh, hello." But clearly there are boundaries between styles. The sequence "A: Hi, Bill—B: Good morning," Professor Zooks immediately suggests either a power relationship (B is being respectful) or, if the speakers are peers, unwillingness on the part of B to accept the intimacy A wants to establish. When interlocutors are strangers, they must introduce themselves in certain circumstances. Whether to do so, and how to do so, is also rule-governed. One would not usually introduce oneself when asking directions of a stranger or a policeman. Here the attention-getter "Excuse me" is more appropriate than "Hello", and B's response will usually be a minimal "uhm uhm" or "yes?".

Conversational endings, like openings, usually involve a paired exchange. Socially, endings are somewhat problematic, because the person initiating the ending is in effect choosing silence over continued talk. In many communities, once a conversation is started, silence is felt to be unwelcome. Silences of more than a few seconds are seen as signs of some problem in the communication, indicating disapproval, irritation, boredom, or incomprehension. This is by no means true of all cultures; in fact Anglo-American culture is somewhat notorious for its intolerance of silence. Given this intolerance, in initiating an ending, A (the initiator) has to find a way to arrange for silence without creating disapproval or a sense of failure on B's part. Endings are usually prefaced by a transition like "Well ..." "So ..." "OK ..." followed by such devices as a return to the beginning of the conversation ("Well, I'm really glad I ran into you; So, we agree on that election question), an excuse concerning other obligations (I have to go, the library closes in an hour), or an oblique suggestion that B should go do something ("Well, have a good time at the concert tonight" or "Don't work too hard"). B can refuse the closing by initiating again

("Listen, before you go, I must tell you ..."), or B can agree to close, usually by saying "OK" and possibly referring to a next encounter ("See you soon"), followed by "A: Goodbye—B: Goodbye". Conversational endings are particularly difficult to achieve appropriately if the initiator of the ending is not going to physically leave the scene. For example, between adjacent passengers on a train or bus, once a conversation is begun, one usually does not terminate it explicitly until the end of the trip. To arrange for silence in these circumstances, A's usual recourse is to indicate through gesture (looking away, picking up a book) or unresponsiveness that silence is desired, and then hope B will pick up the clues.

(Elizabeth Traugott and Marry Pratt, *Linguistics for Students of Literature*, pp. 242-243)

 Food for Thought

(1) What implications does this passage have for us students of English?
(2) Are there individual differences in the way of opening a conversation?
(3) Are there similar markers of ending a conversation in Chinese?

 Reading 2

## Conversation Analysis

There are many metaphors used to describe conversation structure. For some, conversation is like a dance, with the conversational partners coordinating their movements smoothly. For others it's like traffic crossing an intersection, involving lots of alternating movement without any clashes. However, the most widely used analytic approach is based, not on dancing (there's no music) nor on traffic flow (there are no traffic signals), but on an analogy with the workings of a market economy.

In this market, there is a scarce commodity called the floor which can be defined as the right to speak. Having control of this scarce commodity at any time is called a turn. In any situation where control is not fixed in advance, anyone can attempt to get control. This is called turn-taking. Because it is a form of social action, turn-taking operates in accordance with a logical management system that is conventionally known by members of a social group. The local management system is essentially a set of conventions for getting turns, keeping them, or giving them away. This system is needed most at those points where there is a possible change in who has the turn. Any possible change-of-turn point is called a Transition Relevance Point, or TRP. Within any social group, there will be features of talk (or absence of talk) typically associated with a TRP.

This type of analytic metaphor provides with a basic perspective in which speakers having a conversation are viewed as taking turns at holding the floor. They accomplish change of turn smoothly because they are aware of the local management system for taking those turns at an appropriate TRP. The metaphor can be applied to those conversations where speakers cooperate and share the floor equally. It can also be used to describe those conversations where speakers seem to be in competition, fighting to keep the floor and preventing others from getting it. These patterns of conversational interaction differ substantially from one social group to another.

(George Yule, *Pragmatics*, pp. 71-72)

 **Food for Thought**

(1) Do you think there are also problems with comparing the operation of conversation to that of a market economy?

(2) Are there signals at all in conversation? How are the signals, if at all, similar to and different from traffic signals?

**Appendix: Conversational notations**

| Symbol | Meaning |
| --- | --- |
| [ | simultaneous start of speech |
| ] | simultaneous end of speech |
| (0.3) | duration of a pause |
| . | falling tone |
| , | level tone |
| ? | rising tone |
| ↑ | sudden rise of tone |
| ↓ | sudden fall of tone |
| <u>he</u> | emphasis |
| : | lengthened syllable |
| ((laugh)) | non-verbal behavior |
| (?) | inarticulate speech |
| 2 | line number |

# Unit 11

## The Use of English (IV)

11.1 Comparison-based tropes in English
11.2 Association-based tropes in English
11.3 Repetition-based rhetoric in English
11.4 Omission-based rhetoric in English
11.5 Contrast-based rhetoric in English

> *The skillful use of language became increasingly important in society. In the Greek legal system, there were no professional lawyers. People brought charges and defended themselves in person …*
> —Gorgias

## Pre-Class Reading

### 11.1 Comparison-based tropes in English

In English, quite a few **rhetorical devices** or **figures of speech** are based on the comparison of things due to the similarity of one kind or another between them. The most common ones include **metaphor**, **simile**, **analogy**, **personification**, **parody**, **onomatopoeia**, among others.

A metaphor is "an imaginative way of describing something by referring to something else which is the same in a particular way" (*Collins Cobuild*), as in "Life is a journey" and "The economy of the country is going uphill". As a rhetorical device, a metaphor puts two things together, leaving the readers to figure out their similarities.

Sometimes, a metaphor can be extended to develop ideas in a paragraph or a passage, thus an **extended metaphor**. Take Dorothy Aldis' *Brooms* for example:

> On stormy days
> When the wind is high
> Tall trees are brooms
> Sweeping the sky
>
> They swish their branches
> In buckets of rain,
> And swash and sweep it
> Blue again.

In the poem, such verbs as "sweep", "swish" and "swash" are collocates of the word "broom" used metaphorically here.

Unlike a metaphor, a simile makes direct comparison between two things, as indicated by the use of words such as "like", "as", "than", and "resemble". Also unlike a metaphor, which often suggests subtle comparison, a simile presents more explicit comparison, as in "The international situation was as tense as a ballgame tied up in the final minute" and "Charity is like molasses, sweet and cheap".

An analogy as a figure of speech is also based on similarity or comparison. Unlike a metaphor or a simile that generally focuses on one dimension for comparison, an analogy often explores two or more similarities between things under description. Take F. W. Bourdillon's poem, *Light*, for example:

> The night has a thousand eyes,
> And the day but one;
> Yet the light of the bright world dies
> With the dying sun
>
> The mind has a thousand eyes,
> And the heart but one;
> Yet the light of a whole life dies
> When love is done.

In the above poem, what the mind is to heart is described as analogous to what the night is to the day; what the sun is to the world is seen as what love is to a whole life.

Sometimes, though, an analogy is employed in proverbs, sayings, mottos, etc., as in "A woman needs a man like a goldfish needs motorbike".

Personification is a figure of speech that attributes a certain feature or property of human beings to something unhuman, like animals, vegetables, objects, abstract concepts, as in "The baby crocodile thought hard. Then he had a good idea" and "Justice is blind and, at times, deaf".

Both parody and onomatopoeia are figures of speech that are motivated by imitation on the basis of some kind of similarity between two things. Parody often refers to satiric or ironic imitation for the purpose of making fun of, or commenting on the subject, author, style, or some other target of an original work, e.g. "Beauty is more than skin deep" (c.f. "Beauty's but skin deep") and "A friend in need is a friend to be avoided" (c.f. "A friend in need is a friend indeed").

Onomatopoeia refers to the use of a word that phonetically imitates, resembles or suggests the source of the sound that it describes. For example,

> The crowd began to hiss and boo him for his unsportsmanlike conduct, but he sat unmoved. Another great outburst of applause was Danny's as he walked back across the ring.
> When Danny stirred, there were "ohs!" and "ahs!" of delight.

In the above excerpt from *The Mexican*, Jack London used four onomatopoeic words: hiss, boo, oh, ah.

## 11.2　Association-based tropes in English

The second set of tropes in English includes **metonymy**, **synecdoche**, **antonomasia**, **allusion**, **euphemism**, etc., which are basically based on association between things.

Metonymy is a figure of speech in which a thing or concept is called, instead of by its own name, by the name of something associated in some way with that thing or concept. The association or **contiguity** may include at least the following common categories.

　　a. material for the object: *The bronze* was unearthed last month.
　　b. instrument for user: *The scalpel* is a butcher.
　　c. brand for product: I use a *Samsung*.
　　d. author for work: Do you have *Jack London*?
　　e. feature for person: *The blonde* has not paid.
　　f. container for content: *The kettle* is boiling.
　　g. location for establishment: *The Wall Street* is closed today.
　　h. capital for central government: *Washington* will sign a treaty with *Beijing* tomorrow.

Synecdoche, sometimes subsumed under the category of metonymy as a specific type of it, refers to the use of a specific part of something to refer to the whole, or the whole to a specific part, as in "We are currently short of *hands*" and "Great *minds* think alike". Sometimes, synecdoche also includes the use of a specific concept for an abstract concept, as in "Jack has a sweet *tongue*", or the other way round, as in "*The authorities* were greeted".

Antonomasia, by which we refer to the use of a common noun for a proper noun or the other way round, is also treated as a specific type of metonymy. In "The party met its *Waterllo* in the last election", "Waterloo" is used to mean "defeat"; in "At the Presidential Debate, *The Donkey* and The *Elephant* Had a Fight", "the donkey" refers to American Democatic Party, whereas "the elephant" refers to American Republican Party.

Allusion is a figure of speech in which the speaker or writer makes mention of some name or object from a legend, a fable, a mythological story, a literary work, a historic event, etc., as in "Will rider safety be *the Achilles' heel* for Uber?" and "Kangroo Island ... you can escape from the rush of life and become a modern-day *Crusoe*".

Euphemism is a figure of speech that involves speaking with good words. Two types of euphemism are differentiated: traditional euphemism and stylistic euphemism. In the first type, we use mild expressions to refer to taboo topics related to bodily parts or functions, disease or death, God, etc. In the second type, we use elegant expressions to refer to some less attractive professions, industries, educational topics, political acts, etc. The following are some examples:

| Traditional euphemism | | Stylistic euphemism | |
|---|---|---|---|
| death | fall asleep, pass away, go to heaven, join the majority, etc. | hair dresser | beautician |
| | | whore | working girl, street walker, call girl, etc. |
| | | death penalty | capital punishment |
| urinate | go to stool, wash one's hands, go to the bathroom, answer nature's call, etc. | invasion | involvement |
| | | striking | industrial movement |
| | | poor | needy, underprivileged |
| God | the Almighty, the Supreme Being, the Eternal, Holy One, the Creator, etc. | economic crisis | recession, depression |

## 11.3  Repetition-based rhetoric in English

In English, a variety of rhetorical devices are based on repetition, such as **alliteration**, **consonance**, **assonance**, **tautology**, and **parallelism**.

Alliteration and assonance both involve the repetition of sounds. In the case of alliteration, the initial consonant(s) in a sequence of words in a phrase or sentence, or the same kind of sound in stressed syllables in a phrase or sentence, is repeated, as in "Peter Piper picked a peck of pickled peppers". In the case of consonance, the final consonant(s) in a sequence of words in a phrase or sentence is repeated, as in "As the wind will bend". In the case of assonance, the same vowel is repeated in neighboring words or in rhyming lines, as in "come"—"love".

Tautology, sometimes called epanalepsis, refers to the repetition of the same thing in the subject and the predicative positions, as in "Wars are wars" and "Boys will be boys".

Parallelism concerns repetition of a certain type of lexical unit or a particular syntactic structure leading to intensified force. It is often found in poems, drama, prose, speeches and so on. Look at the following example:

> With this faith, we will be able *to work together*, *to pray together*, *to struggle together*, *to go to jail together*, *to stand up for freedom together*, knowing that we will be free one day.

In the above example taken from Martin Luther King's *I Have a Dream*, parallelism stems from the repetition of the "to-do-something (together)" structure.

## 11.4  Omission-based rhetoric in English

In English, some rhetorical devices, such as **ellipsis**, **sentence fragment**, and **aposiopesis**, are based on omission of some kind.

Ellipsis involves the deletion of some elements of a sentence that convey information known to the hearer/reader. It is used for the purpose of being economical of words, as in "Women are the opposite of clocks: clocks serve to remind us of the hours; women to make us forget them".

Sentence fragment also results from the omission of words, but in this case, only one element, say the subject, the predicative, or the object, is left alone, as in "I used to eat at a restaurant where she sang. She was vital. Fascinating. Tremendous." The rhetorical use of sentence fragments is for the purpose of giving stress or emphasis, or describing an after-thought.

Aposiopesis occurs when a speaker or writer halts halfway in a sentence, omitting words that might express unpleasant, sensitive, inappropriate ideas. Look at the following example:

**Crofts**: (*starting, with a suppressed oath*) Who told you?
**Vivie**: Your partner. My mother.
**Crofts**: (*black with rage*) The old—

In the above excerpt, Crofts under Bernard Shaw's pen does not finish his sentence in his second turn. We could guess that he has refrained from uttering a complete curse.

## 11.5 Contrast-based rhetoric in English

Finally, let's turn to a set of figures of speech that are based on contrast, notably **antithesis**, **oxymoron**, **paradox**, and **irony**.

Antithesis is a figure of speech that involves apparently contradictory ideas, words, clauses, or sentences within a balanced grammatical structure, as in "Man proposes, God disposes". The following excerpt from Charles Dickens's *A Tale of Two Cities*, is a good example of antithesis:

> It was the best of times, it was the worst of times, it was the age of wisdom, it was the age of foolishness, it was the epoch of belief, it was the epoch of incredulity, it was the season of Light, it was the season of Darkness, it was the spring of hope, it was the winter of despair, we had everything before us, we had nothing before us, we were all going direct to Heaven, we were all going direct the other way ...

Oxymoron is a figure of speech that involves the combination or collocation of two contradictory terms in meaning, as in "open secret", "organized mess", and "alone in a crowd". In *Romeo and Juliet*, Shakespeare employs a series of oxymoron expressions, as shown below:

> O heavy lightness! Serious vanity!
> Mis-shapen chaos of well-seeming forms!
> Feather of lead, bright smoke, cold fire, sick health!

Paradox is a figure of speech in which an apparently absurd or self-contradictory statement, contrary to expectation, makes perfect sense, as in "Failure is the mother of success" and "More haste, less speed".

Irony is a figure of speech in which the speaker says the opposite of what he or she actually means, as in "You're such a good friend" when the addressee spoils something the speaker is doing. In the following example, "This hard-working boy seldom reads more than an hour per week", "hard-working" cannot be interpreted literally, either. Clearly, it is also a case of irony.

State whether each of the following statements is True or False.
(1) Metaphor and simile differ only in whether words like "as" and "like" are used.
(2) Synecdoche is treated as one type of metonymy by some researchers.
(3) Tautology is always an instance of bad language use.
(4) Sentence fragment can be rhetorical in literary writing.
(5) Oxymoron occurs when we say something opposite to what we actually mean.

## In-Class Activities

1. English makes use of a lot of alliteration in all sorts of communication, especially in classic English poetry and plays. The following excerpts come from Shakespeare's *A Midsummer Night's Dream* (V. i. ) and Tennyson's *The Brook* respectively:

### Excerpt 1
Anon comes Pyramus, sweet youth and tall,
And finds his trusty Thisby's mantle slain;
Whereat, with blade, with bloody blameful blade,
He bravely broach'd his boiling bloody breast;
And Thisby, tarrying in mulberry shade,
His dagger drew, and died.

### Excerpt 2
I slip, I slide, I gloom, I glance,
Among my skimming swallows;
I make the netted sunbeam dance
Against my sandy shallows.

Alliteration is also widely found in English proverbs, as shown below:

Praise is not pudding.
Plenty is no plague.
Health is happiness.
Fortune favors fools.

**ask**

(1) What are likely positive effects of using alliteration? Use one of the poetic examples for illustration.

(2) Is there a similar use of alliteration in Chinese?

2. Read the following poem by X. J. Kennedy:

### A Water Glass of Whisky

Through the hill by the Rite Nite Motel
Not a picture unbroken can reach:
An old famous head in the screen
Facelifted, falls halt in its speech

As if no line cast from the set
Could fix with a definite hook
Into any live lip going by.
There is no good book but the Good Book.

No use. Try the window instead
But the near-beer bar's sign is no more.
As far as the breeze stretches off
Only outer space answers your stare.

You don't die for want of TV
But even so, here lies a lack
As though more than night or a hill
Had walled you in, back of its back.

**ask**

(1) What words are in assonance in this poem?

(2) How is assonance used to stress the sense of superficiality and lack of meaning the poet is trying to convey here?

Unit 11　The Use of English (Ⅳ) 　167

3. Rhyming occurs when the words or lines of verse use the same terminal sounds (i.e. the nucleus and the coda of the final syllable of the words are identical). For instance, the phrase "fair and square" has an internal rhyme because "fair" and "square" use the identical final vowel. From a very early age, children learn that certain words rhyme.

　　(1) What is the stylistic effect of rhyming?
　　　　Rhyming is widely found in English proverbs, as shown below:
　　　　Haste makes waste.
　　　　Health is better than wealth.
　　　　Forbearance is not aquittance.
　　(2) Can you find more proverbs that involve internal rhyming?

4. In public speeches as well on other occasions, speakers or writers often resort to **parallelism**, a rhetorical device that derives power and impact from the use of repetition. Read the following excerpt from President Obama's victory speech in 2012.

　　If there is anyone out there who still doubts that America is a place where all things are possible, who still wonders if the dream of our founders is alive in our time, who still questions the power of our democracy, tonight is your answer.
　　It's the answer told by lines that stretched around schools and churches in numbers this nation has never seen, by people who waited three hours and four hours, many for the first time in their lives, because they believed that this time must be different, that their voices could be that difference.
　　It's the answer spoken by young and old, rich and poor, Democrat and Republican, black, white, Hispanic, Asian, Native American, gay, straight, disabled and not disabled. Americans who sent a message to the world that we have never been just a collection of individuals or a collection of red states and blue states.
　　We are, and always will be, the United States of America.
　　It's the answer that led those who've been told for so long by so many to be cynical and fearful and doubtful about what we can achieve to put their hands on the arc of history and bend it once more toward the hope of a better day.

　　(1) How is parallelism used in this excerpt?

(2) What other figures of speech do you think there are in it?

5. In English, we may sometimes ask questions that are rhetorical by nature. The so-called **rhetorical questions** are not intended to seek answer from the hearer or reader, but rather are used for emphasis or convey strong emotion. Here are two examples:

   A. O, Wind, if winter comes, can spring be far behind? (Shelly)
   B. Can't you do anything right?

   (1) Do rhetorical questions have special phonetic or syntactic features?
   (2) Are there other types of rhetorical questions besides the ones exemplified above?

6. Many great writers like Shakespeare are good at using **puns**, a rhetorical device that plays on ambiguity that results from the sound or meaning of a word, or the structure of a sentence. The following joke involves a pun depending on phonetic identity.

   A Swedish explorer, Leif, returned from his voyage to the New World, only to find that his name had been removed from his hometown register. He complained bitterly to the leader of the town council. After investigating the oversight the council leader apologized, admitting he must have taken Leif off his census.

   (1) Where does the pun lie in this short passage?
   (2) What does the council leader intend to mean?

**Presentation Topics**

1. Metaphors in English sport reports
2. Parralelism in English speeches
3. Rhetorical devices in English proverbs

Unit 11　The Use of English (IV)

### Task 1　Reference Search

Find in the library or online some information about the following themes:
(1) personification
(2) irony
(3) euphemism
(4) synaesthesia
(5) dead metaphor

### Task 2　Term Definition

Study the following definitions and then discuss how they combine to help you understand the terms.

**hyperbole**: a figure of speech which gently exaggerates the truth [*Longman Modern English Dictionary*]

**understatement**: a statement that expresses an idea, etc. too weakly [*Oxford Advanced Learners' Dictionary*]

**zeugma**: a word is used to modify or govern two or more words although its use is grammatically or logically correct with only one [*The American Heritage Dictionary of the English Language*]

**periodic sentence**: a sentence in which the meaning is suspended till the close of the sentence [*Encyclopedia of English*]

### Task 3　Study Questions

1. Are there cultural differences in the formation of metaphors? Use one type of metaphor for illustration.

2. There seems to be cultural differences in the formation of euphemisms, like those in English and Chinese for death. Discuss possible causes for the differences.

3. There is abundant use of rhetorical devices in English songs. Read the following one and point out the figures of speech used in it.

**Yesterday Once More**

*Carpenters*

When I was young I'd listen to the radio
Waiting for my favorite songs
When they played I'd sing along
It made me smile
Those were such happy times and not so long ago
How I wondered where they'd gone
But they're back again just like a long lost friend
All the songs I love so well
Every shalala every wo'wo still shines
Every shing-a-ling-a-ling that they're starting to sing so fine

When they get to the part
Where he's breaking her heart
It can really make me cry
Just like before
It's yesterday once more
(shoobie do lang lang)
Looking back on how it was in years gone by
And the good times that had
Makes today seem rather sad
So much has changed

It was songs of love that I would sing to them
And I'd memorize each word
Those old melodies still sound so good to me
As they melt the years away
Every shalala every wo'wo still shines
Every shing-a-ling-a-ling that they're starting to sing so fine

All my best memorise come back clearly to me
Some can even make me cry

Unit 11 The Use of English (IV)

       Just like before
      It's yesterday once more
      (shoobie do lang lang)
    Every shalala every wo'wo still shines.

  Every shing-a-ling-a-ling that they're starting to sing so fine
     Every shalala every wo'wo still shines

4. Read the following excerpt from Lewis Carrol's *Alice's Adventures in Wonderland*. Discuss the figures of speech used in it.

  The Hatter shook his head mournfully: "Not I!" he replied. "We quarreled last March just before he went mad, you know." (*pointing with his teaspoon at the March Hare*) "It was at the great concert given by the Queen of Hearts, and I had to sing
     'Twinkle, twinkle, little bat!
     How I wonder what you're at!'
You know the song, perhaps?"
  "I've heard something like it," said Alice.
  "It goes on, you know," the Hatter continued, "in this way:—
     'Up above the world you fly,
     Like a tea tray in the sky.
     Twinkle, twinkle—'"

5. Discuss the use of figures of speech in the following slogans of car companies.
  A. The relentless pursuit of perfection. (Lexus)
  B. Not all cars are created equal. (Mitsubishi)
  C. Don't dream it. Drive it. (BMW)
  D. Buick—your key to a better life and a better world. (Buick)
  E. We would never say the new Audi A4 is the best in its class. We don't have to. (Audi A4)
  F. Life is a journey. Enjoy the ride. (NISSAN)
  G. Engineered to move the human spirit. (Mercedes-Benz)

6. Metaphors are also extensively used in English poetry. Look at the following classic excerpt and discuss how the use of metaphors enhances the effect of the poetic communication.
  **Hamlet:** To be, or not to be: that is the question.

Whether 'tis nobler in the mind to suffer
The slings and arrows of outrageous fortune,
Or to take arms against a sea of troubles,
And by opposing end them?                    (Hamlet III. i. 57-61)

##  Task 4    Mini-Project

Collect some data to show that English advertisements, newspaper headlines, English songs, and presidential addresses sometimes make use of alliteration and rhyming.

# Unit 12

# The Cognitive Study of English

* 12.1 Cognitive approach to language
* 12.2 Conceptual metaphors in English
* 12.3 Conceptual metonymies in English
* 12.4 Categorization and prototypes in English

> *Cognitive science is a new field that brings together what is known about the mind from many academic disciplines: psychology, linguistics, anthropology, philosophy, and computer science. It seeks detailed answers to such questions as: What is reason? How do we make sense of our experience? What is a conceptual system and how is it organized? Do all people use the same conceptual system? If so, what is that system? If not, exactly what is there that is common to the way all human beings think? The questions aren't new, but some recent answers are.*
> 
> —George Lakoff

## Pre-Class Reading

## 12.1 Cognitive approach to language

**Cognitive linguistics** as an influential paradigm of linguistic research today explores the relation between language and cognition. In particular, it seeks to reveal how our experience of the world and the way we perceive and conceptualize it affect the way language is structured and shaped. Thus, it is different from the more traditional "logical" approach to language that places emphasis on the knowledge of logical rules and objective semantic features stored in our memory (thus "cognitive" in a different sense for being related to knowledge).

Cognitive linguists assume that language is not an endowed ability but rather acquired after birth. The **faculty of language** (FL), or **linguistic competence**, is an inseparable part of our general cognitive abilities instead of an independent module. Language is not assumed to be autonomous but dependent on our experience of the world. It is not just logical, but also experiential.

There are three major views of language in Cognitive Linguistics: the **experiential view**, the **prominence view**, and the **attentional view**.

According to the experiential view, linguists need to emphasize how people's observations, impressions, and associations about an object, an event, etc. affect how language is formed and used as opposed to stressing the role of theoretical considerations and logical introspection about the attributes of the object, event, etc. The experiential view is superior to the logical view in that it can provide a richer and more subtle description of language and enable us to understand a lot of figurative language. For instance, when understanding "Hearing the news, Jane collapsed", we call forth our own experiences to conjure up a scene of how one feels disappointed or disillusioned and breaks down like a collapsed building. We would not derive a picture in which, by logical analysis, Jane fell into parts or broke up.

According to the prominence view, the more prominent an entity is, the more likely it will be highlighted in language structures. Take the choice of the subject of a sentence for example. Generally, the subject position is filled by something that is most salient. Compare "The man jumped over the fence" with "The fence was jumped over by the man". Clearly, the former sentence sounds more natural than the latter one because the concept encoded by "the man" is more salient than that encoded by "the fence". Yet, it is to be noted that salience can be subjective in context, depending on how the viewer conceptualizes the world. This explains why we can say "Perkins murdered John yesterday" and "John was murdered by Perkins yesterday" in an equally natural though experientially different way.

According to the attentional view, not everything in our observation or experience gets encoded in language now that our attentional resources are limited and therefore selective. In other words, we only express whatever parts of an object, an event, etc. that attract our attention. This does not affect human comprehension because given limited information, we can rely on our experiences to enrich the linguistic description for a fuller picture of the object, event, etc. Or we make do with a non-detailed description for a rough idea. Still take "Perkins murdered John yesterday" for example. A lot of information are left unsaid here: where the murder took place; what tool Perkins used to murder John; why Perkins murdered John; what time of yesterday the murder took place; etc.

Fundamentally, these three views can help account for various semantic phenomena in language, such as **conceptual metaphors**, **conceptual metonymies**, and **prototypes**, which we are going to discuss here, and syntactic phenomena, which readers may find elsewhere.

## 12.2 Conceptual metaphors in English

As we discussed in Unit 11, metaphor has long been regarded as a figure of speech that directly compares without using "like" or "as" two subjects that are seemingly unrelated but have very similar qualities. In the simplest case, metaphor takes the form "A is B". Thus, A can be economically and artistically described because implicit and explicit attributes from B are used to describe A. Naturally, this device has extensive usage in literature, especially in poetry, where with few words, emotions and associations from one context are associated with objects and entities in a different context (as in "The rain came down in buckets" and "All the world's a stage"). It is also commonly held that metaphor is a figure of speech that we can do without; we use it for special effects, and it is not an inevitable part of everyday human communication. Importantly, metaphor is deemed to be a conscious and deliberate use of words, and you must have a special talent to be able to do it and do it well. For instance, Aristotle makes the following statement: "The greatest thing by far is to have command of metaphor. This alone cannot be imparted by another; it is the mark of genius." Thus, it seems that only great poets or eloquent speakers, such as Shakespeare and Churchill, can be its masters.

However, with the introduction of the cognitive linguistic approach, marked by George Lakoff and Mark Johnson's *Metaphors We Live by* (1980), metaphor is no longer seen as purely about language, but rather it is also seen as about thought. Specifically, metaphors are about how human beings conceptualize their worlds and function within them. When we use metaphors, we are using them to structure our way of thinking, reflecting how we get around in the world, and how we relate to other people.

Typically, conceptual metaphors bring two distant **conceptual domains** (or concepts) into correspondence with each other. One is called the **source domain**: the conceptual domain from which we draw metaphorical expressions; the other is the **target domain**: the conceptual domain that we try to understand. One of the domains is typically more physical or concrete than the other (which is thus more abstract). Each cognitive domain contains some conceptual schemes based on the experience. The metaphor is gained by **mapping** the source domain onto the target domain. Thus, we understand an idea from one conceptual domain in terms of an idea from another. For example, when we say "Prices are rising", we are seeking to understand quantity in terms of directionality.

Many everyday metaphors, including the so-called metaphors like "the foot of the mountain" and "head of department", are conceptual in nature; that is, they are not mere words used non-literally. Rather, they are exploited to do important cognitive jobs. One of these jobs that conceptual metaphors do is "create", or constitute social, cultural, and psychological realities for us, as in Shakespeare's "All the world's a stage".

Below is a list of the main metaphorical source domains, with one or more linguistic examples illustrating each conceptual metaphor:

- Anger is a hot fluid in a container: She is **boiling** with anger.
- Anger is fire: He is doing **a slow burn**. His anger is **smoldering**.
- Anger is insanity: The man was **insane** with rage.
- Anger is an opponent in a struggle: I was **struggling** with my anger.
- Anger is a captive animal: He **unleashed** his anger.
- Anger is a burden: He **carries** his anger around with him.
- Angry behavior is aggressive animal behavior: Don't **snarl at** me!
- Anger is a physical annoyance: He's **a pain in the neck**.
- Anger is a natural force: It was **a stormy** meeting.
- An angry person is a functioning machine: They really **got** him **going**.
- Anger is a social superior: His actions were completely **governed** by anger.

To summarize, the cognitive approach to metaphor yields the following findings:

a. Metaphor is a property of concepts, not just of words.
b. The function of metaphor is to better understand certain concepts, not just for some artistic or esthetic purpose.
c. Metaphor may not always be based on similarity.
d. Metaphor is used effortlessly in everyday life by ordinary people, not just by special, talented people.
e. Metaphor, far from being a superfluous though pleasing linguistic ornament, is an inevitable process of human thought and reasoning.

## 12.3 Conceptual metonymies in English

Also as discussed in Unit 11, metonymy has long been considered as a rhetorical device, a trope based on association like proximity and correspondence. Thus, when this figure of speech is used, one word or phrase is substituted for another with which it is closely associated, as in "Arafat: a gun in one hand and an olive branch in the other", where "the gun" stands for "military power" and "olive branch" for "peace".

In the cognitive approach to metonymies, we take it to be conceptual in nature. In other words, we conceptualize one thing in terms of another on the basis of **contingency** or **proximity**, **contiguity**. For example, when we use "The rose died" to describe a girl holding a rose, "rose" here is meant to refer to the girl holding a rose, which is a contingent fact. If she were holding a banana, we would say "The banana died".

Like conceptual metaphors, conceptual metonymies can be **conventionalized**. Thus, our use of some metonymies seems to be automatic, unconscious, and effortless because they have become established as a mode of thinking. Unlike conceptual metaphors that are based on conceptual mapping across different cognitive domains or models, however, conceptual metonymies involve mapping within the same domain or model; namely, one category within a certain domain is **conceptualized** or **construed** to represent another from the same domain. Thus, the cognitive job conceptual metonymies do is to activate or highlight one cognitive entity by picking up another entity within the same domain. For instance, when we say "The company needs good heads", we suggest that the company need people who are smart or intelligent rather than those who are physically strong.

## 12.4 Categorization and prototypes in English

Human beings are subject to the so-called **principle of cognitive economy**, which states that human beings try to gain as much information as possible about its environment while minimizing cognitive efforts and resources. This cost-benefit balance drives category formation. In other words, rather than storing separate information about every individual stimulus experienced, humans can group similar stimuli into categories, which maintains economy in **cognitive representation**.

As we human beings recognize and differentiate experiences and concepts, we are involved in the job of **categorization**. Specifically, we classify these experiences and concepts into **cognitive categories**, usually for some specific purpose, based on their commonalities. Indeed, categorization reflects human beings' ability to identify perceived similarities (and differences) between entities and thus group them together. We benefit from the fact that the world around us has correlational structures. For instance, it is a fact about the world that wings most frequently co-occur with feathers and the ability to fly (as in birds), rather than with fur or the ability to breathe underwater. Thus, humans rely upon correlational structures of this kind in order to form and organize categories.

Categories are generally organized into levels of categorization: **superordinate level**, **basic level** and **subordinate level**. Firstly, categories at the superordinate level are the most general ones. Secondly, categories at the basic, generic, or middle level are perceptually and conceptually more salient. As members of superordinate-level categories, categories of the generic level tend to elicit the most responses and richest images. Finally, categories at the subordinate level are the most specific ones. As members of the basic-level categories, they have many individuating specific features. The following table exemplifies the differences of the three levels of categorization:

| Superordinate level | Basic level | Subordinate level |
| --- | --- | --- |
| FURNITURE | CHAIR | KITCHEN CHAIR |
|  |  | LIVING-ROOM CHAIR |
|  | TABLE | KITCHEN TABLE |
|  |  | DINING-ROOM TABLE |
|  | LAMP | FLOOR LAMP |
|  |  | DESK LAMP |

One important concept in categorization is **prototype**. Scholars find that not all members of a set share the same attributes; rather, some categories are defined by the best exemplar or prototype of the set or by **family resemblance**. An example of family resemblance is the notion of games. One game may resemble at least one game, although not all of them have to be alike at the same time. In "Natural categories" (1973), Eleanor Rosch defined the term "prototype" as a stimulus which takes a salient position in the formation of a category as it is the first stimulus to be associated with that category. Later, she redefined it as the most central member of a category, in the sense that it assembles the key attributes or features that best represent instances of the given category. It provides structures to and serves to organize a given category. An important consequence of this is that categories exhibit typicality effects.

There are some basic rules underlying categorization, as listed below:
a. Categories are defined in terms of family resemblances rather than by means of a set of necessary and sufficient features. For instance, ostriches and penguins can not fly and are not small in size, but they nevertheless belong to the category of birds because they share some other key features like having feather and laying eggs. By contrast, a robin has all features that define the category of birds and therefore it is considered a prototype of the category.
b. Membership in a category is determined by the perceived distance of resemblance of the entity to the prototype. There is no clear-cut boundaries. But there is a continuum, such that the borderline between and among the members is often fuzzy. The system of colors is a typical example.
c. All members of a category are not equal in terms of prototypicality and thus in status. Therefore, some members are core ones whereas some others are peripheral ones.
d. Many categories are not monocentric but polycentric in the sense that they may have more than one prototype instead of just one. For instance, in Chinese, both pears and peaches are likely to be thought of as prototypes of fruit.

## Check your understanding

*State whether each of the following statements is True or False.*
(1) Cognitive linguistics denies that metaphor is rhetorical.
(2) Metonymy is based on mapping of entities from different conceptual domains.
(3) For any category there is always one and only one prototype.
(4) For the same category, the prototype is the same across cultures and languages.
(5) The basic level of categories is the superordinate one.

## In-Class Activities

1. In English, there are many so-called **orientational metaphors**: expressions containing prepositions such as "up" and verbs such as "rise" denote positive meanings whereas expressions involving the use of "down" and verbs like "fall" convey the opposite meanings. Here are some examples:

- low/high spirits
- spirits rise
- have control over somebody
- on top of the situation

fall into depression
get the upper hand of
under control

(1) Do the orientational metaphors make sense to you?

(2) What about Chinese? Do we have similar metaphors?

2. By means of **metaphorical mapping**, certain objects, ideas, or events from one domain are described with words from a different domain of objects, ideas, and events. An interesting case is the metaphorical extension of words from the physical domain of food and digestion into the mental domain of ideas and interpersonal exchange of ideas. For example, consider the following cases:
- Let me chew on these ideas for a while.
- They just wouldn't swallow that idea.
- She'll give us time to digest that idea.
- Will you stop feeding me that old line?
- You'd better cook up a good story this time!
- Her proposal left a bad taste in my mouth.
- She's really hungry for knowledge.

(1) In what ways are communicating ideas similar to food intake and digestion?

(2) Can you give two more expressions involving similar metaphors?

3. In our daily life we like to think and talk metaphorically about things. For example, we may say "Time is money". Such metaphorical way of thinking and talking about time has produced a lot of expressions, as illustrated below:

budget one's time   waste one's time   save one's time

(1) What else do we compare "time" to? What related expressions do we have?

(2) Do we use the same kind of metaphors in English and in Chinese? Give some examples that show their convergence and divergence.

(3) What metaphors do you know that relate to the following themes?

        language    life    books

4. Newspaper headlines employ a lot of metonymies. Here are some examples from *The Washington Post*:

   **A.** White House Softens Tone on Embryo Use
   **B.** List of Top Pentagon Orders Reveals Strategy Shift
   **C.** Bush Pollution Curbs Are Rated Equal to Clinton's
   **D.** Microsoft Confirms It Will Offer Device to Battle the iPod

(1) What are the metonymies used in these headlines?

(2) Why are they used? For effectiveness or for economy?

5. Iconicity of language is an aspect of language where form echoes meaning. Onomatopoeia, also known as "sound symbolism", is one type of iconicity. Some researchers have found other evidence of iconicity. For example, words beginning with the sound combination "sl-" in English often have an unpleasant sense, as in "slithering", "slimy", "slugs".

(1) Is the "unpleasant" sense actually true of all, or even most, words beginning with "sl-" in English?

(2) Are there any other sounds or sound combinations that you associate

with particular meanings?

(3) How about the vowel sounds in words that identify near-to-speaker concepts (this, near, here) versus far-from-speaker concepts (that, far, there)? What is the difference? Is it a general pattern distinguishing terms for things that are near versus far in English? What about the case in Chinese?

6. English has a number of expressions such as "chit-chat" and "flip-flop" which never seem to occur in the reverse order (i.e. chat-chit, flop-flip). Here are more examples of this kind:

| | | |
|---|---|---|
| criss-cross | hip-hop | riff-raff |
| dilly-dally | knick-knacks | see-saw |
| ding-dong | mish-mash | sing-song |
| fiddle-faddle | ping-pong | tick-tock |
| flim-flam | pitter-patter | zig-zag |

(1) Can you think of a phonetic description of the regular pattern in these expressions?
(2) Can you think of any possible explanation for the observed pattern?

1. Metaphors of time in English and Chinese
2. Functions of metonymy
3. Prototypes of vegetables in English and Chinese

# Exercises

## Task 1  Reference Search

Find in the library or online some information about the following themes:
(1) gastalt
(2) mental space
(3) conceptual blending
(4) Charles Fillmore
(5) George Lakoff
(6) Ronald Langacker

## Task 2  Term Definition

Study the following definitions and then discuss how they combine to help you understand the terms.

**schema**: A mental construct of reality as culturally ordered and socially sanctioned: what people in a particular community regard as normal and predictable ways of organizing the world and communicating with others. [Henry Widdowson]

**schema**: An abstract characterization that is fully compatible with all the members of the category it defines (so membership is not a matter of degree); it is an integrated structure that embodies the commonality of its members, which are conceptions of greater specificity and detail that elaborate the schema in contrasting ways. [Ronald Langacker]

**prototype**: What members of a particular community think of as the most typical instance of a lexical category, e.g. for some English speakers "cabbage" (rather than, say, "carrot") might be the prototypical vegetable. [Henry Widdowson]

**prototype**: We can apply the term to the central member, or perhaps to the cluster of central members, of a category. Thus, one could refer to a particular artifact as the prototype of CUP. Alternatively, the prototype can be understood as a schematic representation of the conceptual core of a category. On this approach, we would say, not that a particular entity is the prototype, but that it instantiates the prototype. [John Taylor]

**prototype**: A typical instance of a category, and other elements are assimilated to the category on the basis of their perceived resemblance to the prototype; there are degrees of membership based on degrees of similarity. [Ronald Langacker]

**frame**: any system of linguistic choices—the easiest case being collections of words, but also including choices of grammatical rules or linguistic categories—that can get associated with prototypical instances of scenes [Charles Fillmore]

**frame**: a data-structure for representing a stereotypical situation [Minsky]

**frame**: a pre-existing knowledge structure with a fixed static pattern [George Yule]

**script**: a pre-existing knowledge structure for interpreting event sequences [George Yule]

**trajactor**: the figure or most prominent element in any relational structure [F. Ungerer and H. J. Schimdt]

**landmark**: the other entity in a relation which is a reference point for orientation [F. Ungerer and H. J. Schimdt]

## Task 3  Study Questions

1. In many of the world's languages there are so-called nursery names for parents. In English, for example, corresponding to the word "mother" is the nursery name "mama", and for father one finds "dada" and "papa". There is remarkable similarity across different languages in the form of these nursery names for parents. For example, in Chinese and Navajo "ma" corresponds to English "mama". Why do you think that this is the case?

2. Study the following sentences:
   A. Jane went *into* the room.
   B. The information goes *into* the computer.
   C. They have made up their mind to go *into* business.
   
   How would you understand the use of "into" in the different contexts? What is the nature of X in "into X"? Use a couple of other examples to illustrate.

3. Saying that "Time is money" is attempting a conceptual metaphor. Most metaphors, indeed, are conceptual. When we argue with others, we often do so as if we were fighting a war. Such conceptualization gives rise to many expressions like "win an argument" and "indefensible arguments". Do you know other similar expressions? Is the same kind of metaphorizing employed in Chinese?

4. Words referring to spending and finance (such as "cost", "spend", "invest", "buy", "sell") also have abstract metaphorical uses, as in "That mistake will cost you a lot", "He invested a lot of time in the project", "He paid dearly for his ways", "You're only buying trouble if you do that". List three additional examples of the metaphorical use of words from the realm of spending and finance and discuss how the metaphorical uses are related to the concrete (financial) meanings. Also, is the same kind of metaphorizing employed in Chinese?

5. The words in the following list are all related in terms of the superordinate term "tableware":

| glass | cup | plate | cutlery | napkin | tumbler |
| fork | goblet | teaspoon | flatware | bowl | crockery |
| tablecloth | wineglass | ladle | dish | saucer | spoon |
| tray | knife | mug | linen | bottle | pan |
| salt-shaker | peppermill | bread-basket | candlestick | table-mat | |

Can you work out what the prototype item of tableware is? One research procedure would be to create a list of these terms down one side of a page, with a scale beside each term. The scale would go from 5 ( = excellent example of "tableware") to 1 ( = not really an example of "tableware"). Make copies of your list (plus scale) and ask people to indicate their choices on the scale. The highest score would presumably be the prototype. What do you think of this procedure?

6. The following English words are what we call onomatopoeic words, words that are characterized by a natural correspondence between their physical property (like sound or form) and their content or meaning. Does the existence of onomatopoeic words overthrow the claim that language is arbitrary?

bang   bark   crash   hiss

Task 4   Mini-Project

Collect a set of metaphors from a literary discourse and analyze it in terms of how they contribute to thematic development or characterization.

# Recommended Readings

## Reading 1

### Good Examples, Bad Examples and Category Boundaries

As the categorization of colours, shapes, birds and vehicles suggests, category membership is not, as was for a long time assumed by philosophers and linguists, a yes-or-no distinction. Rather it involves different degrees of typicality, as is supported by goodness-of-example ratings, recognition, matching and learning tasks.

Rosch's main concern was to prove that categories are formed around prototypes, which function as cognitive reference points. As far as the boundaries of categories are concerned, she leaves us with the impression that at some unspecified point or area beyond their periphery the categories somehow fade into nowhere. This is not the idea we have when we talk about categories in a naive way. Normally, we tend to imagine them as boxes, drawers or some sort of fenced compound—certainly as something which has boundaries. With regard to the category BIRD, the allocation of boundaries seems to be easy enough, even though a little knowledge of zoology might be required. Yet our confidence will be undermined when they follow the philosopher Max Black and consider the imaginary chair museum he invented. According to Black, it consists of

> a series of chairs differing in quality by least noticeable amounts. At one end of a long line, containing perhaps thousands of exhibits, might be a Chippendale chair; at the other, a small nondescript lump of wood. Any "normal" observer inspecting the series finds extreme difficulty in "drawing the line" between chair and non-chair.
>
> (Black 1949:32)

What Black's interpretation of his chair museum suggests is that the collection of chairs could and should be regarded as a continuum with a kind of transition zone between chairs and non-chairs but no clear-cut boundaries. This view seems to be in conflict with what we observed at the beginning of the chapter: that concrete objects like houses, books and also chairs are clearly delimited and easy to identify, and that vague boundaries and transition zones are restricted to items like knees, fog and valleys and to scales like length, temperature and colour.

Here we must be careful not to confuse two different types of boundaries and transition zones. One type of transition zone arises from the observation that some concrete entities do not have clear-cut boundaries in reality—this is the case with knees and other body parts, it applies to fog, snow and similar weather phenomena and to landscape forms like valleys or mountains. In Black's chair museum, however, the visitor is confronted with a different type of transition zone, since each exhibit in the museum is an entity with absolutely clear boundaries. In the chair museum, it is not entities that merge into each other, but categories of entities, and these categories are the product of cognitive classification. Consequently, it is not the boundaries of entities that are vague, but the boundaries of these cognitive categories (here: chairs and non-chairs). To distinguish the two types of vagueness we will restrict the terms vague entity and vagueness to the first type (knees, fog, valleys) and use fuzzy category boundaries or fuzziness for the second, i.e. for the category boundaries of CHAIR, etc.

(F. Ungerer and H. J. Schimdt, *An Introduction to Cognitive Linguistics*, pp. 14-15)

 Food for Thought

(1) How is category membership traditionally defined?
(2) How is category membership newly defined?
(3) What is the difference between vagueness and fuzziness?

 Reading 2

## Basic Category Words

If the sense of words like "horse", "pig" and "bird" is little more than the fact of having a certain denotation, there must be some other role for all the information which seems to attach to these words. The point is easily illustrated with "bird".

BIRD    1. flies, has wings
          2. sings sweetly
          3. is small and light
          4. lays eggs in a nest
          5. is timid

Points 1-3 are quite likely to come to mind as components of the sense of "bird", particularly because these properties are the basis of metaphors and similes such as "fly/

sing like a bird". Although these seem to be obvious bird properties, not all birds have them. Many birds do not fly (kiwi, ostrich, emu, pukeko, moa, takahe, penguin), many birds are not small and light (Emperor penguin, moa, ostrich, emu) and many birds do not sing sweetly. Not all birds are timid—swans, geese and magpies can be very aggressive.

The properties of birds contrast strongly with semantic components such as MALE/FEMALE and ADULT/JUVENILE, which are always present in any use of a word containing them. "This is a stallion" entails "This is juvenile". The bird features, on the other hand, are not always present with the word—"This is a bird" does not entail "This flies" or "This sings sweetly". The contrast indicates that the bird features listed in [the example] are features of a cognitive concept, not semantic features of a word sense.

Findings in cognitive psychology indicate that mental concepts of concrete entities such as birds are structured around prototypes. The central bird prototype, for example, is a generalized average or prototypical bird. The prototypical bird flies and sings, has a fairly small roundish body and round head, a small beak, short legs and dull-coloured plumage. Real birds fall at various distances from the prototype depending on their similarity to that prototype. Thrushes, sparrows, starlings and blackbirds are close to the prototype. Birds like parrots, turkeys, emus, flamingos, cranes, kiwis and penguins are further from the prototype in features like size, body shape, colour and lack of flight.

If you are asked to quickly visualize a bird, the chances are that you will visualize something near the prototype, such as a sparrow, or the prototype itself, which isn't any particular bird species. If you are shown pictures of assorted objects including birds and asked to pick out those that are birds, it takes a moment longer to recognize non-prototypical birds, such as flamingos or penguins, as birds, even though they are well-known. The prototype is like a mental template for recognizing birds which works better (or faster) for some birds than for others.

Were we to identify conceptual prototypes with word senses, we would be led to conclude that senses themselves reflect the inner grading which ranks sparrows and thrushes as more birdlike than emus and turkeys. One might say that a sparrow is 100 per cent a bird but a turkey is only 70 per cent a bird, or that the statement "This turkey is a bird" is only 70 per cent true.

However, this conclusion seems to confuse prototypes with vague predicates, such as "bald", "crowd" or "orange". How many hairs can a bald man have and still be bald? How small can a group of people be and still be a crowd? Vague predicates have undefined boundaries. Suppose you have a colored ribbon which is red at one end and yellow at the other, changing gradually from one shade to the other through the length of the ribbon. The middle zone is orange. There is no clear-cut boundary between orange and red or between orange and yellow. The region bordered by yellow on one side and orange on the other is likely to be called "yellowy-orange" or "orangey-yellow" or "halfway between yellow and orange". It isn't quite true to call the color "yellow" but it isn't quite false either—it's yellow to some extent.

Birds are different. A turkey is a bird—it is 100 per cent a bird. If it were only 70 per cent a bird, what would the other 30 per cent of it be? Either a thing is a bird or it isn't. The slight delay in recognizing a turkey as a bird compared with recognizing a sparrow is not like the decision of whether or not orangey-yellow is yellow. Despite the momentary hesitation, once you realize that a turkey is a bird you are absolutely certain of it, but you cannot ever be certain that orangey-yellow is not yellow, or that it is yellow—there is no sure conclusion to be reached.

The mental concept BIRD may be compared to the dictionary entry for horse quoted earlier. Both the concept and the dictionary entry give information about a word's denotation or information about a kind and its instances, but these are not the same as senses. For words like these a sense distinct from denotation is very difficult to define. To know further facts about those objects, such as that "horses are used for riding upon", is to have more general knowledge about the world. Searching for the senses of many categorematic words leads us to mental concepts, which are not themselves senses, or to denotations. The pure sense, if any, is elusive.

(Kate Kearns, *Semantics*, pp. 11-13)

 **Food for Thought**

(1) Can you find any flaw with the prototype theory?
(2) Is there any overlapping between different categories?
(3) Is there any category that is vague in its boundaries?

# Unit 13

## The Varieties of English (I)

* 13.1 Regional dialects of English
* 13.2 Social dialects of English
* 13.3 Styles of English
* 13.4 Genres and registers of English

> *No human language can be said to be fixed, uniform or unvarying: all languages, as far as anyone knows, show internal variation in that actual usage varies from speaker to speaker. For example, speakers of English differ in their pronunciation of the language, in their choice of vocabulary words and the meaning of those words, and even in their use of syntactic constructions.*
> —Adrian Akmajian et al

## Pre-Class Reading

## 13.1 Regional dialects of English

When groups of speakers differ in noticeable ways in their use of a language, they are often said to speak different dialects of the language. It is notoriously difficult, however, to define with any precision what dialect is, even though many examples of dialectal differences can be readily given. Also, it is difficult to draw a demarcation line between the concept of language and that of dialect. However, people generally agree that a language may have some dialects. Transition from one dialect to another is gradual rather than abrupt. Two neighboring dialects are often mutually intelligible.

Like other languages, English may vary in its use in different places and at different historical times. The former results in **regional** or **geographical dialects**. Although a regional dialect is often associated with a certain accent, it is in fact more complex than that.

In British English, a well-known dialect goes by the name of London Cockney. Representing the broadest form of London local accent, it is characterized by its own special vocabulary and usage. The glottal stop is also considered particularly characteristic of Cockney, as manifested in different ways such as "t" glottalling in final position.

cat = [kæʔt]　up = [ʌʔp]　sock = [sɒʔk]

Also, "h" dropping at the beginning of certain words is highly frequent in Cockney. For examples:

house = 'ouse　hammer = 'ammer

Another major characteristic of Cockney is "th" fronting, which involves the replacement of the dental fricatives, [θ] and [ð], by labiodentals [f] and [v] respectively. Here are some examples:

thin = fin [fɪn]　brother = bruvver [brʌvə]　three = free [friː]

Finally, Cockney is known for its rhyming **slang**. Here are a couple of examples:

*north and south*: mouth
*two and eight*: state (as in "he's in a bit of a two and eight")
*trouble*: wife (from trouble and strife = wife, as in "going home to the trouble")
*plates*: feet (from plates of meat = feet, as in "you've got big plates")

Now, we take a look at a well-known American regional dialect: New York English. It is characterized by the stable peripheral position of the high and mid vowels /iy, ey, uw, ow/ (corresponding to /iː/, /eː/, /uː/, /əu/ respectively), which are typical of the North dialect region of America. The everyday speech of the city exhibits consistent vocalization of postvocalic /r/ except for the mid-central vowel in "bird", and when a final /r/ is followed by a vowel in the next word. Other phonetic features are listed below:

1. /a/ [corresponding to /æ/] is used for /ɑ/ [corresponding to /ɑː/], as in "father", "spa";
2. /ɑɪ/ [corresponding to /ɑːi/] is used for /aɪ/, as in "lightening", "right";
3. /oh/ [corresponding to /ɔː/] is raised to mid and high position;
4. dropping of "g" in -ing participles, as in "finding", "thinking".

The intonation typical of New York English involves a bit of a heavier drop off at the end. It is relatively monotone.

It is worth noting that the social value of a regional dialect or variety reveals the social status of its speakers. Also, a speaker with a large linguistic repertoire is likely to be more successful in his future career. For example, the ability to speak different dialects is often advantageous in job hunting.

## 13.2 Social dialects of English

English also varies with the social attributes of its speakers, resulting in what is called **social dialects** (also termed "**social-class dialects**", "**sociolects**", or "**class dialects**"). Often, they arise from the separation brought about by different social conditions. Apart from the well-known role of RP as a high-status marker, a study by Trudgill (1974) (refer to Wardhaugh 2000, p.167) is worth mentioning. It examined the percentage of speakers using [n] for [ŋ] in Norwich in England and revealed the findings in Table 13.1:

Table 13.1   Social classes and pronunciation

| Social classes | In casual speech | In formal speech |
| --- | --- | --- |
| Middle middle class (MMC) | 31% | 3% |
| Lower middle class (LMC) | 42% | 15% |
| Upper working class (UWC) | 87% | 74% |
| Middle working class (MWC) | 95% | 88% |
| Lower working class (LWC) | 100% | 98% |

In 1966 William Labov did a survey of New York City which covered r- pronunciation, among other things. It was found that while people in higher social classes had mostly shifted from r- dropping to r- pronunciation, other people were pronouncing r's only in their careful speech.

Labov conducted the survey like this: he went into a store and asked various employees where certain items were, items which he knew were on the fourth floor. The idea was to hear how the employees said "fourth floor" in spontaneous speech. He did this in three department stores, which catered to different social classes. In Table 13.2, the numbers outside of parentheses indicate the percentages of people who pronounced the r in both words. The numbers in parentheses indicate percentages of people who pronounced the *r* in at least one word.

Table 13.2   Labov's department store survey results

| Age groups | Saks (Upper-Middle) | Macy's (Lower-Middle) | Klein's (Working) |
|---|---|---|---|
| 15-30 | 67(78) | 21(47) | 10(25) |
| 35-50 | 26(65) | 26(56) | 0(15) |
| 55-70 | 13(48) | 39(58) | 4(23) |

Thus, Labov found that in the 1960's the amount of *r-* use increased on the whole by social class and formality of style in New York. Based on this study and that of *th-* pronunciation as in "three" and "thing" (see Fasold, 1990: 224), Labov concluded that there was a sharp break or stratification in linguistic behavior between working-class groups and middle-class groups.

## 13.3   Styles of English

English, like Chinese, makes a distinction between two **styles** (also called **registers**, though the latter term has another reading to be discussed later): **formal style** and **informal style**. Formal English occurs in social contexts that are formal, serious, often official in some sense, in which one has to mind one's language and in which the manner of saying or writing something is regarded as socially important. These contexts include formal job interviews, giving formal lectures, standing before a court of law, and so forth, as far as the spoken form of the style is concerned. When it comes to written communication, formal contexts include writing business letters, drafting academic papers, composing diplomatic memos, and the like. Informal English also has two forms, written and spoken. The spoken type occurs in casual, relaxed social settings in which speech is spontaneous, rapid, and uncensored by the speaker. Social settings for this style of speech include chatting with close friends and interacting in an intimate or family environment or in similar relaxed settings. The written type of informality occurs in the writing of personal letters, short text messages, lecture notes, daily emails, and the like.

Most, if not all, native speakers of English or any language have at their disposal a number of language styles, whether they are aware of it or not. For instance, one might offer coffee to a guest by saying "May I offer you some coffee?" Or "Would you care for some coffee?" in a formal setting. By contrast, in an informal setting, one might say

"Want some coffee?" or even "Coffee?" Some educated speakers of English equate the formal language style with the so-called standard language whereas the informal style is dubbed a form of sloppy speech or even slang. Actually, the informal style is equally rule-governed and has its own social functions.

## 13.4 Genres and registers of English

English is characterized by its variability in different **genres**. A genre is a particular class of speech events which are considered by the speech community as being of the same type. Traditionally it is classified according to purpose and other criteria; novels, newspaper articles, and business letters each belong to separate genres, for instance. Examples of culturally recognizable genres are prayers, sermons, conversations, songs, speeches, poems, letters and novels. They have particular and distinctive characteristics. For example, narration is paramount in the genre of fiction; argument-commentary is paramount in the genre of editorials; description is paramount in travelogue writing.

A domain of activity may allow different kinds of genres, as listed below:

- Genres in the domain of law: cases, judgments, ordinances, contracts, agreements, etc.
- Genres in the domain of business: memos, reports, case studies, letters, etc.
- Genres in the domain of public administration: government documents, political communication, news reports, policy statements, international treaties, memoranda of understanding, etc.
- Genres in the domain of mass media: editorials, news reports, review articles, advertisements, sports reports, letters to the editor, etc.

A functional approach to English variation with its use in different contexts is attempted by M. A. K. Halliday's **register theory**. A register has three components, as defined below:

**Field of discourse**: This is related to what is going on, the purpose and the subject matter of communication; it answers the questions of why and about what communication takes place; it can be technical, like linguistic lectures, and specialist communication, or non-technical, like shopping, chatting, etc. It largely determines the vocabulary used.

**Tenor of discourse**: This answers the question of whom the speaker is communicating to, determines the level of linguistic formality and the relationship between the language users.

**Mode of discourse**: This has to do with the medium used, whether it is spoken or written, spontaneous or non-spontaneous; it answers the question of how communication takes place.

These three components correspond to the three metafunctions of language mentioned in Unit 1. Using these categories, we can analyze the register of a classroom lecture on linguistics as follows:
- Field of discourse: pedagogical (linguistic)
- Tenor of discourse: teacher-students (formal, polite)
- Mode of discourse: oral (prepared)

## Check your understanding

State whether each of the following statements is True or False.
(1) A language often has some dialects.
(2) London Cockney is very prestigious in Britain.
(3) Different social classes often have their own dialects.
(4) Spoken English is informal in style.

## In-Class Activities

1. Regional dialects used to coincide with geographical barriers, like mountains and rivers. However, as modern communications technology develops, such physical barriers seem to disappear.

(1) Do you speak any local dialect(s)? Demonstrate a little bit.
(2) What do you think about the future of dialects? Should we take measures to protect our dialects?

2. **Temporal dialects** are also one dimension of linguistic variation. For example, English has gone through several major stages of development, from Old English, through Middle English, to Modern English. Study the following passage from Shakespeare's *Hamlet*, Act IV, Scene iii.

**Hamlet:** A man may fish with the worm that hath eat of a king, and eat of the fish that hath fed of that worm.

**King:** What dost thou mean by this?

**Hamlet:** Nothing but to show you how a king may go a progress through the guts of a beggar.

**King:** Where is Polonius?

**Hamlet:** In heaven. Send thither to see. If your messenger find him not there, seek him in the other place yourself. But indeed, if you find him not within this month, you shall nose him as you go up the stairs into the lobby.

## ask

(1) Can you identify any linguistic difference between Elizabethan and current Modern English? (e.g. in line 3, "thou" is now "you".)

(2) Since Shakespeare (1564-1616), do you think the English grammar has changed profoundly? Justify your judgment with evidence from the above excerpt.

(3) How does Modern English differ from Old English and Middle English?

3. The speech of an individual may develop into a personal style or an **idiolect**, characterized by some linguistic pattern unique to him or her. Thus we may talk about Shakespeare's language or Lu Xun's language. Study the following excerpts from two well-known authors.

**Excerpt 1** (Opening paragraph of Chapter 1 of Mark Twain's *The Adventures of Huckleberry Finn*)

YOU don't know about me without you have read a book by the name of *The Adventures of Tom Sawyer*; but that ain't no matter. That book was made by Mr. Mark Twain, and he told the truth, mainly. There was things which he stretched, but mainly he told the truth. That is nothing. I never seen anybody but lied one time or another, without it was Aunt Polly, or the widow, or maybe Mary. Aunt Polly—Tom's Aunt Polly, she is—and Mary, and the Widow Douglas is all told about in that book, which is mostly a true book, with some stretchers, as I said before.

Now the way that the book winds up is this: Tom and me found the money that the robbers hid in the cave, and it made us rich. We got six thousand dollars apiece—all gold. It was an awful sight of money when it was piled up. Well, Judge Thatcher he took it and put it out at interest, and it fetched us a dollar a day apiece all the year round—more than a body could tell what to do with. The Widow Douglas she took me for her son, and

# Unit 13  The Varieties of English (I)

allowed she would sivilize me; but it was rough living in the house all the time, considering how dismal regular and decent the widow was in all her ways; and so when I couldn't stand it no longer I lit out. I got into my old rags and my sugar-hogshead again, and was free and satisfied. But Tom Sawyer he hunted me up and said he was going to start a band of robbers, and I might join if I would go back to the widow and be respectable. So I went back.

**Excerpt 2** (Opening paragraph of Chapter 1 of Henry James' *The Portrait of a Lady*)

Under certain circumstances there are few hours in life more agreeable than the hour dedicated to the ceremony known as afternoon tea. There are circumstances in which, whether you partake of the tea or not—some people of course never do—the situation is in itself delightful. Those that I have in mind in beginning to unfold this simple history offered an admirable setting to an innocent pastime. The implements of the little feast had been disposed upon the lawn of an old English country-house, in what I should call the perfect middle of a splendid summer afternoon. Part of the afternoon had waned, but much of it was left, and what was left was of the finest and rarest quality. Real dusk would not arrive for many hours; but the flood of summer light had begun to ebb, the air had grown mellow, the shadows were long upon the smooth, dense turf. They lengthened slowly, however, and the scene expressed that sense of leisure still to come which is perhaps the chief source of one's enjoyment of such a scene at such an hour. From five o'clock to eight is on certain occasions a little eternity; but on such an occasion as this the interval could be only an eternity of pleasure. The persons concerned in it were taking their pleasure quietly, and they were not of the sex which is supposed to furnish the regular votaries of the ceremony I have mentioned. The shadows on the perfect lawn were straight and angular; they were the shadows of an old man sitting in a deep wicker-chair near the low table on which the tea had been served, and of two younger men strolling to and fro, in desultory talk, in front of him. The old man had his cup in his hand; it was an unusually large cup, of a different pattern from the rest of the set and painted in brilliant colors. He disposed of its contents with much circumspection, holding it for a long time close to his chin, with his face turned to the house. His companions had either finished their tea or were indifferent to their privilege; they smoked cigarettes as they continued to stroll. One of them, from time to time, as he passed, looked with a certain attention at the elder man, who, unconscious of observation, rested his eyes upon the rich red front of his dwelling. The house that rose beyond the lawn was a structure to repay such consideration and was the most characteristic object in the peculiarly English picture I have attempted to sketch.

(1) What style or idiolect do you think characterizes Mark Twain? Justify

yourself with evidence from the text.

(2) What style do you think characterizes Henry James? Justify yourself with evidence from the text.

4. One important difference between formal style and informal style of English is that the former uses a lot of complete, long and complex sentences while the latter employs a great deal of elliptical, short, and simple sentences. Compare the following conversational fragments with the examination regulations of a Hong Kong university.

A. What, me worry?
B. What, John get a job? (Fat chance!)
C. My boss give me a raise? (Are you joking?)
D. Him wear a tuxedo? (He doesn't even own a clean shirt!)

---

**Regulations Governing Conduct at Examinations**

(1) These regulations cover examinations for any degree, diploma, certificate or other academic distinction or award granted by the University. For the purpose of these regulations, examinations include written, practical and oral tests; continuous assessment; submission of any form of work; any other means of assessment as specified by the examiners; and any combination of the above.

(2) A candidate shall not introduce or cause to be introduced into the place of examination, or remove or cause to be removed there from, any printed or written matter or any other form of recorded matter or any blank writing paper or blotting paper or any blank recording material save with the express permission of the Examiners previously conveyed by the Examinations Secretary.

(3) A candidate shall write only on his own answer book and on any supplementary answer books or sheets provided for the purpose. He shall not mutilate his answer book or any supplementary answer books or sheets, and shall give up all such materials on leaving the place of examination.

(4) A candidate shall not obtain or seek to obtain advantage in the examination by having or seeking access to unauthorized information or material or by copying or attempting to copy from, or by communicating or attempting to communicate with any other person during the time appointed for an examination.

*(Continued on next page)*

Unit 13  The Varieties of English (I)

(5) A candidate shall not impersonate another candidate, nor shall he permit himself to be impersonated at any examination.

(6) A candidate shall not engage in plagiarism nor employ nor seek to employ any other unfair means at an examination or in any other form of work submitted for assessment as part of a University examination. Plagiarism is defined as the unacknowledged use, as one's own, of work of another person, whether or not such work has been published.

(7) In conducting research, a candidate shall not engage in any misconduct. which shall include, but not limited to, fabrication; falsification; plagiarism; infringement of another person's intellectual property rights; misleading ascription of authorship including the listing of authors without their permission, attributing work to others who have not in fact contributed to the research, or the lack of appropriate acknowledgement of work primarily produced by another person; and other practices which seriously deviate from those commonly accepted within the academic community for proposing, conduction or reporting research.

(1) How would you express each of the conversational fragments in formal English? Do these informal sentences express any feeling or idea that is not expressed in the formal style?

(2) How is the language of administrative regulations different from that of the conversational fragments?

(3) Look at the following picture. Which style does the language used belong to, formal or informal? Why?

5. English also varies with the gender of its speakers. It is found that women are more status-conscious in the English-speaking society. They use more standard language. They tend to use polite language. Their speech is characterized by greater variation in intonation than male speech. There are a lot of tag questions in their speech. The following is an excerpt from Chapter III of Jane Austen's *Pride and Prejudice*.

"Oh! my dear Mr. Bennet," as she entered the room, "we have had a most delightful evening, a most excellent ball. I wish you had been there. Jane was so admired, nothing could be like it. Everybody said how well she looked; and Mr. Bingley thought her quite beautiful, and danced with her twice. Only think of that my dear; he actually danced with her twice; and she was the only creature in the room that he asked a second time. First of all, he asked Miss Lucas. I was so vexed to see him stand up with her; but, however, he did not admire her at all: indeed, nobody can, you know; and he seemed quite struck with Jane as she was going down the dance. So, he enquired who she was, and got introduced, and asked her for the two next. Then, the two third he danced with Miss King, and the two fourth with Maria Lucas, and the two fifth with Jane again, and the two sixth with Lizzy, and the Boulanger—"

"If he had had any compassion for **me**," cried her husband impatiently, "he would not have danced half so much! For God's sake, say no more of his partners. Oh! that he had sprained his ankle in the first dance!"

"Oh! my dear," continued Mrs. Bennet, "I am quite delighted with him. He is so excessively handsome! And his sisters are charming women. I never in my life saw any thing more elegant than their dresses. I dare say the lace upon Mrs. Hurst's gown—"

Here she was interrupted again. Mr. Bennet protested against any description of finery. She was therefore obliged to seek another branch of the subject, and related, with much bitterness of spirit and some exaggeration, the shocking rudeness of Mr. Darcy.

"But I can assure you," she added, "that Lizzy does not lose much by not suiting **his** fancy; for he is a most disagreeable, horrid man, not at all worth pleasing. So high and so conceited that there was no enduring him! He walked here, and he walked there, fancying himself so very great! Not handsome enough to dance with! I wish you had been there, my dear, to have given him one of your set-downs. I quite detest the man."

(1) How does Mrs. Bennet's speech reflect the general characteristics of women's language? Justify your answer with examples.

(2) What other features may characterize feminine discourse?

Unit 13  The Varieties of English (I)   201

6. The genre of public signs has its own linguistic features. Study the following signs:

(1) How would you describe public signs as a unique genre?

(2) Are there features of signs that are not captured by these pictures?

7. Cyber language is a particular kind of dialect used by young netizens. Study the following samples carefully.

| | | | |
|---|---|---|---|
| **2B or not 2B** | To Be Or Not To Be | **GL** | Good Luck |
| **AFAIC** | As Far As I'm Concerned | **IDK** | I Don't Know |
| **AFK** | Away From Keyboard | **IMO** | In My Opinion |
| **4ever** | Forever | **J/K** | Just Kidding! |
| **ASAP** | As Soon As Possible | **LTNS** | Long Time No See |
| **B4** | Before | **NOYB** | None Of Your Business |
| **BTW** | By The Way | **OMG** | Oh My Gosh |
| **F2F** | Face-to-Face | **TY** | Thank You |
| **FYI** | For Your Information | **TYVM** | Thank You Very Much |

(1) What stylistic features can you associate with cyber language as shown here?

(2) Can you give a few samples of Chinese cyber language?

8. A genre may have sub-genres. For example, narrative as a genre may include travelogues, diaries, and stories. The following is a story from *The Fables of Aesop*.

### The Leopard and the Fox

A leopard and a fox were arguing about which of them was the better animal.

"My spotted coat is the most beautiful fur in the world," said the leopard.

"You cannot see my beauty," said the fox, "for it is inside my head. But it is better to be wise than beautiful in the forest, my friend."

*Cleverness is more useful than beauty.*

(1) How would you characterize the genre of fables as a sub-genre of narrative?

(2) How is this genre different from that of children's stories?

1. Weather forecast English

2. Online American university introductions

3. Teachers' language in class

 Task 1   Reference Search

Find in the library or online some information about the following themes:

(1) speech community

(2) argot

(3) vernacular

(4) repertoire

(5) taboo

(6) William Labov

Unit 13  The Varieties of English (I)   203

## Task 2  Term Definition

Study the following definitions and then discuss how they combine to help you understand the terms.

**dialect**: the variety of a language spoken in a particular area (regional dialect) or by a particular social group (social dialect) [Ronald Wardhaugh]

**dialect**: A dialect is a variety of a language associated with a particular group of speakers and mutually intelligible with other varieties. [Ronald Wardhaugh]

**dialect**: A dialect is a speech variety used by a community comprising some of those who speak a particular language. [Stuart Poole]

**idiolect**: the language or dialect of an individual speaker [Ronald Wardhaugh]

**idiolect**: An idiolect is the speech variety of an individual. [Stuart Poole]

**slang**: Slang is a variety of speech that may be used to reinforce the identity of a section of society. [Stuart Poole]

**slang**: very informal language employing vigorous and generally evanescent words and expressions [Ronald Wardhaugh]

**slang**: a kind of jargon marked by its rejection of formal rules [Bernard Spolsky]

## Task 3  Study Questions

1. America has four major dialect regions: Inland North, South, West, and Midlands. Look for information about each. How about China? How many major dialect regions are there? Which region do you belong to? What are the characteristics of your dialect?

2. English words fall into different classes of formality and therefore are used in different genres or by different speakers. Look at the following.

| | |
|---|---|
| steed (poetic) | residence (formal) |
| horse (general) | abode (poetic) |
| nag (slang) | home (general) |
| gee gee (baby language) | domicile (very formal, official) |
| throw (general) | tiny (colloquial) |
| chuck (casual, slang) | diminutive (very formal) |
| cast (literal, biblical) | wee (colloquial, dialectal) |

Can you give more examples? Does Chinese make similar distinctions? Use at least two examples to justify your judgment.

3. People of different ages may speak English somewhat differently. Old people, for example, tend to frequently use level tone and slow tempo in thein speech. They may cling to old-fashioned words. They like long and complete sentences. How about youngsters? Collect some data to illustrate how the old and the young differ in their use of English. Make the same comparison with regard to speakers of Chinese, old and young.

4. English use also varies with occupation to a large extent, which gives rise to the concept of jargon. Collect some data about doctor-patient conversations and lawyer-client conversations to discuss the effect of occupation on the use of English. For comparison, collect some data from films or novels about the use of language, English or Chinese, by members of some underground society. Characterize their argot, a specialized vocabulary or set of idioms used by the particular group.

5. Sports announcers on TV and radio use a style of English that is both colorful and unique. Listen to a variety of sports broadcasts, paying careful attention to the language, and try to characterize as precisely as you can how this language differs from the formal style or standard language. To get started, you might consider the following sample of sportscaster language: "Smith on third. Jones at bat. Mursky winding up for the pitch." Also, read the following football commentary.

(1) And the ball goes out of play for a goal-kick to Arsenal. (2) Gould, the Arsenal goalkeeper, places the ball, runs up and boots it well upfield to Smart, the outside-left. (3) Smart traps it neatly and sets off at a cracking pace up the left wing. (4) Hunt's there with him now, out on the left, on the far side of the field. (5) And at the moment the Wolves' defense is looking rather disorganized. (6) Smart to Hunt. (7) Hunt takes the ball forward quickly, cutting inside towards the Wolverhampton goal. (8) The centre-half comes across and tries to intercept him, but Hunt slips past and quickly pushes the ball out to Smart again, who's still making ground up the left wing. (9) Now Smart. (10) He gathers the ball right on the touchline and brings it almost to the corner-flag. (11) Wolves' right-back is with him now. (12) Tackles; but Smart beats him, brings the ball clear, and now he's looking for the centre-forward. (13) He's still holding on to it. (14) What's he going to do? (15) He'll lose it if he's not careful. (16) No! (17) He swings it across the

goalmouth, hard and high a beautiful centre. (18) And Johnson's right there: the center-forward's there; and he's unmarked; and he jumps; he gets his head to it and—Oh! What a goal! (19) What a beautiful goal! (20) The Wolves' goalie just didn't stand a chance with that one. (21) Johnson took it beautifully. (22) Headed it like a bullet into the top left-hand corner of the net. (23) Well, there's the first goal. (24) Arsenal have opened scoring, and as they make their way back to the centre-spot the crowd are still roaring their approval.

What linguistic features characterize this fragment of football commentary?

6. Study the following pictures. Discuss their differences in terms of genre features.

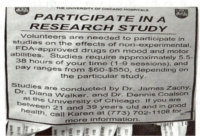

7. Find a recipe, a resume, and the acknowledgments of an academic thesis and discuss their genre characteristics.

 Task 4  Mini-Project

A social being has a variety of rights and obligations which are encoded or reflected in his or her way of using language. Collect some data in which the same person under study carries out different social roles. Conduct a contrastive study of how the role influences one's way of speaking.

 Recommended Readings

 Reading 1

### Speech and Identity

When you greet someone you don't know and ask formulaic questions, you are not only establishing lines of communication and setting up social roles, you are also finding out something about where the person is from and perhaps also what the person's socio-economic status is—or at least what he or she would like you to think it is. Dress, style of walk, gesture all indicate such factors too, but language plays a crucial role. Formulaic openings, such as comments on the weather, allow an apparently objective context to reveal delicate differences. Even a formula as simple as

    a. Hi, how are you?

tells a lot about the speaker, revealing, for instance, that the speaker wants to be informal ("Hi" as opposed to "hello"), and is from the United States ("Hi" is rarely used in England), and probably from the Southeast United States. In many other parts of the United States the intonation pattern in the example (a) with rise-fall on "you" can be used only for a real question, not a greeting. Speakers from these regions use an intonation pattern with a rise on "are":

    b. Hi, how are you?

for the greeting. Another greeting formula, "Mornin'", tells something about regional or social background through presence or absence of r, and presence of [in] versus [iŋ], where [in] indicates familiarity, casual speech, or lower-class economic status. There are very few utterances that do not give us at least some extra-linguistic information.

In most speech communities, we find language variation along lines of regional or ethnic origin, socioeconomic status, and also sex, age, and education. All speakers have at least some internalized knowledge of how their language varies along these parameters, and in most cases we find culturally shared attitudes to certain varieties. For instance, in England before the Second World War, a social dialect known as the King's or Queen's English was the high prestige variety, mandatory for anybody aspiring to a civil service or academic post, and speakers of this variety were socially approved of while non-speakers were not. This attitude was immortalized in Shaw's *Pygmalion* and the musical based on it, *My Fair Lady*. Since the 1960s, however, a considerable number of regional and even social varieties have become widely acceptable in England. Indeed, many prospective professors who twenty-five years ago would have cultivated "the Queen's English" now studiously avoid it and announce their social and regional origins proudly (in some cases we may even find a "reverse snobbism", the adoption of a variety typical of a socioeconomic class lower than that into which the speaker was born). This cultural attitude depends for its existence on the knowledge that language varies, and that language varieties can have social meaning. That is, they can function as indicators of social identity.

In sum, when we consider why people speak the way they do, all of the following factors must be considered separately in addition to the structure of the code itself:

1. type of speaker (regional and ethnic origin, socioeconomic status, education, sex, age)
2. type of addressee
3. topic of speech (politics, sex, linguistics, a drunken brawl)
4. genre (sermon, casual talk, interview)
5. medium (spoken, written; radio, television)
6. situation (classroom, bar, a walk in the fields)
7. degree of formality (casual, formal )
8. type of speech act (statement, command, question)

These factors form the basis of study in the discipline called "sociolinguistics". All are essential to a full understanding of language as communication and of the structures that control it.

(Elizabeth Traugott and Marry Prattt, *Linguistics for Students of Literature*, pp. 309-311)

 Food for Thought

(1) Is the discussion of greeting forms also true of Chinese?
(2) Do we have a Chinese equivalent to Queen's English?
(3) Why is there the emergence of the "reverse snobbism", as mentioned in the passage?

## Speech Community

To understand what the ethnography of communication is all about, it is necessary to understand some fundamental concepts. It is one of Hymes's emphases that ways of speaking can vary substantially from one culture to another, even in the most fundamental ways. For example, it has been pointed out (for instance, Schegloff 1972) that most middle-class white Americans (and possibly members of other Western societies as well), have a "no gap, no overlap" rule for conversational turn-taking. If two or more people are engaged in conversation and if two speakers start to talk at the same time, one will very quickly yield to the other so that the speech of two people does not "overlap". On the other hand, if there is a lull in the conversation of more than a few seconds' duration the participants become extremely uncomfortable. Someone will start talking about something unimportant just to fill the "gap" or the group will break up.

So profoundly ingrained is this rule for speakers who have it that they can hardly imagine a conversation being carried on in any other way. But Reisman (1974) found that it was quite the usual practice for Antiguans to carry on discussions with more than one speaker speaking simultaneously. On the other hand, Saville-Troike (1982) reports that there are American Indian groups where it is common for a person to wait several minutes in silence before answering a question or taking a speaking turn. Reisman (1974:112) tells the following story about his experiences in a Lapp community in northern Sweden, where conversational gaps are part of the ordinary way people talk:

> We spent some days in a borrowed sod house in the village of Rensjoen ... Our neighbors would drop in on us every morning just to check that things were all right. We would offer coffee. After several minutes of silence the offer would be accepted. We would tentatively ask a question. More silence, then a "yes" or a "no". Then a long wait. After five or ten minutes we would ask another. Same pause, same "yes" or "no". Another ten minutes, etc. Each visit lasted approximately an hour—all of us sitting formally. During that time there would be six or seven exchanges. Then our guests would leave to repeat the performance the next day.

Obviously, an ethnography of communication for middle-class white Americans would include the "no gap, no overlap" conversational rule. The corresponding description of Antiguan speech rules would not include the "no overlap" rule. And a description of the American Indian groups Saville-Troike refers to, or the Lapps that Reisman lived near, would not include the "no gap" rule.

If the rules for speaking can be different from one social group to the next, how do we decide what a social group is for purposes of ethnographic description? It is clear that it cannot be all citizens of the same country; American middle-class whites and some American Indians have different rules for conducting conversations. It cannot be decided on the basis of speaking the same language, either. In England, for example, conversations in public places like restaurants are subdued such that people who are not in the conversing group cannot hear what is being said. American public conversations can easily be overheard by anyone else in the same average-sized room unless what the group has to say is particularly personal or secret. Yet the two nations share the English language. It is necessary, then, for ethnographers of communication to develop the concept of speech community: the group to which a particular ethnographic description applies.

Defining "speech community" has proved to be far from easy. Numerous definitions have been proposed, most of them at least slightly different from the next. Hymes (1972b: 53-55), for example, insists that all members of a speech community share not only the same rules for speaking, but at least one linguistic variety as well. Suppose people in a Czech village and people in an Austrian village just across the border were to have the same rules for how to greet other people, how many people can and must be speaking at a time and so forth; but suppose Austrians spoke only German and the Czechs spoke only Czech. They would not, according to Hymes, be members of the same speech community. Saville-Troike (1982:20) speaks of a level of analysis at which a speech community need not share a language. By all definitions, though, a speech community must at least share rules for speaking.

(Ralph Fasold, *The Sociolinguistics Language*, pp. 40-41)

  **Food for Thought**

(1) Does the "no gap, no overlap" rule apply to the conversation among your classmates?
(2) How would you define a speech community?
(3) Why is it difficult to define the notion of a speech community?

# Unit 14

# The Varieties of English (Ⅱ)

* 14.1 African-American Vernacular English
* 14.2 Pidgin English and Creole
* 14.3 British English and American English
* 14.4 Bilingualism and diglossia
* 14.5 English as a lingua franca

> *There is a lively controversy about whether or not these "world Englishes", as they are sometimes called, should be understood and taught as legitimate entities, or whether the standards in force in English-speaking countries should be taught in other places in the world and, if so, to what extent.*
>
> —Ralph Fasold

## Pre-Class Reading

## 14.1 African-American Vernacular English

African-American Vernacular English (AAVE for short) (also referred to as **Black English**, though less preferably today) is a dialect or group of similar dialects spoken in ghettos in large urban areas of the United States. Look at the following examples:

① She the first one started us off.
② He fast in everything he do.
③ I know, but he wild, though.
④ You out the game.

Unit 14   The Varieties of English (Ⅱ)

⑤ We on tape.
⑥ But everybody not black.
⑦ They not caught.

Clearly, AAVE is characterized, among other things, by the omission of the verb "to be". In the examples cited, the correspondence between SE (**standard English**) and AAVE is partly as follows:

| SE: Contraction | AAVE: Deletion |
| --- | --- |
| She's the first one … | She the first one … |
| He's fast … | He fast … |
| You're out … | You out … |
| They're not caught. | They not caught. |

Note that the deletion of "is" or "are" in AAVE is not arbitrary. Rather, it follows the same regular rules as standard English contraction. In both AAVE and SE, the verb "to be" (as well as other auxiliary verbs) becomes reduced in casual speeches when it is unstressed. Thus, it is wrong to say that AAVE is a kind of defective dialect that violates rules of grammar or, even worse, has no rules of grammar.

## 14.2   Pidgin English and Creole

**Pidgins** are mixed or blended languages used by people who speak different languages for restricted purposes such as trading. Originally "pidgin" referred to Chinese Pidgin English and was a modification of the word "business". As might be expected, pidgins, given their limited vocabulary and reduced grammar, typically serve limited functions, especially in their early stages. They identify social groupings (who is in and who is out), differentiate speech functions (for example, statement, question, command, request, and naming of trade objects and body parts), and specify immediate local contexts (trading post, ship, harbor, or road). They are often extensively supplemented by gestures.

When a pidgin has become the primary language of a speech community and is acquired by the children of that speech community as their mother tongue, it is said to be a **Creole**. The original pidgin is expanded in terms of its grammar and vocabulary. Examples are English-based Creole in Jamaica and the French-based Creole in Haiti. "Creole" originally meant a white colonist born in the tropical colonies; later it applied to slaves and other residents of these colonies, and later still to the contact languages spoken especially in colonial situations. As a native or home language, a creole clearly has more linguistic functions than a pidgin and therefore is more varied in structure.

## 14.3 British English and American English

English is a national language as well as an official language in many countries. We may speak of different varieties of English rather than dialects of it. Thus, we have **American English**, **British English**, **Australian English**, and **Canadian English**. While they are fundamentally similar, each variety has its own characteristics.

Take American English and British English for example. There are a lot of differences between the two varieties at the phonetic, lexical, and syntactic levels. Phonetically, different values are assigned to certain vowels, particularly conspicuous in the tense vowels and diphthongs of the variety of British English known as **Received Pronunciation** (RP). Different phonemic choices are also apparent, as exemplified in "bath", "either", "clerk", "fertile" and in the pronunciation of z (as /ziː/ in America and as /zed/ in Britain). Stress patterns differ, as do the number of syllables in words such as "medicine", "necessary", "laboratory", and "missionary", and the intonation contours for sentences. British English is more varied in the use of pitch, while American English is more monotonous, using level intonation.

Vocabulary may be the area of the biggest difference between the two varieties. Here are some pairs for contrast:

| British English | American English |
| --- | --- |
| autumn | fall |
| lift | elevator |
| angry | mad |
| film | movie |
| garden | yard |
| ill | sick |
| lorry | truck |

American English and British English also employ different spellings for a large number of words, as exemplified below:

| British English | American English |
| --- | --- |
| colour | color |
| humour | humor |
| neighbour | neighbor |
| skilful | skillful |
| fulfil | fulfill |
| grey | gray |
| programme | program |
| cheque | check |

Most subtle differences are syntactic ones. British English has a preference for the use of "have" as a full verb in "Haven't you any?" as opposed to an American preference for "Don't you have any?" The tendency to add particles to verbs as in "visit with" and "call up" is an American usage, whereas the use of "those" and "ones" together in "Give me those ones" is a British usage.

## 14.4 Bilingualism and diglossia

**Bilingualism**, often a result of immigration and foreign language learning, refers to a phenomenon where two languages are used side by side with each other, each having a different role to play. Some individuals are bilingual, so are some communities or even the whole nations.

In most bilingual communities, some speakers (balanced bilinguals) have equal control of two languages, while some have full control of one and limited control of a second. A bilingual's degree of bilingualism can be assessed in the four skills of listening comprehension, speaking, reading comprehension and writing. There are many possible combinations of abilities in these skills. Many children of immigrants, for instance, possess all four skills solely in the official language of their country of residence (for example, English in Australia), while they may be able to understand only the spoken form of their parents' language (for example, Chinese) and barely able to speak it.

Which language is used on a given occasion will in part be determined by the relative competence of the speakers concerned. But no matter how extensive a person's knowledge of both languages is, very rarely will the person use both equally in all situations. This is also true of how the languages are used in the community as a whole. One language (say English) might be used on the job and for writing, another (say Chinese) might be used at home. One language is nearly always the public, **official language**, while the other the language of intimacy. Since this is the case, the use of one language over another on a given occasion will also depend on the topic and the context.

When drastically different functions are served by two varieties of the same language in one speech community, we have a "diglossic" situation. The term "**diglossia**" was originally coined by Charles Ferguson to refer to situations where different varieties of the same language were used with markedly different functions. For example, in contemporary Arabic-speaking countries, Classical Arabic and Modern Arabic are both in use, each with a different range of functions, as contrasted below:

| High Variety (Classical Arabic) | Low Variety (Colloquial Arabic) |
|---|---|
| poetry | conversation with family, friends |
| news broadcast | radio soap operas |
| personal letters | instructions to servants, waiters |
| political speeches | captions on political cartoons |

## 14.5 English as a lingua franca

A **lingua franca** is a language commonly used by people who speak different first languages. Theoretically, any language can be a lingua franca. Latin and French used to serve more or less as a lingua franca in their history. Today, in China, Mandarin Chinese, or *Putonghua*, functions as a lingua franca for its peoples of over fifty nationalities. More globally, English is predominently a lingua franca.

The term "**English as a world language**" (EWL) or "**English as an international language**" (EIL) emphasizes the fact that English is now used all over the world or serves the purpose of international communication. **English as a lingua franca** (ELF) is defined by the fact that the English language is used as a common means of communication for speakers of different first languages, not only in the domain of trade but also in many other areas like education, politics, traveling, etc.

Unlike **English as a foreign language** (EFL), English as a lingua franca makes no reference to the linguistic, cultural, and communicative norms of native speakers of English like Americans and Canadians. The use of ELF takes place among non-native speakers of English, as in a chat between a Chinese and a Japanese. Naturally, when they talk, they concentrate on communicative function rather than linguistic form. In other words, in the context of ELF interaction, communicative efficiency (i.e. getting the message across) and fluency are more important than grammaticality and idiomaticity.

To ensure the success of communication, ELF speakers are generally found to accommodate to each other's linguistic habits and cultural backgrounds. They look more tolerant and empathetic. They adhere to "linguistic equality or neutrality" in the sense that neither side would claim a privilege or advantage in the mastery and use of language, which might be found in the communication between a native speaker and a non-native speaker. Likewise, they assume cultural equality, instead of having to follow the cultural pattern of native speakers of English.

Unit 14　The Varieties of English (II)

## Check your understanding

*State whether each of the following statements is True or False.*

(1) African-American Vernacular English is an inferior dialect of English.
(2) Pidgin English no longer exists today.
(3) Some people speak a creole as their mother tongue.
(4) British English and American English are identical in grammar but different in vocabulary.

## In-Class Activities

**1.** In recent years African-American Vernacular English has attracted a good deal of attention from linguists, whose investigations have shown quite clearly that AAVE is as rule-governed and logical as Standard English. Study the following excerpt from Chapter IV of Harriet Beecher Stowe's *Uncle Tom's Cabin*.

　　"Well, now, I hopes you're done," said Aunt Chloe, who had been busy in pulling out a rude box of a trundle-bed; "and now, you Mose and you Pete, get into thar; for we's goin' to have the meetin'."

　　"O mother, we don't wanter. We wants to sit up to meetin', —meetin's is so curis. We likes 'em."

　　"La, Aunt Chloe, shove it under, and let 'em sit up," said Mas'r George, decisively, giving a push to the rude machine.

　　Aunt Chloe, having thus saved appearances, seemed highly delighted to push the thing under, saying, as she did so, "Well, mebbe 't will do 'em some good."

　　The house now resolved itself into a committee of the whole, to consider the accommodations and arrangements for the meeting.

　　"What we's to do for cheers, now, I declar I don't know," said Aunt Chloe. As the meeting had been held at Uncle Tom's weekly, for an indefinite length of time, without any more "cheers", there seemed some encouragement to hope that a way would be discovered at present.

　　"Old Uncle Peter sung both de legs out of dat oldest cheer, last week," suggested Mose.

　　"You go long! I'll boun' you pulled 'em out; some o' your shines," said Aunt Chloe.

　　"Well, I'll stand, if it only keeps jam up agin de wall!" said Mose.

(1) What phonetic features can you spot as typical of AAVE rather than SE?

(2) What grammatical feature(s) may look unusual to you? Is it systematically distributed?

2. A pidgin may be roughly defined as a language that is nobody's native language. It arises in situations where speakers of mutually unintelligible languages come together, typically as social subordinates to a socially dominant minority who speak yet another language.

(1) Can we find such pidgin English in China? Can you provide a couple of examples?

(2) What linguistic features can be said to be typical of such pidgin English?

3. Creoles, as developed on the basis of pidgins, are by no means chaotic. They are nearly as much rule-governed as standard varieties of natural languages like English. Here are some data for comparison (Yule, 1996).

|   | Hawaii's Creole English | Standard English Equivalents |
|---|---|---|
| 1 | Us two bin get hard time raising dog. | The two of us had a hard time raising dogs. |
| 2 | John them stay cockroach the kaukau. | John and his friends are stealing the food. |
| 3 | He lazy, "a" swhy he no like play. | He doesn't want to play because he's lazy. |
| 4 | More better I bin go Honolulu for buy om. | It would have been better if I'd gone to Honolulu to buy it. |
| 5 | The guy gon' lay the vinyl bin quote me price. | The man who was going to lay the vinyl had quoted me a price. |
| 6 | Bin get one wahine she get three daughter. | There was a woman who had three daughters. |
| 7 | She no can go, she no more money, "a" swhy. | She can't go because she hasn't any money. |

Unit 14　The Varieties of English (II)  217

(1) Can you list a couple of features typical of Hawaii's Creole English?

(2) In what ways is the creole recognizable as regularly patterned?

4. **Language policy and language planning** (LPLP or LPP for short), as a branch of study, offers advice on a number of issues including how the language factor (including L1 and L2) affects at least the following to varying degrees in different historical periods:
   A. the economic and educational systems of a nation;
   B. the modernization and internationalization of a nation;
   C. the cultural identity and unity of a nation;
   D. the fate of the mother tongue and dialects of a nation.

(1) Do you find problems with any English-related policies currently practiced in China? What policies do you recommend regarding English education in our country?

(2) Do you think China will turn into a bilingual society in the near future? Do you wish to see that happen?

5. In bilingual communities, a great deal of switching back and forth from one language to another may be observed. This "**code-switching**" may at first look random, but is actually highly systematic and based upon particular appropriateness conditions.

(1) Can you give an example of code-switching?

(2) Under what circumstances do people code-switch?

(3) In a broad sense, code-switching also includes the shift from one dialect to another and that from a dialect to a standard variety. Do we switch for the same reason on such occasions as we do from one language to another?

6. **Code-mixing** refers to the use of two languages or one language plus a dialect in a unit of linguistic expression or discourse, as in the sentence "I'm very 快乐". Some local newspapers and anchors of recreational programs are often found to use it.

(1) Do you sometimes use code-mixing?
(2) What is your attitude towards the practice of code-mixing?

1. Indian English
2. China English
3. Australian English

 Task 1　Reference Search

Find in the library or online some information about the following themes:
(1) lingua franca
(2) speech community
(3) code-mixing
(4) bilingualism
(5) language planning

 Task 2　Term Definition

Study the following definitions and then discuss how they combine to help you understand the terms.

**pidgin**: A pidgin is a means of communication between people with different first languages. [Stuart Poole]

**pidgin**: A variety of a language (e.g. English) which developed for some practical purpose, such as trading, among groups of people who had a lot of contact, but who did not know each other's languages. As such, it would have no native

Unit 14  The Varieties of English (II)   219

speakers. The origin of the term "Pidgin" is thought to be from a Chinese Pidgin version of the English word "business". [George Yule]

**pidgin**: a variety of language that is not a native language of anyone, but is learned in contact situations [Bernard Spolsky]

**creole**: A Creole is a variety that has developed from a pidgin to the extent that it serves as the principal language of a community. [Stuart Poole]

**creole**: Creoles arise when a pidgin language becomes the native language of a new generation of children. [Ralph Fasold]

**creole**: a pidgin which has expanded in structure and vocabulary to express the range of meanings and serve the range of functions required of a first language [Janet Holmes]

**diglossia**: a situation when two distinct varieties of the same language are used, side by side, for two different sets of functions. [Bernard Spolsky]

**diglossia**: A relatively stable language situation in which, in addition to the primary dialects of the language (which may include a standard or regional standards), there is a very divergent codified (often grammatically more complex) superposed variety, the vehicle of a large and respected body of written literature, either of an earlier period or in another speech community, which is learned largely by formal education and is used for most written and formal spoken purposes but is not used by any sector of the community for ordinary conversation. [Charles Ferguson]

**diglossia**: A situation that exists in a society when it has two distinct codes which show clear functional separation; that is, one code is employed in one set of circumstances and the other in an entirely different set. [Ronald Wardhaugh]

 Task 3  Study Questions

1. The following is an excerpt from Chapter 2 of Mark Twain's *The Adventures of Huckleberry Finn*. Underline any part that characterizes African-American Vernacular English.

WE went tiptoeing along a path amongst the trees back towards the end of the widow's garden, stooping down so as the branches wouldn't scrape our heads. When we were passing by the kitchen I fell over a root and made a noise. We scrouched down and laid still. Miss Watson's big nigger, named Jim, was setting in the kitchen door; we could see him pretty clear, because there was a light behind him. He got up and stretched his neck out about a minute, listening. Then he says:

"Who dah?"

He listened some more; then he come tiptoeing down and stood right between us; we could a touched him, nearly. Well, likely it was minutes and minutes that there warn't a sound, and we all there so close together. There was a place on my ankle that got to itching, but I dasn't scratch it; and then my ear begun to itch; and next my back, right between my shoulders. Seemed like I'd die if I couldn't scratch. Well, I've noticed that thing plenty times since. If you are with the quality, or at a funeral, or trying to go to sleep when you ain't sleepy—if you are anywheres where it won't do for you to scratch, why you will itch all over in upwards of a thousand places. Pretty soon Jim says:

"Say, who is you? Whar is you? Dog my cats ef I didn' hear sumf'n. Well, I know what I's gwyne to do: I's gwyne to set down here and listen tell I hears it agin."

So he set down on the ground betwixt me and Tom. He leaned his back up against a tree, and stretched his legs out till one of them most touched one of mine. My nose begun to itch. It itched till the tears come into my eyes. But I dasn't scratch. Then it begun to itch on the inside. Next I got to itching underneath. I didn't know how I was going to set still. This miserableness went on as much as six or seven minutes; but it seemed a sight longer than that. I was itching in eleven different places now. I reckoned I couldn't stand it more'n a minute longer, but I set my teeth hard and got ready to try. Just then Jim begun to breathe heavy; next he begun to snore—and then I was pretty soon comfortable again.

......

Some thought it would be good to kill the FAMILIES of boys that told the secrets. Tom said it was a good idea, so he took a pencil and wrote it in. Then Ben Rogers says:

"Here's Huck Finn, he hain't got no family; what you going to do 'bout him?"

"Well, hain't he got a father?" says Tom Sawyer.

"Yes, he's got a father, but you can't never find him these days. He used to lay drunk with the hogs in the tanyard, but he hain't been seen in these parts for a year or more."

They talked it over, and they was going to rule me out, because they said every boy must have a family or somebody to kill, or else it wouldn't be fair and square for the others. Well, nobody could think of anything to do—everybody was stumped, and set still. I was most ready to cry; but all at once I thought of a way, and so I offered them Miss Watson—they could kill her. Everybody said:

"Oh, she'll do. That's all right. Huck can come in."

2. **Look for information about the features of Australian English, and Canadian English.**

3. How does bilingualism differ from diglossia? Do you think the phenomenon of diglossia exists in China?

4. Language contact is inevitable in the world today. What might happen to English and Chinese respectively, now that China is engaged in the opening-up policy which promotes the contact between the two languages? Use specific examples to prove your speculation.

5. What advantages does a bilingual or even multilingual person have over a monolingual person?

6. Is code-switching rule-governed? Collect some data to prove your answer.

## Task 4　Mini-Project

Conduct a survey among university students about their attitudes toward the popularization of English in China. You may compare the responses from different groups of gender, specialization, family background.

## Recommended Readings

### Reading 1

### Networks and Repertoires

Another way of viewing how an individual relates to other individuals in society is to ask what "networks" he or she participates in. That is, how and on what occasions does a specific individual A interact now with B, then with C, and then again with D? How intensive are the various relationships: does A interact more frequently with B than with C or D? How extensive is A's relationship with B in the sense of how many other individuals interact with both A and B in whatever activity brings them together? If, in a situation in which A, B, C, D, and E are linked in a network, as in the following figure 14.1, are they all equally linked as in (1) in that illustration; strongly linked but with the link through A predominant, as in (2); weakly linked, with the link to A providing all the connections, as in (3);

or, as in (4), is the link from A to E achieved through C?

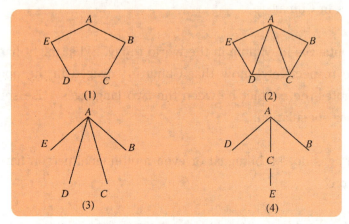

Figure 14.1   Links in a Network

You are said to be involved in a "dense" network if the people you know and interact with also know and interact with one another. If they do not the network is a "loose" one. You are also said to be involved in a "multiplex" network if the people within it are tied together in more than one way, i.e. not just through work but also through other social activities. People who go to school together, marry each other's siblings, and work and play together participate in dense multiplex networks. In England these are said to be found at the extremes of the social-class structure. On the other hand, middle-class networks are likely to be loose and simplex. Much linguistic behavior seems explicable in terms of network structure and we will see in chapters 7 and 8 how valuable the concept of "social network" is when we consider matters of language variation and change.

It is quite apparent that no two individuals are exactly alike in their linguistic capabilities, just as no two social situations are exactly alike. People are separated from one another by fine gradations of social class, regional origin, and occupation; by factors such as religion, sex, nationality, and ethnicity; by psychological differences such as particular kinds of linguistic skills, e.g., verbality or literacy; and by characteristics of personality. These are but some of the more obvious differences that affect individual variation in speech. Any individual has a "speech repertoire"; that is, he or she controls a number of varieties of a language or of two or more languages. Quite often, many individuals will have virtually identical repertoires. In this case it may be possible to argue, as Platt and Platt (1975, p. 35) do, that "A speech repertoire is the range of linguistic varieties which the speaker has at his disposal and which he may appropriately use as a member of his speech community".

The concept of "speech repertoire" may be most useful when applied to individuals rather than to groups. We can use it to describe the communicative competence of individual speakers. Each person will then have a distinctive speech repertoire. Since the Platts find both a community's speech repertoire and an individual's speech repertoire worthy of sociolinguistic consideration, they actually propose the following distinction (p. 36):

> We ... suggest the term speech repertoire for the repertoire of linguistic varieties utilized by a speech community which its speakers, as members of the community, may appropriately use, and the term verbal repertoire for the linguistic varieties which are at a particular speaker's disposal.
>
> In this view each individual has his or her own distinctive verbal repertoire and each speech community in which that person participates has its distinctive speech repertoire; in fact, one could argue that this repertoire is its defining feature.

Focusing on the repertoires of individuals, and specifically on the precise linguistic choices they make in well-defined circumstances does seem to offer us some hope of explaining how people use linguistic choices to bond themselves to others in very subtle ways. A speaker's choice of a particular sound, word, or expression marks that speaker in some way. It can say "I am like you" or "I am not like you". When the speaker also has some kind of range within which to choose, and that choice itself helps to define the occasion, then many different outcomes are possible. A particular choice may say "I am an X just like you" or it may say "I am an X but you are a Y". It may even be possible that a particular choice may say "Up till now I have been an X but from now on you must regard me as a Y", as when, for example, someone pretends to be something he or she is not and then slips up. However, it also seems that it is not merely a simple matter of always choosing X rather than Y—for example, of never saying "singin'" but always saying "singing". Rather, it may be a matter of proportion: you will say "singin'" a certain percent of the time and "singing" the rest of the time. In other words, the social bonding that results from the linguistic choices you make may depend on the quantity of certain linguistic characteristics as well as their quality.

We have seen that "speech community" may be an impossibly difficult concept to define. But in attempting to do so, we have also become aware that it may be just as difficult to characterize the speech of a single individual. Perhaps that second failure follows inevitably from the first. We should be very cautious therefore about definitive statements we may be tempted to make about how a particular individual speaks, the classic concept of "idiolect". Just what kinds of data should you collect? How much? In what circumstances? And what kind of claims can you make? We will need to find answers to questions such as these before we can proceed very far. Any attempt to study how even a single individual speaks in a rather limited set of circumstances is likely to convince us rather quickly that language is rather "messy" stuff. For certain theoretical reasons it might be desirable to ignore a lot of that mess, as Chomsky insists that we do; but it would be unwise for sociolinguists always to do so since that is, in one sense, what sociolinguistics is all about: trying to work out either the social significance of the various bits and pieces of language or the linguistic significance of the various bits and pieces of society.

(Adapted from Ronald Wardhaugh, *An Introduction to Sociolinguistics*, pp. 126-129)

Food for Thought

(1) How is a social network different from a speech community?
(2) Are there any problems with the notion of social networks?
(3) Do you think there are still alternatives to the concept of social networks as a way to capture the speech of a community?

Reading 2

## Language Policy and Language Planning

The very centrality of language to social life, the value of language as a means of access to power and influence, and the symbolic value of language in establishing social class and ethnic identity, all produce conditions where people want to engineer language or language choice itself.

We will look at a number of kinds of language planning or policy activities. These terms represent fashion rather than other differences. When sociolinguists started to be involved in the 1950s and 1960s, they preferred the term language planning as the term for any effort to modify language form or use. In the late 1980s, the regular failure of national planning activities seems to have encouraged the more neutral seeming term, language policy.

Exactly where these activities arise depends in large measure on the perceived language situation of the social organization involved. For instance, in a situation where there are seen to be two or more languages available, any attempt to set up norms or rules for when to use each is what is called status planning. A decision to make one language official, or to ban another from use in school, or to conduct church services in a third, are cases of status planning. The most studied cases are in deciding on official or national languages for a newly independent state.

Once a language has been fixed as appropriate for use in a specific situation (i.e. as the official language, or in printing books, or in schools), any effort to fix or modify its structure is called corpus planning. The coining of new terminology for languages coping with modernization, or the Young Turk policy to remove Arabic words from Turkish, or the French efforts to rid the language of English words, or the Dutch decisions to change spelling, are all cases of corpus planning.

One aspect of corpus planning is the process of language standardization, which consists of attempting to standardize grammar and pronunciation towards some norm that is discovered or invented by some officially appointed or self-proclaimed group of language guardians. This process may be called normativism or prescriptivism by linguists who study it, or "keeping the language pure" by those who carry it out.

A language status decision often produces a situation that some people need learn a language that they do not normally speak. In Finland, for instance, the decision to recognize both Finnish and Swedish as official languages means that Finns must learn Swedish and Swedes Finnish. Sometimes called language acquisition planning, this process of language education policy is also involved when a government decides which foreign languages are to be taught in school or through other means. Similarly, a national policy to develop literacy in a language might be considered a kind of language acquisition policy.

For various reasons, a country or other social group may wish to encourage other people to learn their language. Language diffusion policy is sometimes associated with religious missionary work, as Islam spread Arabic, or with the national concerns of imperialist powers, as in Soviet activities to spread Russian throughout the USSR and Soviet-dominated Eastern Europe, or the French policy to spread *la francophonie*.

In countries where there is clear recognition of the existence of two or more respected languages and associated ethnic groups, such as Belgium, Switzerland, or Canada, status planning is an important activity. This is also the case in newly independent states where there exists a myriad of languages that must be chosen between, as in postcolonial India, Indonesia, or Nigeria. In a country where there is believed to be only one important language, and where other indigenous languages tend to be marginalized, the principal activity tends to be some aspect of corpus planning, such as the purification of the standard language.

(Bernard Spolsky, *Sociolinguistics*, pp. 66-67)

**Food for Thought**

(1) Why is language planning important?

(2) What suggestions do you have for language planning in China?

(3) What can we learn from the experience of other countries?

# Unit 15

# The Acquisition of English

* 15.1  Study of English in China
* 15.2  Factors in English learning
* 15.3  Aspects of learners' English
* 15.4  Learners' English errors

> As never before, people have had to learn a second language, not just as a pleasing pastime, but often as a means of obtaining an education or securing employment.
>
> —Rod Ellis

**Pre-Class Reading**

## 15.1  Study of English in China

English has become part of education for modern Chinese. It is one of the most important subjects in the middle school. Also, at least two years of English study is required for college students, whatever their majors. For further education and degree application, English is still a must for them. It is, therefore, very natural that Chinese pupils in primary schools begin their study of English in their third grade or even much earlier stage.

What is, by nature, the study of English for Chinese learners? It is the learning of a second language in a non-native or non-natural environment. In most, if not all, cases, these learners have basically completed their acquisition of their first language, i.e. Chinese. When they embark on English, they have had a great deal of experience, as well as relatively mature cognitive capacities, in learning a natural language. They know, for example, language is governed by rules, despite a few exceptions; it works essentially on vocabulary and grammar; learning errors are inevitable and yet practice makes perfect. Such experience will contribute explicitly or implicitly to their learning of a second language. They do not have to start from scratch, as in the case of their first experience with language. Moreover, they have mentally set up a world which they may use Chinese to represent and talk about. There is a natural connection and correspondence between the world and their mother tongue.

However, Chinese learners of English suffer some serious disadvantages. They generally do not have a natural English environment. Although nowadays they are privileged with such aids as English video tapes, English TV or radio channels, English newspapers and magazines, the input they receive every day is still very much impoverished, compared with that available to native children learners. They have no native speakers around to talk with them in English; they are under no pressure, nor are they highly motivated,to communicate in English. What surrounds them most of the day is only the sounds and scripts of Chinese. They have a strong inclination to think and speak in Chinese. Its use gives them ease and comfort. The only thing they have to fight for is to pass (largely written) English exams.

## 15.2 Factors in English learning

What determines the success of English study on the part of Chinese learners? The following briefly outlines some important factors, external and internal, that are found to be relevant.

### A The input issue

It seems self-evident that **second language acquisition** (SLA for short) is impossible without access to **L2 input**, whether in the form of exposure in natural settings or in the form of formal instruction. A question of importance and interest is what type of input effectively or even best facilitates L2 learning. Do learners benefit more from simplified input or from genuine, natural input? An influential claim regarding the input issue is the hypothesis that there must be sufficient, comprehensible input available to L2 learners, as captured by the "i + 1" formula. That is, the learner needs input that contains exemplars of the language forms which, according to the natural order, are due to be acquired next. A necessary (but not sufficient) condition to move from stage "i" to stage "i + 1" is that the learner understands (the meaning of) the input that contains "i + 1". It may not be the case that the larger the amount of input or the more complex and genuine the input, the better or the quicker the learning outcome. Given its determining role in L2 acquisition, one has to consider its suitability for the target learners. The provision of input has to consider the learners' existing L2 proficiency, mental abilities and life experiences. This provides justification for the use of **foreigner talk** and **teacher talk** (which corresponds to motherese or caretakerese in the case of children's L1 acquisition), a kind of simplified and properly adjusted input for L2 learners. There has been considerable evidence that this simplified portion of the total input, as occurs in interactional settings, is useful and necessary.

Note that not all the input (made) available to the learners is actually processed, either because some of it is not comprehensible or because some of it is not noticed. Only the part of the input that is processed will count as effective or valid input, thus called "**intake**". **Noticing** is a necessary condition for L2 acquisition. It is an important notion, since much of the time one spends on the study of English is not rewarding owing to the lack of adequate attention and concentration.

### B The output issue

The development of English learners' linguistic and communicative competence does not depend on sufficient **comprehensible input** alone: the learners' output also has an independent and indispensable role to play. It has been found that **L2 output** may trigger certain cognitive processes necessary for second language learning. It helps language learners notice the gaps in their linguistic knowledge as a result of **external feedback** (**clarification requests**, **modeling**, **overt correction**, etc.) or **internal feedback** (**monitoring**) of language they have produced. By making learners consciously aware of their own language production, output can help them internalize linguistic forms, test hypotheses about the language, and increase control over previously internalized forms. Thus, the claim that humans acquire languages in only one way—by understanding a message, or by receiving "comprehensible input"—is inadequate. English learners should not rest content with the input made available to them. They also need to put what they learned into active use. It is said that output facilitates L2 acquisition; particularly it positively affects learners' accuracy.

Both the input issue and the output issue have a frequency aspect. For the former, the more frequently an item is input, the greater the number of opportunities for noticing and acquisition. For the latter, it seems likely that practice makes perfect, though an upper limit must be set so as not to dampen the learners' enthusiasm.

### C The motivation issue

Here, the notion of "**motivation**" is an inclusive one. It has to do with why one learns a foreign language like English and how much effort one is willing to invest in the learning process. Some aspects of motivation are internal, like interest in English. Some aspects of motivation are external, like the instrumental need to use English as the medium of learning other things or, as commonly found in China, the overwhelming pressure to pass exams in order to procure opportunities for university admission, degree application, or professional promotion. In both cases, those with strong and enduring motivation are generally found more likely to become successful learners.

L2 learners are said to possess a sort of "**socioaffective filter**" governing how much of the input made available to them gets through to their language processing mechanisms. Some learners, owing to their lack of (strong) motivation, are "closed" to the L2 input. Once they have obtained sufficient L2 knowledge to meet their communicative and emotional needs, they may stop learning, resulting in so-called **fossilization** or **backsliding**. No matter how much input they receive and no matter in what form the input is provided, the learners do not learn. A limited few who have no interest in the language or recognized need for it at all, or those who have certain hatred for the nation(s) speaking the language, or even for the teacher(s) of the foreign language will fail to master the language to any satisfying degree.

### D The strategy issue

The serious study of **learner strategies** dates back to the 1980s. Three types of strategies have been distinguished: **learning strategies**, **production strategies**, and **communication strategies**. Learning strategies, are "the special thoughts or behaviors that individuals use to help them comprehend, learn, or retain new information". Three subtypes of the category were extensively studied: **metacognitive strategies**, **cognitive strategies**, and **social mediation strategies**. Various lines of research have revealed that beginners employ more learning strategies than intermediate learners; cognitive learning strategies are utilized more often than the other two types; good language learners are more conscious of and effective in taking advantage of all sorts of learning strategies. There is, therefore, sufficient justification for the training of learners, as well as language teachers, in terms of learning strategies.

### E  Other learner-related issues

There are other factors that underlie individual differences with regard to English learning outcomes. For example, age is an important variable. It has been suggested that young learners are better at the acquisition of an L2 like English than old ones. Although it is hard to pinpoint any " **critical period** ", as in the case of L1 acquisition, it seems very likely, though yet to be confirmed, that the earlier an adult starts to learn an L2, the better. But whether adults are less successful L2 learners than children remains to be explored. It has been demonstrated that students in their early teens are quicker and more effective L2 learners than, for example, seven-year-olds. After all, adults enjoy a greater memory capacity and are more capable of focusing on the formal features of L2 input and output. What is more, the acquisition of an L2 requires a combination of factors. The optimal age may be during the years from ten to sixteen when the "flexibility" of the language acquisition faculty has not been completely lost, and the maturation of cognitive skills allows a more effective "working out" of the regular features of the L2 encountered.

Another variable worthy of mention and research is gender. It is a common belief, perhaps an observation, too, that female students are better learners of L2, as well as L1, than male ones. Comprehensive and conclusive evidence is still called for, though. More factors documented in the literature include aptitude, cognitive style, and personality. Do people differ so significantly in these regards? Again, we need evidence.

## 15.3  Aspects of learners' English

There are different ways of looking at Chinese learners' mastery of English. The first perspective entails a distinction between English competence and performance. Take vocabulary knowledge for example. Chinese learners, whether they are intermediate or advanced, generally have a much bigger receptive vocabulary (which they can only use in reading and listening) than productive vocabulary (which they can also use in writing and speaking).

Another way of addressing Chinese learners' English involves a distinction between **declarative knowledge** and **procedural knowledge**, both of which are essential for the use of English. The former refers to their static knowledge of words, grammar rules, and pragmatic conventions, whereas the latter refers to their ability and facility regarding how to put such knowledge into actual use. Understandably, many Chinese learners are unable to use English comfortably despite their substantial knowledge of vocabulary and grammar. Indeed, with adequate practice, they can improve their ability to use the language once some automaticity accrues with the increase of procedural knowledge.

A further way of characterizing Chinese learners' English calls for meticulous analysis of their output, written or spoken, in terms of **accuracy**, **complexity**, **fluency**, and **idiomaticity**. We can measure the **accuracy rate** of their use of a certain linguistic item or **type** by dividing the number of correctly used **tokens** by the total number of tokens used. To calculate the **error rate**, one just divides the number of wrongly used tokens by the total number of tokens used. In order to measure the complexity of their output, one can resort to such indices as the proportion of complex clauses, T-unit complexity ratio (the number of clauses divided by the total number of T-units; a T-unit is defined as one main clause plus a subordinate clause attached to or embedded in it), or the average complexity of sentences in terms of verb patterns. The fluency of Chinese learners' English is often measured by counting the number of clauses or sentences produced within a certain period of time (say, per minute), or counting the frequency of disfluency markers such as pauses, repairs, repetitions within a certain period of time. Finally, idiomaticity can be measured in terms of the frequency of formulaic expressions or prefabricated chunks used within the output of a certain length or duration.

## 15.4 Learners' English errors

An important part of English learners' production is the errors. What attitudes do people take towards learner errors? Earliest structuralist views (prior to 1960) treated errors as evidence of bad learning to be avoided, corrected, and not allowed to occur. Post-structuralist views, influenced by the idea that learning a language involves making constant hypotheses about the structure of the target language, believed that errors are evidence of learners' incorrect hypotheses, or evidence for "**interlanguage**", which has features of both the first and second languages but is neither. Thus errors are evidence of the learners' active learning process. Indeed, some errors, like the misspelling of irregular verbs, are developmental: they will disappear eventually in the course of maturation, whether they are corrected or not.

Learner errors fall into two major types: competence-related errors, which are inevitably made owing to the lack of adequate lexical, grammatical or pragmatic information, and performance-related errors or lapses, which are induced by anxiety, carelessness, insufficiency of time, energy, attention, and the like.

Some competence errors are of a universal type characterizing L2 acquisition. For example, L2 learners, whatever their L1, are more or less likely to transfer bits of their mother tongue to their L2 production. On the other hand, some competence errors are particular to Chinese learners. For instance, due to the lack of morphological marking, Chinese learners, beginners in particular, persist in dropping such markers as those of the past tense and plurality.

Competence-related learner errors arise for a variety of reasons. Some stem from the learners' **overgeneralization** and **overextension**. For example, Chinese students may over-apply the rule of un-affixation so as to yield words like "uncapable" and "unevitable". Or, they may assign too broad a range of meanings to some words like "finger" so that they use it for "toe" and "thumb". Another root cause for learner errors is the improper use of **cross-association**, lexical or structural. For lexical cross-association a case in point is the spelling of "develope" based on the association between "develop" and "envelope". For structural cross-association, a related case is the use of "It is sure to rain tomorrow" based on the association between "It is certain to rain tomorrow" and "I'm sure it will rain tomorrow". Lastly, perhaps most seriously, learners commit errors because of the interference of their L1. We often speak of Chinglish, which pertains to the perceptible traces of negative Chinese influence in the production of sentences, particularly by those prior to advanced stages of learning, to the detriment of idiomaticity or even intelligibility.

It is worth mentioning that Chinese learners vary among themselves in terms of the errors they commit. In other words, the chances of error-making are also affected by some other factors. For example, the marking of S-V agreement in number is found to be easier in a simple sentence than in a complex one involving the agreement between an antecedent and the finite verb in the relative clause. Also, in a narrative of a past event, one is more likely to be correct at the beginning of a sentence, a paragraph, or an essay than in the later part of the sentence, the paragraph or the essay.

## Check your understanding

*State whether each of the following statements is True or False.*

(1) Learning English is too difficult for Chinese students to be successful.
(2) The more input of English a Chinese student obtains, the more he will learn.

(3) Boy students can never learn English as well as girl students in China.
(4) All errors learners commit in English production must be corrected.
(5) Learners' first language is an obstacle to their L2 acquisition.

## In-Class Activities

1. The title of this unit is "The Acquisition of English" rather than the "learning" of it. The title is used in a loose sense. Technically, the term "acquisition" (of language) refers to the gradual development of ability in a language by using it naturally in communicative situations, whereas the term "learning" applies to a conscious process of accumulating knowledge of the vocabulary and grammar of a language. Activities traditionally used in language class tend to result in knowledge "about" the language studied. Those whose L2 experience is primarily a learning one tend not to develop the proficiency of those who have had an acquiring experience like young children.

(1) Are there any activities in your English class that are more like those for acquisition than for learning?
(2) What are the advantages and disadvantages of acquisition and learning respectively?

2. L2 learning seems to differ from L1 acquisition in that the former often involves a lot of grammar learning. Chinese students are often said to know more about English grammar than ordinary native speakers. However, many teachers and learners today deem it unnecessary to emphasize the role of grammar. Rather, they accord a more central position to fluency.

(1) Do you think grammar lessons are necessary and important?
(2) Suppose you are a judge in a national English speaking contest. Three contestants are PKing for the entry into the final. Comparatively speaking, one is very fluent, one has a good pronunciation and intonation, and the other is grammatically accurate. As a judge, which of them would you vote for? Why?

Unit 15　The Acquisition of English  235

3. Another respect in which L1 acquisition and L2 learning are clearly different is that adult L2 learners already have a fully developed grammar of their first language. They—especially at the beginning stages of acquiring their L2—seem to rely on their L1 grammar to some extent. This is shown by the kinds of errors they make, which often involve the transfer of collocational patterns and grammatical rules from their L1.

(1) Is L1 always a bad influence on L2 learning? Use some evidence to prove your point.

(2) Do you think some languages are easier to learn than others? Why might that be the case?

4. The term "input" is used to describe the language that the learner is exposed to. To be beneficial for L2 learning, that input has to be comprehensible. An input is comprehensible if it is simple in structure and vocabulary. Native speakers of English may try to ask a Chinese student "How are you getting on in your studies?" but, if not understood, can switch to "English class, you like it?" Foreigner talk of this type may be beneficial, not only for immediate communicative success, but also for providing the beginning learner with clearer examples of the basic structure of the L2 as input.

(1) Can you give more examples of foreigner talk? Is there anything negative about it?

(2) When you talk to someone with a much lower English proficiency, say someone you meet at an English corner, do you consciously use "comprehensible input"?

5. "SLA is just one aspect of acculturation and the degree to which a learner acculturates to the TL group will control the degree to which he acquires the second language" (Schumann, 1978:34). By **acculturation**, Schumann means the social and psychological integration of the learner with the target language group. It consists of the following social and affective factors.

Acculturation
- Social factors
  - Social dominance patterns
  - Integration patterns (assimilation, preservation, adaptation)
  - Enclosure, attitude, intended length of residence, etc.
- Affective factors
  - Language shock
  - Cultural shock
  - Motivation
  - Ego-permeability

It is suggested that success in language learning—both the rate of SLA and ultimate level of achievement will be improved where the social (group) and psychological (individual) distance between learner and target language community is lessened. Distance or diminished contact will reduce the quantity and quality of language input, and thus support less learning.

(1) In order to study English well, we need narrow our distance, social or affective, from the culture of the native speakers of English. Do you agree?

(2) Do you think there is the need to maintain our cultural identity?

6. Learning strategies are an important part of L2 acquisition. There are many articles published and theses written regarding the issue.

(1) What are some common vocabulary learning strategies used by English learners? How about your own case?

(2) Do you know any reading strategies? Elaborate on one of them.

7. Communication strategies, or strategies of second language communication, often refer to those employed when things go wrong, or when the L2 learner has difficulty communicating in the foreign language. Essentially, L2 learners have problems in expressing something because of the more limited resources they possess in the L2 as compared with L1 learners. More often than not, they take an alternative form of expression for the intended meaning. Here are some common communication strategies:

A. Avoidance: The learner avoids the communication problem by means of topical avoidance, message abandonment (i.e. give up speaking halfway), etc.

B. Paraphrase: The learner compensates for an L2 word that is not known by means of approximation, word coinage, circumlocution, etc.
C. Conscious transfer from L1: The learner resorts to the mother tongue by means of literal translation, language switch, etc.
D. Appeal for assistance: The learner turns to the interlocutor for help.
E. Mime: The learner uses a certain non-verbal activity such as a gesture, a facial expression, a movement, etc.

(1) Do you often employ communication strategies when you speak English? Which of the strategies do you use most often? Can you give an example for each type of communication strategy?
(2) Do you use any of the strategies in your English writing?
(3) Does any of your English teachers encourage or discourage your use of communication strategies?

8. Chunks are rote-learned or imitated linguistic items of unanalyzed language (You may refer to Unit 3). In production, they are recalled as a whole, rather than generated from individual items plus linguistic rules. Language fluency and accuracy are achieved largely by using and retrieving ready-made chunks of language. The following is an extract from a spoken corpora built out of the oral production of the Chinese EFL learners.

　　I think it's hard to say. It depends on the surroundings and environment. If they are bad, it is appropriate for college students to rent apartments outside the campus and live there. But if the situation are good, it's not appropriate. Generally speaking, I don't think the answer is bad. There are three reasons. The first, safety problems. If you live in campus, there are many students live together, so you can go to university, classrooms, libraries together. You can do many things together. If you are ill, or have some unusual things, they can help you. And if they can't help you, they can tell the teachers about these things. But you live alone outside campus, nobody can do this. The second, convenient problems. If you live in the campus, you'll be more convenient to study, to go to classrooms, to computer rooms, to library rooms. You don't have to go out or come in to study. The third, you can feel the lives together. In the groups, you can feel the relationships. In fact, it has no relationships but because you live together, do everything together, you will become more close to each other. It's like a big home. If you live outside the campus, you won't feel this thing. I think it is better to live inside the campus. (224 words)

The following is an extract from a native speaker's monologue about renting apartments off campus. Underline the phrases that are prefabricated chunks.

I think the idea of college students' renting apartments off campus is a great thing in certain schools. You don't have to struggle with the getting to school in the morning and finding parking which, according to most students with cars, it's difficult, although I think if you can compare that to some other universities our ten minutes walk is very little. But I think for certain students it is a good idea and something that works for them, in a sense that they like having a place to go home to at the end of the day, that's not on campus, and to get away from kind of the stress of Davidson and pressure cooker and bubble that we live in. But for me, personally I think that would be a poor decision because I would probably never come out of that apartment most times. It's difficult enough to drag yourself from down the hill, up the hill for a party or class or get-together, and I think being off campus I will just kind of hold up in my apartment and not leave very often which may be great for my work ethic, but probably not good for my social life. But I do have a friend that is living off campus now and she loves it. She and her roommates cook dinner every night. They hang out there and have parties over there and gather some dinner parties. But she does admit that she doesn't get so much time with people living on campus as she did in previous years, and you also have to get the whole idea if something goes wrong in your apartment, you need to call a plumber, call an electrician, and whereas on campus you simply have to put in a work order and someone comes over for free to fix whatever the problem there is. But no matter where you live, an apartment is a good experience to have before entering the real world after graduation. (336 words)

### ask

(1) How many chunks are used in each of the data? Underline the chunks used and then compare the two data.

(2) What implication can you draw after comparing the different frequencies in the two sets of data that are supposedly representative of native and non-native speech?

9. Schmidt (1990) states that noticing is a necessary condition for L2 acquisition. He identifies three aspects of consciousness involved in language learning: awareness, intention and knowledge. Above all, awareness embraces noticing. Noticing turns the input into an intake, as shown by the following figure (see Ellis 1997a):

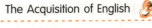

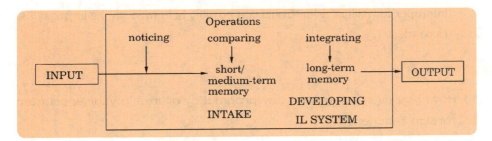

(1) Why is noticing so important? Do we have any evidence to support this hypothesis?

(2) How can the noticing hypothesis be used to explain the phenomenon of incidental vocabulary learning (e.g. we may pick up some words without deliberately paying attention to them while watching English TV programs or reading English newspapers)?

(3) Does noticing place an important role in the process of output, written or spoken? Can you support your answer with some evidence?

10. In the area of pragmatics, the concept of appropriateness plays a role somewhat analogous to the role played in syntax by the concept of grammaticality. When appropriateness conditions are violated, pragmatic failures will result. Chinese learners of English often commit such failures that have to do with inappropriateness in terms of social conventions, cultural differences, manner of talking, and so on. They are often treated as "behaving badly" rather than "speaking badly". Two major types of pragmatic failures have been identified:

A. **Pragma-linguistic failures**
   a. mother tongue interference (as in the use of "What do you want?" by a salesgirl to an approaching customer)
   b. poor command of the target language (as in the use of "Never mind" in response to an expression of thanks)

B. **Socio-pragmatic failures**
   a. improper compliment/response (like the rejection of a compliment)
   b. inappropriate addressing (like the use of "Teacher" as a form of direct address for a foreign teacher)
   c. starting taboo topics like income, religious belief, etc.

d. improper formality (as in "Could you possibly help me with the luggage?" said to a close friend)

(1) Have you ever committed any pragmatic failures in your encounters with foreign teachers?
(2) Are there any other types of pragmatic failures that Chinese learners may bump into unawares?

1. Teacher talk
2. Strategies for vocabulary learning
3. Chinglish

Find in the library or online some information about the following themes:
(1) input hypothesis
(2) noticing hypothesis
(3) interaction hypothesis
(4) pragmatic competence
(5) pragmatic failure

Study the following definitions and then discuss how they combine to help you understand the terms.

**interlanguage**: The term coined by Selinker (1972) refers to the systematic knowledge of a second language which is independent of both the learner's first language and the target language. [Rod Ellis]

**interlanguage**: A linguistic system that results from a second language learner's attempt to produce the target language. It is considered to be a separate linguistic system from the native language and the target language. [J. Michael O'Malley and Anna Chamot]

**transfer**: The process of using knowledge of the first language in learning a second language. Transfer can be positive, when a first-language pattern identical with a target-language pattern is transferred, or it can be negative, when a first-language pattern different from the target-language pattern is transferred. In either case, L1-induced errors occur. [Rod Ellis]

**transfer**: use of previous linguistic knowledge or prior skills to assist comprehension or production [J. Michael O'Malley and Anna Chamot]

**fossilization**: Selinker (1972) finds most L2 learners fail to reach target language competence. That is, they stop learning when their internalized rule system contains rules different from those of the target language. This is referred to as "fossilization". [Rod Ellis]

**fossilization**: It is a process that sometimes occurs in second language learning in which incorrect linguistic features become a permanent part of the way a person speaks or writes in the target language. [Stephen Krashen]

## Task 3  Study Questions

1. As the learner's interlanguage develops, there is a need for more interaction and the kind of negotiated input that arises in conversation. Negotiated input is L2 material that the learner can acquire in interaction through requests for clarification and active attention being focused on what is said. Collect some data from your English conversation class to illustrate the negotiated input.

2. L2 acquisition does not just involve the transfer of L1 properties to the L2 interlanguage. Rather, there is a strong creative component to L2 acquisition. Many things specific to L1 grammar generally do not transfer. Whereas L2 learners are likely to transfer structures in which the semantic relations are transparent, they are less likely to transfer irregular, infrequent, or semantically difficult items in their L2 production. For example, they will not typically transfer L1 idioms, such as "He hit the roof" meaning "He got angry". Collect some data to prove the point.

3. As an English student, which do you think is the most difficult part: pronunciation, vocabulary, grammar, or something else? Why do you think so? Is there any factor responsible for it (e. g. the teacher, the textbook, the physical setting, lack of time, other students, or anything else)?

4. Do you believe there is a "best age" for beginning to learn English or any other second language? Why?

5. Do you think there exists a "best personality" for learning a foreign language? If so, what is it? Why?

6. Underline in the following learner productions the expressions (collocations and sentence structures) that you consider to be typical of Chinglish.

Passage 1

### Get Ready for Tomorrow's Rain

Some people think we should save money today for tomorrow. Some think we should use money today from tomorrow. Although the two opinions both have own advantage, but in my opinion, I think save money today is more reasonable.

Save money today can make you ready for tomorrow's rain. In case you meet some unexpected thing, for example, your car suddenly go wrong, your family member get ill without any preparation, your children bring some serious trouble to you, and so on. All these kinds of things need enough money to deal with. Using tomorrow's money is enjoyable now, but what we do when we meet with those things? Life is not kind enough to us. You never know which moment he will make fool of you. So we should have money in our hand.

And also, as a common woman, I will have my family and children. I have the responsibility to give them good life and should not get them into trouble. Because of this reason, I must save a lot of money.

So I will save money, instead of use tomorrow's money.

Passage 2

### Education as a Lifelong Process

Education is a lifelong process. At school, students should learn the knowledge from books and teachers. When they become adult, they also should learn from the society by themselves. In a word, learning is endless.

The world is big and the society is varying and improving. So one man can't say "I will also be a wise man 10 years later". We don't know how the world will be like when we are 30 or 40, just as my grandma didn't know every child could play computer today. I'm an English major in XXX University now, but I don't know whether 10 years later I still can get a good job as an English major for more and more people can speak English well in China.

Though we still in campus we should get in touch with the society, notice new things and top technology and important international news, at last we should make us proper for the society. Also we should remember learning is not a temporal work, but need patience and determination.

There is an old saying in China: Growing a big tree needs 10 years while educating a good man needs 100 years. This old saying needs us to learn all our life.

7. There are two tendencies in Chinese learners' use of English: either they are too formal in their oral English, or they are too informal in their written English. Illustrate each of the two tendencies based on the following learner production data.

### Education as a Lifelong Process

Education is not only going to school. Actually, you are getting it just from the moment you were born. Your first teachers are your parents. No matter if they got good educated, they will teach you a lot of things, such as eating, dressing. Then you go to school. School time is just a part of your education period. You will get more and more advanced and useful knowledge in school. At the meanwhile, you will be taught to be a citizen in the society, and a person on the earth. Then, you can secure a good job which can give you more chance to be a brilliant man. If you are successful, you shouldn't be proud, because the world is changing every moment. If you think you are so brilliant that you can give up education, the God will give up you. For example, Michael Jordan is a brilliant person. But if he was too proud to crow over, he would find that more and more skillful young players could play basketball better. So the audience would abandon him. And if he was too proud to be rude to journalists and fans, he would be not worthy of respect. So the society would abandon him. In a word, if a successful man give up education, he will lose way and don't know how to keep it and how to be a real man, he will fail at last.

While, when you are in trouble, please don't worry. What you need is chances, confidence and, what is most important, education. What you should do is to get advanced education which can teach you how to catch chances, how to get confidence.

What I want to say at last is that education is a key to leading a real and happy life.

### Renting Apartments?

In my opinion, it is not appropriate for college students to rent apartments outside the campus. First, I think there will be a lot of inconvenience. First is the money problem. Compared with 800 *yuan* a year to live on the campus in the dormitory, usually all students have to pay 300 to 500 *yuan* a month to rent apartment outside, which is a big sum of money for our students who have no regular jobs. Secondly, I think if the students live outside the campus, they cannot use a lot of facility on the campus, for example, the student dining hall, and the library. They have to cook the food themselves, because dining in the restaurant must be very expensive. Above all, if he lives outside the campus, it may be a reason for his being regularly late for class. The third major reason for my argument that it is not appropriate to rent apartment outside is that it will cause the problem of communication. Living outside, his communication with classmates and his teacher must be reduced, and especially for those students who are hunting jobs, the information is really important for them. Living outside will block their access to the information of some important good job. Furthermore, his relationship with his classmates will become not so good. If he lives in the dormitory, because there will be a lot of encounter, they can talk with his classmates in the dormitory about a lot of things and it will give him ideas or opinions from different aspects. The last reason I think is the security problem. Especially those girls have to take the safe problem into consideration by themselves.

8. L2 acquisition is not simply that of L2 linguistic knowledge but also involves the development of **communicative competence**, which can be defined as the ability to use the L2 accurately, appropriately, and flexibly. The first component is grammatical competence which involves the accurate use of words and structures in the L2. Concentration on grammatical competence only, however, will not provide the learner with the ability to interpret or produce language appropriately. This ability is called sociolinguistic competence. It enables the learner to know when to say "Can I have some water?" versus "Give me some water!" The third component is called strategic competence. This is the ability to organ-

ize a message effectively and to compensate, via strategies, for any difficulties. Are communicative competence and pragmatic competence the same thing? Do you think there is a positive correlation among the three components as far as their development is concerned?

## Task 4   Mini-Project

Interview three experienced Chinese English teachers and three foreign English teachers, asking them about their ideas on successful ways to learn English in China. Then interview three excellent learners and three poor learners on the same questions. Compare these people's responses for some interesting findings.

Reading 1

### Is L2 Acquisition the Same as L1 Acquisition?

With some exceptions, adults do not simply "pick up" a second language. It usually requires conscious attention, if not intense study and memorization, to become proficient in a second language. Again, with the exception of some remarkable individuals, adult second language learners(L2ers) do not often achieve nativelike grammatical competence in the L2, especially with respect to pronunciation. They generally have an accent and they may make syntactic or morphological errors that are unlike the errors of children acquiring their first language(L1ers). For example, L2ers often make word order errors, especially early in their development, as well as morphological errors in grammatical gender and case. L2 errors may fossilize so that no amount of teaching or correction can undo them.

Unlike L1 acquisition, which is uniformly successful across children and languages, adults vary considerably in their ability to acquire an L2 completely. Some people are very talented language learners. Others are hopeless. Most people fall somewhere in the middle. Success may depend on a range of factors, including age, talent, motivation, and whether you are in the country where the language is spoken or sitting in a classroom five mornings a week with no further contact with native speakers. For all these reasons, many people, including many linguists who study L2 acquisition, believe that second language acquisition is something different from first language acquisition. This hypothesis is referred to as the fundamental difference hypothesis of L2 acquisition.

In certain important respects, however, L2 acquisition is like L1 acquisition. Like L1ers, L2ers do not acquire their second language overnight; they go through stages. Like L1ers, L2ers construct grammars. These grammars reflect their competence in the L2 at each stage and so their language at any particular point, though not nativelike, is rule-governed and not haphazard. The intermediate grammars that L2ers create on their way to the target have been called interlanguage grammars.

### A Critical Period for L2 Acquisition?

Age is a significant factor in L2 acquisition. The younger a person is when exposed to a second language, the more likely she is to achieve nativelike competence.

In an important study of the effects of age on ultimate attainment in L2 acquisition, Jacqueline Johnson and Elissa Newport tested several groups of Chinese and Korean speakers who had acquired English as a second language. The subjects, all of whom had been in the United States for at least five years, were tested on their knowledge of specific aspects of English morphology and syntax. They were asked to judge the grammaticality of sentences such as:

The little boy is speak to a policeman.
The farmer bought two pig.
A bat flewed into our attic last night.

Johnson and Newport found that the test results depended heavily on the age at which the person had arrived in the United States. The people who arrived as children (between the age of three and eight) did as well on the test as American native speakers. Those who arrived between the ages of eight and fifteen did not perform like native speakers. Moreover, every year seemed to make a difference for this group. The person who arrived at age nine did better than the one who arrived at age ten; those who arrived at age eleven did better than those who arrived at age twelve and so on. The group that arrived between the ages of seventeen and thirty one had the lowest scores.

Does this mean that there is a critical period for L2 acquisition, an age beyond which it is impossible to acquire the grammar of a new language? Most researchers would hesitate to make such a strong claim. Although age is an important factor in achieving nativelike L2 competence, it is certainly possible to acquire a second language as an adult. Indeed, many teenage and adult L2 learners become quite proficient, and a few highly talented ones even manage to pass for native speakers.

Unit 15  The Acquisition of English    247

It is more appropriate to say that there is a gradual decline in L2 acquisition abilities with age and that there are "sensitive periods" for the nativelike mastery of certain aspects of the L2. The sensitive period for phonology is the shortest. To achieve nativelike pronunciation of an L2 generally requires exposure during childhood. Other aspects of language, such as syntax, may have a larger window.

(Victoria Fromkin et al., *An Introduction to Language*, pp. 379-384)

 Food for Thought

(1) What may cause or prevent fossilization?
(2) Do you agree that some L2ers are more talented than others in learning the L2?
(3) Do you find the research findings reported here highly credible?

 Reading 2

## Learning Strategies

**Metacognitive Strategies**

Metacognitive strategies "are higher order executive skills that may entail planning for, monitoring, or evaluating the success of a learning activity"; in other words they are strategies about learning rather than learning strategies themselves. They are divided into nine types:

- advance organizers: planning the learning activity in advance at a general level—"You review before you go into class";
- directed attention: deciding in advance to concentrate on general aspects of a learning task;
- selective attention: deciding to pay attention to specific parts of the language input or the situation that will help learning;
- self-management: trying to arrange the appropriate conditions for learning—"I sit in the front of the class so I can see the teacher";
- advance preparation: planning for and rehearsing linguistic components necessary to carry out an upcoming language task;
- self-monitoring: checking one's performance as one speaks—"Sometimes I cut short a word because I realize I've said it wrong";
- delayed production: deliberately postponing speaking so that one may learn by listening—"I talk when I have to, but I keep it short and hope I'll be understood";

- **self-evaluation**: checking how well one is doing against one's own standards;
- **self-reinforcement**: giving oneself rewards for success.

### Cognitive Strategies

Cognitive strategies "operate directly on incoming information, manipulating it in ways that enhance learning". They recognize 16 cognitive strategies:

- **repetition**: imitating other people's speech, silently or aloud;
- **resourcing**: making use of language materials such as dictionaries;
- **directed physical response**: relating new information to physical actions, as with directives;
- **translation**: using the first language as a basis for understanding and/or producing the L2;
- **grouping**: organizing learning on the basis of "common attributes";
- **note-taking**: writing down the gist of texts;
- **deduction**: conscious application of L2 rules;
- **recombination**: putting together smaller meaningful elements into new wholes;
- **imagery**: turning information into a visual form to aid remembering it—"Pretend you are doing something indicated in the sentences to make up about the new word";
- **auditory representation**: keeping a sound or sound sequence in the mind—"When you are trying to learn how to say something, speak it in your mind first";
- **key word**: using key-word memory techniques, such as identifying an L2 word with an L1 word that sounds similar;
- **contextualization**: placing a word or phrase in a meaningful language sequence;
- **elaboration**: relating new information to other concepts in memory;
- **transfer**: helping language learning through previous knowledge—"If they're talking about something I have already learnt (in Spanish), all I have to do is remember the information and try to put it into English";
- **inferencing**: guessing meanings by using available information—"I think of the whole meaning of the sentence, and then I can get the meaning of the new word";
- **question for clarification**: getting a teacher to explain, help, and so on.

### Social Mediation Strategies

- **Social mediation strategies**, or **social/affective strategies**: "represent a broad grouping that involves either interaction with another person or ideational control

over affect". In O'Malley et al. (1985a) only one is listed:
- cooperation: working with fellow-students on a language task.

The list in O'Malley and Chamot (1990) differs in that "delayed production", "self-reinforcement", and "directed physical response" are dropped; the "advance preparation" strategy is renamed "functional planning"; the last cognitive strategy, *question for clarification*, is reclassified under social mediation; and the following cognitive strategy is added:
- summarizing: making a summary of new information received.

......

Some additional strategies were added to the list, namely the cognitive strategy:
- rehearsal: going over the language needed for a task;

and the social/affective strategy:
- self-talk: boosting one's confidence to do a task more successfully.

Like the ESL students, the foreign language students "reported using far more cognitive strategies than metacognitive ones" (O'Malley and Chamot, 1990, p. 127). Beginners relied most on "repetition", "translation" and "transfer", while advanced learners used "inferencing" more.

A further experiment reported in O'Malley and Chamot (1990, pp. 133-143) looked at the strategies reported for the same tasks by 19 learners over a period of four "semesters". This experiment yielded another metacognitive strategy to add to the list:
- problem identification: identifying important points of learning task.

(Adapted from Vivian Cook, *Second Language Learning and Language Teaching*, pp. 114-115)

 Food for Thought

(1) Which strategies do you use most in your study of English?
(2) Are you satisfied with the classification of the strategies? Do you think there are more strategies than those included here?

# Appendix I

# Empirical Studies of English

## 1. Defining linguistic research

What is research? Research can be defined as a systematic approach to finding answers to questions. Reflecting on one's experience and feelings, or giving unwarranted judgments and groundless viewpoints, is NOT true research.

Linguistic research is the systematic study of language, usually with respect to a particular aspect of it. It can be categorized into conceptual research (or theorizing) and empirical research. The former depends heavily on speculation/deduction, e.g. the study of the origin of language. The latter, characterized by the use of induction and the process of hypothesis formation-confirmation, can be further classified into quantitative research (like an experiment and a survey) and qualitative research (like field work and case study), each type having its advantages and disadvantages. Quantitative research is empirical research where the data are in the form of numbers. Qualitative research is empirical research where the data are not in the form of numbers. Here is a tentative summary of their differences:

Table 1  Quantitative vs. qualitive research

|  | Quantitative | Qualitative |
|---|---|---|
| Objective | Testing hypotheses from experiences, observations, other studies, etc. | Generating hypotheses for later confirmation |
| Research questions | Specified before data-collection | Gradually specified in the process |

*(Continued on next page)*

|  | **Quantitative** | **Qualitative** |
|---|---|---|
| Sampling | A large sample | A small sample |
| Data-collection | Use questionnaires, pre-/post-tests, testing instruments, etc. | Use interviews, think-aloud, observation, diaries, writing tasks, field work, etc. |
| Data-analysis | Statistical | Non-statistical and/or statistical |
| Findings | Generalizable | Ungeneralizable |

A typical research project is characterized by "PPP": Purpose (answerable questions), Process (a systematic approach), and Product (valid answers). Research varies along these dimensions. For instance, a study may be carried out to describe, explain, predict, or control. A study may be theoretical or applied. A theoretical study can be descriptive, interpretive, or explanatory.

A good study needs to (1) have good questions (those that are theoretically and/or practically significant, original, and answerable); (2) employ a systematic approach; and (3) obtain valid answers.

One starts a study by finding a research topic (e.g. Chinese learners' ways of performing requests in English) in a subfield (e.g. interlanguage pragmatics) of a general field (e.g. pragmatics) in a discipline (e.g. linguistics). Then, for the research topic, one may ask a certain general question, one that may provide the direction for research, but may not be directly answerable, e.g. "How do Chinese university students perform requests in English?" Next, one has to break down the general questions into specific questions, those that are answerable, that is, those that can be tackled by the researcher within the time and resources available, and those that can be further narrowed down into specific sub-questions. For instance,

—How do Chinese university students make requests to their peers and superiors in English respectively?
—How do Chinese university students make requests involving real face threat in English respectively?
—Does English proficiency have any effect on the way Chinese university students make requests in English?

To effectively narrow down a research topic and break down a general research question, one may ask the following types of questions:

<u>Who questions</u>: Who are the learners? (middle school students or university students;

English majors or non-English majors; freshmen, sophomores, juniors or seniors)

What questions: What do the learners do?

Why questions: Why do the learners do some things (but not others)?

How questions: How do the learners undertake a certain learning task?

All research must have its object of study and its research objectives or goals. A study may be undertaken to reveal the features, functions, patterns, and causes of a certain independent object of study, like those of conversational repairs in a Chinese learners' spoken English corpus. Or, a study may be directed to finding out the relation between two or more variables, of which one is the central object of study. For instance, one may study how English proficiency may relate to the use of conversational repairs. In this case, the English proficiency is an independent variable, whereas the use of conversational repairs (including their frequency, types, functions, etc.) is a dependent variable because it is "affected" by the former. The way one variable affects another may be causal (as shown in the relation between one's English proficiency and one's grammatical repairs in conversation) or just correlational (that is, one variable can be used to predict another, as shown in the relation between English proficiency and the use of content repair). A study often includes one or more variables that have an effect on the causal or correlational relation. For instance, one may consider the influence of gender and task type on the causal relation between English proficiency and the use of grammatical repair and their influence on the correlational relation between English proficiency and the use of content repair. We call such factors moderator variables.

Clearly, research into some topics like Chinese learners' use of conversational repairs through the analysis of a corpus is very time-consuming or even too costly to be practical. To serve the same purpose, we can study a few samples of Chinese learners and then draw generalizable conclusions based on inferential statistics. The critical part here is that the sampling of subjects must be randomly executed so as to be representative of the population of Chinese learners and the number of samples must be big enough. For instance, if we want to answer the question of whether high-proficiency Chinese learners differ significantly from low-proficiency Chinese learners in the use of conversational repairs, we need to have at least 30 high-proficiency Chinese learners' conversational data (at least for a complete record of a speech event) and 30 low-proficiency Chinese learners' conversational data (also at least for a complete record of a comparable speech event occurring in a similar context or setting), although the number of subjects may come down somewhat if each subject produces more than one complete set of data. Basically, the larger the number of the subjects and their data, the more valid the inference for the whole population from which the subjects are taken.

After deciding on variables to be investigated, we may formulate some hypotheses about their relations. Hypotheses are tentative answers to research questions. There are different types of hypotheses to choose from. For instance, regarding the research question of "Is there any relation between the English proficiency of Chinese learners of English and their use of conversational repairs?", we can hypothesize in any of the following ways:

A. $H_o$ = null hypothesis: There is no relationship between the English proficiency of Chinese learners of English and their use of conversational repairs.

B. $H_1$ = positive, directional hypothesis: There is relation between the English proficiency of Chinese learners of English and their use of conversational repairs. (i.e. the more proficient, the more likely to repair)

C. $H_2$ = negative, directional hypothesis: There is some relationship between the English proficiency of Chinese learners of English and their use of conversational repairs. (i.e. the more proficient, the less likely to repair)

D. $H_3$ = non-directional hypothesis: There is some relationship between the English proficiency of Chinese learners of English and their use of conversational repairs, but the direction is not specified.

However, for a very specific research question like "Do high-proficiency Chinese learners of English differ significantly from low-proficiency learners in the frequency of using conversational repairs?", we tend to use either a null hypothesis like "High-proficiency Chinese learners of English do not differ significantly from low-proficiency learners in the frequency of using conversational repairs" or the opposite one like "High-proficiency Chinese learners of English differ significantly from low-proficiency learners in the frequency of using conversational repairs".

To verify or nullify a hypothesis, data collection and data analysis are inevitable. Two types of data are frequently used: descriptive data and numeric data. Descriptive data are narrative information or statements of opinions or attitudes recorded in an interview, a think-aloud, and a diary. Numeric data are those obtained from responses to questionnaires, performances in (pre-/post-) tests (which may include descriptive data, though, as in the case of writing tasks). To facilitate calculation, we may use different scales for the collected data. A nominal scale is used to name objects or classify objects. An ordinal scale provides information about the relative amount of some trait possessed by objects. An interval scale can provide information about the distance between any two attributes. Here are examples for the different scales:

Table 2  Different scales of data

| | |
|---|---|
| **Nominal scale** | Sex: 1 =male  2 = female<br>Marital status: 1 =single  2 =married  3 =divorced<br>4 =widowed/widower |
| **Ordinal scale** | Performances in a contest: first, second, third, etc.<br>Frequency of strategy use:<br>1 =never  2 =seldom  3 =sometimes  4 =usually  5 =always |
| **Interval scale** | Performances in a contest: 80, 85, 90, 95, 100 |

After the data are collected and assigned values, we can start statistic processing. There are two levels of statistics: descriptive statistics and inferential statistics. In the former case, the researcher is interested only in describing the features of the group(s) from which the data are gathered. In the latter case, the researcher's interest goes beyond describing the group(s) and he or she tries to draw inferences about the population from which the group(s) were selected.

Suppose we have a set of numeric data: 58, 65, 84, 70, 90, 75, 86, 76, 80, 82, 83, 84, 69, 84, 85, 86, 72, 89, 75, 92. Then, the descriptive statistics may cover the following aspects:

(1) Determining the range of the raw data;

(2) Determining the number of classes;

(3) Determining the width of the class interval;

(4) Determining the mode of the raw numbers;

(5) Determining the median of the raw data;

(6) Determining the mean of the data.

The following tables employ two different class intervals and thus demonstrate different frequencies and percentages:

Table 3  Class intervals(1)

| Class internals | Frequencies | Percentages |
|---|---|---|
| 50-under 65 | 1 | 5% |
| 65-under 80 | 7 | 35% |
| 80-under 95 | 12 | 60% |
| Total | 20 | 100% |

Table 4  Class intervals(2)

| Class internals | Frequencies | Percentages |
|---|---|---|
| 50-under 60 | 1 | 5% |
| 60-under 70 | 2 | 10% |
| 70-under 80 | 5 | 25% |
| 80-under 90 | 10 | 50% |
| 90-under 100 | 2 | 10% |
| Total | 20 | 100% |

To vividly demonstrate the distributions of frequencies or percentages, we may make use of some diagrams, of which the following are three options:

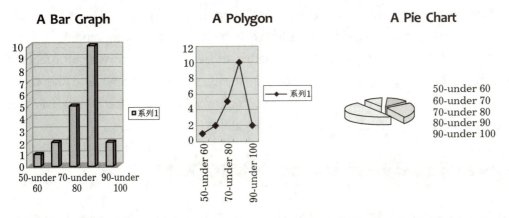

Apart from calculating frequencies and percentages, further dimensions to look at are the mean and standard deviation of a certain body of data. By "mean", one refers to the average score (the most frequently used indicator of central tendency of the sample) of the data, whereas by "standard deviation (SD)", one means the average deviation of all the scores from the mean (the most frequently used indicator of variability of the sample). Here is an example:

Table 5  Means of groups

|  | Student 1 | Student 2 | Student 3 | Mean |
|---|---|---|---|---|
| Group One | 68 | 70 | 75 | 71 |
| Group Two | 58 | 67 | 88 | 71 |

Group One: mean =71/SD =3.61   Group Two: mean =71/SD =15.39

Inferential statistics works on the basis of descriptive statistics, especially the notions of frequency, percentage, mean and standard deviation. For example, a *t*-test operation seeks to find out whether there is any significant difference between the means of two comparable independent groups, as used when we want to check whether a high-proficiency learner group differs significantly from a low-proficiency learner group in their frequency of using conversational repairs within the same period of time, or used when we want to figure out whether the same group of subjects perform significantly better in the post-test than in the pre-test after undergoing a certain treatment. When more than two comparison groups are involved at the same time, ANOVA will be necessary to find out whether there are pairs that are statistically different. In both the *t*-test and ANOVA, a significance level must be set before hand, either 0.05 or 0.01. The statistical package will run the data automatically and yield the expected output.

Another frequently used inferential statistical operation is correlational analysis, which aims to find whether two variables are affected implicitly by the same variable. For instance, it is used when we want to check whether those who perform well in a reading test also do well in a writing test. The scores in the two tests are input into the corresponding statistical package and run for their coefficient value. The closer it approximates 1 or $-1$, the higher the correlation, positive or negative.

## 2. Interview-based studies of English

To collect data about the object of study, one common approach adopted is interviewing. In terms of research design, interviewing is often qualitative, aimed at exploring the attitudes, experiences, feelings, beliefs, expectations of the target subject(s), and so forth. There are, according to degrees of formality and research purposes, three types of interviews: (1) Structured: an interview guide is prepared. The questions are asked in the same sequence and the same wording. (2) Unstructured: interview questions are generated spontaneously in the natural flow of an interaction. (3) Semi-structured: an interview guide is prepared before the interview begins. The questions in the schedule need not be taken in any particular order and the actual wording of questions is not determined in advance.

To carry out an interview, we may follow the following procedures:

**Step 1: Preparing an interview guide (if a formal study is called for)**

When we design interview questions, we need to make sure that the questions to be asked to the interviewee will (1) be specific, brief and readily intelligible; (2) be open-ended, unbiased, and capable of obtaining all necessary information if the interview goes properly; (3) involve minimal repetition or face threat. This explains why an interview question like "Do you use conversational repairs because you find something wrong with what you have just said?" must be revised as "Under what circumstances do you use conversational repairs?" In arranging the order of the questions, the easy, interesting ones must come first.

### Step 2: Conducting the interview

When conducting the interview, one needs to take notes. For completeness and greater accuracy, one is advised to use a high-quality tape recorder or video camera, if permitted.

There are some skills for conducting an interview. For example, we can use all sorts of probing strategies: (1) silent probe: remaining quiet and waiting as the interviewee is reflecting and gathering thoughts; (2) verbal probe: giving further guidance when the interviewee arrives at the end of the thought; (3) echo probe: making suitable use of repetition of words to encourage the interviewee to continue, e.g. "I see, you ask your teacher the meaning of the unknown word. Then what else?" (4) uh-huh probe: using affirmative noise to encourage, e. g. "uh-huh", or "yes, I see". While talking, the interviewer had better adopt a conversational style so as to foster a friendly and comfortable atmosphere.

### Step 3: Analyze the interview data

After the interview data is collected, the researcher can move on to analyze the data. Again there are several stages.

### Stage 1: Transcribing tape-recordings

Take down everything you can hear. Ask the subject to clarify the unclear parts, if possible. Make sure to be faithful to the original interview. In order to standardize the process of transcribing, develop a set of codes that can indicate pause, stress, hesitation, and the like.

### Stage 2: Segmenting the data

The data can be segmented with reference to each specific research question so that the irrelevant data can be put aside.

### Stage 3: Displaying the data

Put the segments of the interview data into a file. In a study about why Chinese learners use conversational repair, the obtained interview data can be displayed as follows after they are segmented:

- I found I spoke too fast and my partner seemed to have difficulty understanding me. (Subject 1)
- I used conversational repair because I wanted to express myself precisely. You know, we often make mistakes in conversation. It's inevitable. (Subject 2)
- I didn't realize I made a repair. Maybe I suddenly thought of a better word. (Subject 3)
- Perhaps I have the habit of doing so. When I speak Chinese, I also find I correct myself a lot. Maybe I'm influenced by my Chinese. (Subject 4)
- Of course I must repair. I must give the exact information to my partner. (Subject 5)
- Usually after I said something I noticed I had made a grammatical mistake. My English is not very good. I'm troubled a lot. If I speak fast, I will make mistakes and have to correct them. If I want to be correct, I can't speak fluently. (Subject 6)

**Stage 4: Drawing and classifying categories**

To find patterns or variations, one needs to identify possible categories emerging from the data. Give a name to each of the categories. For instance, we may assign different categories for the various reasons for conversational repairs reflected in the interview data:

(1) Caused by low L2 proficiency (Subject 6)

(2) Motivated by the desire of accuracy (Subject 2, 3, 5)

(3) Influenced by L1 use (Subject 4)

(4) Motivated by interactive considerateness (Subject 1)

Interview-based studies, when used alone, fall under the category of qualitative research. However, such studies are often used as a complement to some quantitative research in second language acquisition. They serve to explain in part why the relation between the variables under study demonstrates a certain pattern.

## 3. Questionnaire-based studies of English

The most frequently used method of data collection in quantitative research is the use of a questionnaire. Compared with an interview addressed to a limited few and intended to gather descriptive data, a questionnaire is administered to a relatively large number of subjects and aimed to gather numeric data. In general, it consists of a heading and two major parts: background information and items aimed at the research questions. Look at the following example.

> **Questionnaire**
>
> (This questionnaire is used for research only; everything you fill in will be kept confidential. Thanks for your cooperation!)
>
> **Part A   Background information**
> Name _____   Sex _____   Score of English in the Entrance Examination:_____
>
> **Part B   Beliefs about learning English**
> Below there are some beliefs that people have about learning English. What are yours? Do you agree or disagree with them? To what extent? Remember that there are no right or wrong answers on this issue. Please write the number which best indicates your opinion in the bracket at the end of each statement. The numbers stand for the following responses:
>
> 1 = I strongly disagree with this statement
> 2 = I disagree with this statement
> 3 = I'm not sure about this statement
> 4 = I agree with this statement
> 5 = I strongly agree with this statement
>
> B01   One must learn a lot of English words by heart in order to use the language. (     )
> B02   One does not have to make a special effort to learn grammar. (     )
> B03   Reading English newspapers every day helps greatly. (     )
> ...

Once one decides on the use of a questionnaire to collect data, the following steps are necessary:

### Step 1: Specifying the kind of data to be collected

There are five common types of data we can collect through a questionnaire: (1) experience/behavior (e.g. I go to the English corner every week in order to improve my oral English); (2) opinions (e.g. I think/believe going to the English corner helps me improve my oral English); (3) feelings (e.g. I feel less confident when having to talk with foreigners); (4) knowledge/abilities (e.g. I can talk fluently with foreigners after the training program); and (5) background (e.g. name, gender, age, etc.).

### Step 2: Deciding on the content of items

What we include as the items of the questionnaire is an essential part of the study. We generally do not use distracters, intentionally or non-intentionally. A good questionnaire must have high validity, which means that the items that make up the questionnaire are expected to be capable of measuring the features of a certain variable or reveal the relation between the variables. We often depend on two sources for items: (1) previous studies; (2) our own interview data. Sometimes, we directly borrow a questionnaire from a study to be replicated, but more often some adaptation will be introduced.

**Step 3: Wording the items**

The items chosen may take the form of statements or questions. In either case, we use ordinary words, avoid biased or misleading questions, and use positive and negative statements with equal numbers. When using the form of a discourse-completion test (DCT), we need to adopt open-ended questions/unstructured questions (like "Why do you use conversation repairs?"). When using structured questions, the respondents have to select one response out of the options provided: (1) multiple choice; (2) dichotomy; (3) scales.

**Step 4: Determining the way to arrange the items**

There are two common types of questionnaires: individual-item-based questionnaires and category-based questionnaires. For the former, we can just list whatever items occur in our mind. For the latter, we may adopt either the top-down approach (categories come before items) or the bottom-up approach (items come before categories). As a rule, background information is placed first. General questions come before specific questions. Questions must be divided into sections and all questions must be numbered. The way the answers are recorded should be convenient for the respondents to write. Here is an incomplete example of the top-down approach:

---

**Part B   Learning beliefs**
1 = I strongly disagree with this statement
2 = I disagree with this statement
3 = I'm not sure about this statement
4 = I agree with this statement
5 = I strongly agree with this statement
B01   Planning your study time is important for success. (     )
B02   Learning a foreign language requires painstaking effort. (     )
B03   It is important to repeat a lot. (     )
...

**Part C   Learning strategies**
1 = This statement is never or almost never true of me
2 = This statement is usually not true of me
3 = This statement is somewhat true of me
4 = This statement is usually true of me
5 = This statement is completely or almost completely true of me
C01   When reading a text, I try to understand everything in it. (     )
C02   I memorize texts. (     )
C03   I talk to myself in English outside of class. (     )
...

### Step 5: Pre-testing the questionnaire

After the questionnaire is drafted, it is necessary to conduct a pilot study to test the appropriateness of the questionnaire. A pilot study is one in which a questionnaire is tested on a small sample of respondents to detect and overcome potential problems. The questionnaire must be modified in content or in language, or both, once inadequacies are found.

## 4. Experiment-based studies of English

An experiment-based study is one in which the researcher manipulates one or more independent variables and measures their effect(s) on one or more dependent variables while controlling the effect of extraneous variables. It is similar to a survey study in that both often depend on quantitative data. It is different, though, because it happens in a human-manipulated environment as opposed to the natural surrounding of a survey, and that it is more powerful in establishing cause-effect relationships than surveys.

An experimental study has the following basic elements:

(1) A treatment in which one or more independent variables are manipulated;
(2) A comparison which involves at least two groups of people or two conditions;
(3) The measurement of one or more dependent variables as the result of the treatment;
(4) Measures that are used to control the effects of extraneous variables.

Three types of experimental studies are identified: (1) pre-experimental (least controlled); (2) quasi-experimental; and (3) truly experimental (most controlled). Here is a comparison:

Table 6  Types of experimental studies

|  | Pre-experimental | Quasi-experimental | Truly experimental |
| --- | --- | --- | --- |
| Control group | No | Yes | Yes |
| Randomization of subject selection | No | No | Yes |

All experiments generally involve a pre-test to identify differences in comparison groups prior to the introduction of intervention or treatment. The post-measurement is obligatory for all experimental studies. The post-test and pre-test should be taken under similar conditions.

The basic criterion for evaluating an experimental study lies in the validity of experimentation. There are two types of validity: internal validity (i.e. To what extent can the cause-effect relation be justified?) and external validity (i.e. To what extent can the research findings be generalized to the population?).

Factors affecting internal validity include the environment (the factors occurring in the environment such as noise, temperature, time of day, etc.), the selection of subjects, measurement, treatment, etc. Factors related to the selection of subjects may concern existing differences (background, opinions on the study, proficiency, etc.) before experiments. Factors related to measurement include testing effects: if the time between the pre-test and the post-test is too short, the subjects may be greatly influenced in the post-test by their performance in the pre-test. There may be the pre-test effect: subjects become aware of the variables the researchers intend to investigate. Problems may arise from the inconsistency or instability of the instrument. Factors related to a treatment cover the length of treatment, the way of treatment, and the people who implemented the treatment.

Factors affecting external validity include those related to environment. For instance, the findings of the study in a language laboratory with highly sophisticated equipment and tightly controlled procedures may not be generalizable to an ordinary classroom. There are factors related to selection of subjects. For example, if you want to study the oral English proficiency of Chinese college students, you should not only choose English major students as your subjects. If you do, findings of your experiment will not be generalized to non-English major students.

Restricting the procedures of the experiment will influence the generalizability. Maximizing external validity will endanger internal validity. Nevertheless, internal validity is prior to external validity.

## 5. Corpus-based studies of English

The latest methodological approach to the study of English is the use of a corpus, thanks to the power of the computer. A corpus, in this context, is a collection of linguistic data, either compiled as written texts or as a transcription of recorded speech. It is considered more or less representative of a language or an interlanguage, usually stored as an electronic database. The data in a corpus may be written or spoken, produced by native speakers or by L2 learners. Currently, the London-Lund corpus, National British Corpus (NBC), and American Spoken English Corpus (ASEC) are some of the frequently used native speakers' corpora. Meanwhile, the much employed Chinese learners' corpora are the Chinese Learners' English Corpus (CLEC) and Spoken and Written English Corpus of Chinese Learners (SWECCL). The data in a corpus are generally tagged with such labels as those for parts of speech, attributes of verbs, identities (like gender, age, proficiency level, nationality, etc.) of the speakers or writers, task types, situations, and the like.

The study of a corpus, or corpus linguistics, is aimed at describing patterns in a language or an interlanguage, for example, to determine the collocation pattern of a certain word. There are many processing operations we can perform on the corpus with the computer, each serving a unique research purpose. The first operation is the frequency check. We can compare, with the tool of a frequency counter, which words rank among the most frequently used ones in two or more corpora, or with what frequency a certain word or a set of words like discourse markers "you know" and "well" occur in each of the corpora. Such a comparison is very helpful in making judgments concerning whether L2 learners underuse or overuse certain lexical items or even syntactic patterns. Incidentally, with the information on how frequently a content word occurs in a single text, one can determine how central it is to the theme of the text.

With the frequency check, we can also perform text analysis in various ways. The following is the result of such an operation (adapted from Sinclair, 1991: 149):

Table 7  Text analysis

| | | |
|---|---|---|
| Length of the text in word-forms | 189 | |
| No. of different word-forms | 113 | |
| Length of the text in characters | 940 | |
| Average word length | 4.97 | |
| Longest word | 15 | |
| Length of the text in sentences | 11 | |
| Average sentence length in word-forms | 17.18 | |
| The longest sentence | 28 | |
| No. of sentences with less than 10 word-forms | 0 | 0.00% |
| No. of sentences with 11-20 word-forms | 7 | 63.64% |
| No. of sentences with 21-30 word-forms | 4 | 36.36% |

We can examine the frequency of use of long sentences and variety of vocabulary in order to determine the readability or difficulty of a single text. The following is the output of the statistical analysis of a text (omitted):

Table 8  Output of a statistical analysis

| | | |
|---|---|---|
| Counts | Words | 980 |
| | Sentences | 50 |
| Averages | Sentences per paragraph | 7.1 |
| | Words per sentence | 19.5 |
| | Characters per word | 4.6 |
| Readability | Passive sentences | 16% |
| | Flesch reading ease | 55.3 |
| | Flesch-Kincaid grade level | 10.3 |

Another useful method of processing we can carry out via a corpus is the concordance check. A concordance is a collection of the occurrences of a word-form, each in its own textual environment. Using a certain key word or phrase, we can search in the corpus for all the lines that contain it. (Depending on the need, there can be a few words preceding or following the key word, or there can be complete sentences; besides, the lines can also be arranged alphabetically according to the word following the keyword). For instance, the diagram below shows just part of the result of a concordance search whose keyword is "get":

| | | |
|---|---|---|
| When we | get | married the relationship will |
| lover or | get | prepared for the meal |
| students to | get | married they may |
| them have | get | a part-time job to |
| money they | get | is really a small |
| not mentally | get | ready for a family |

It is clear that with the help of concordance operation, we can study the collocational properties of a lexical item, the distribution of semantic meanings for a polysemous word, the syntactic behavior of an active verb, the frequency with which a word is used metaphorically, etc. After doing a frequency calculation it is possible to reveal its most frequently co-occurring collocates on the one hand, and judge with much confidence which words cannot, or at least, do not, go together with it.

# Appendix II

# Conceptual Studies of English

## 1. Preliminaries of conceptual research

Doing scientific research entails being original. Whereas empirical research may be original for its choice of a new research topic, new specific research questions, new subjects, new research instrument(s), a new theoretical framework, new statistic tool(s), a new corpus, etc. (each of which may lead to new findings), conceptual research or theorizing may derive its originality from the fact that it discovers a totally new language phenomenon, introduces a new definition, employs a new classification, adopts a new explanatory framework, proposes a new theoretical model, confirms, enriches, amends, or even falsifies an existing theory by presenting new evidence or contrary evidence, etc. The ultimate purpose of conceptual research is to promote our understanding of the object of study either by describing its features as neatly or fully as possible or by uncovering the working or generating mechanism underlying the language phenomenon.

To pursue any conceptual study at a language, we not only have to be observant and sensitive about the language, but also must be well versed in linguistic theories, at least those of the subfield of linguistics to which we belong. Language is everywhere around us. It is free and open for us to study. Although it is rule-governed, its rules seem to have exceptions. To find out a rule which is often implicit, we may need a large body of data for analysis. This may be time-consuming. A short-cut is to observe the language for any irregular, unusual or extraordinary linguistic facts. Here are a few examples:

① Two days **is** not a long time.
② **Boys** are **boys**.

③ **Golf plays** John.
④ Firemen had been **fighting** the forest fire for nearly three weeks.
⑤ Jane's mother is a **woman** athlete.
⑥ John, be a **man**.

Each of the sentences seems to violate some rule or constraint of English, grammatically or semantically. If we have enough "problem consciousness", we would ask ourselves why language users have constructed the sentences in those ways, given that each of them is natural and intelligible.

Observation does not work alone, because the activating of the problem consciousness requires the availability of relevant theoretical knowledge of language. Therefore, we must do extensive and intensive readings in order to arm ourselves with necessary theories and perspectives. Then, we may observe the linguistic data again to find out if there is new evidence to support an existing explanation or theory, or if there is evidence not captured by the existing explanation or theory, or if there is contrary evidence against the existing explanation or theory, etc.

Moreover, while we are studying the existing theories, we may pause to ask if there are ambiguities, inconsistencies, contradictions, etc. in a theoretical model, or we may compare to find out if there are contradictions among the explanations offered by different theories. For instance, there is a lot of criticism of the maxim of relation under the Cooperative Principle proposed by Paul Grice (see Unit 9). The maxim simply goes like this: Be relevant. It is not stipulated at all what kind of response in a conversation counts as relevant. It seems that Grice appeals to our intuitive judgment in this case, which leads to a lot of misinterpretations. Another problem with this maxim is that it seems to overlap with the maxim of quantity under the same principle, because once somebody says more than required, the extra information will be irrelevant. The apparent flaw with the maxim of relation led to a major, systematic revision of the principle by Sperber and Wilson in 1986 by the name of Relevance Theory.

## 2. Defining terms

An important part of conceptual research concerns the definitional job. After we have decided on a language phenomenon as the object of study, we need to define it in strict terms. To quote from *Collins Cobuild*, if we define something, we show, describe, or state clearly what it is and what its limits are, or what it is like.

Still, take the maxim of relation for example. Simply defining it as "be relevant" is somewhat circular because it does not enable us to make easy, straightforward judgment concerning what is relevant and what is not. In the revised theoretical model of communicative relevance, Sperber and Wilson (1995:125) redefine the notion of relevance as follows:

- Extent condition 1: An assumption is relevant in a context to the extent that its contextual effects in this context are large.
- Extent condition 2: An assumption is relevant in a context to the extent that the effort required to process it in this context is small.

When defining a term for a language phenomenon or a theoretical concept, we may take a form-based perspective, specifically what phonetic, phonological, morphological, syntactic or other features are characteristic of it, as shown in the following definition:

clause: A clause is a sequence of words that incorporates a subject and a predicate. It may be a whole sentence (e.g. "He will do it today") or parts of a sentence (e.g. "that he will do it today"). [Stuart Poole]

Sometimes, defining a term for a language phenomenon can be undertaken by considering its functional or semantic properties. For instance,

diminutive: a term used in morphology to refer to an affix with the general meaning of "little", e.g. "-let in English" [David Crystal]

More often than not, a term is defined by combining the formal and functional aspects of the language phenomenon, as shown below:

lexeme: A lexeme is an item of vocabulary which may consist of one or more than one word, e.g. concede, "give" in. The term is often used to denote the basic uninflected form of an item; the lexeme "give" can, for example, be realized by such words as "gives" and "gave". [Stuart Poole]

A very useful approach to defining is the use of illustrative examples. In the above definition, the use of a familiar example immediately gives the reader the idea of what a lexeme is.

Another important strategy in defining terms is to draw distinction between the term in question and some other term(s) that may cause confusion. For example, when we define the basic English sentence pattern SVA, we may describe it as "Subject + Predicate Verb + Adverbial" in which the adverbial is an obligatory constituent. After giving an example like "Jane weighs heavily in John's plan", we may proceed to point out that it is different from "Jane arrived early", which belongs to the basic sentence pattern SV, in that in the former sentence, the deletion of "heavily" would make the sentence grammatically unsound and semantically incomplete while the removal of "early" would not affect the grammaticality and meaningfulness of the latter sentence. Also, it is worth pointing out that a SV sentence may contain an optional adverbial.

When defining a term, we not only need to avoid circularity, as regards the maxim of relation, but also make sure that the metalanguage used is readily understandable and that the description makes it easy for others to recognize and identify the target language phenomenon. Thus, it pays to operationalize the definition.

Finally, it is often beneficial to compare different definitions for the same term(s) by different scholars. It is important to relate a certain definition to its context or the purpose it serves in a given study. For one's own purpose, it may be necessary to establish a working definition.

## 3. Classifying objects

Classifying things works on the principle of similarity. When we put two things into the same class, we do so by identifying features they have in common and ignoring features that distinguish them. For example, when we put such illocutionary acts as requests, orders, advising, and threatening under the category of directives (see Unit 8), we do so because all of these acts are causative in a sense (that is, one causes another to do something). In linguistics, we can also impose an order on things by classifying them in conventionally convenient ways. In the study of conversational repair, for instance, one common classification used in the literature is attempted in terms of who initiates the repair and who does the repair. Thus, we have four types of repair: self-initiated self-repair, self-initiated other-repair, other-initiated self-repair, and other-initiated other-repair. Such a classification is ideal because (1) it follows clearly specified criteria, (2) it is inclusive of all cases of repair, (3) the types classified are mutually exclusive, allowing the least overlapping, (4) the specification of each type is distinct (clearly worded, unambiguous, and identifiable), and so on.

Clearly, an important question to ask is, of course, what common features we are to take as significant. Take any number of things at random and we can always find some common features and therefore some criteria for classifying them as alike. As far as conversational repair is concerned, we may be less interested in who initiates or makes the repair than in what is repaired. Then, a new taxonomy will be necessary; for instance, we may distinguish between formal repairs (of linguistic forms) and content repairs, each of which can be further classified.

A central point worthy of emphasis here is that a classification must be well-principled; i.e. there must be a reasonable and identifiable criterion. Illocutionary acts (refer again to Unit 8) were originally classified by John Austin into verdictives, exercitives, commisives, expositives, and behavitives. Although the taxonomy largely captures our intuitive judgment, it is intrinsically defective because we are not given the criterion used. To remedy the inadequacy, John Searle (Austin's former American student) reformulated the classification as consisting of representatives, directives, commissives, expressives, and declarations, on the basis of clearly stated criteria as well as lucid explanation:

Table 1  Searle's classification of speech acts

| Speech-act categories | Explanation | Illocutionary acts | Relation between "the words" and "the world" | Who is responsible for the relation |
|---|---|---|---|---|
| **Representatives** | Represent some state of affairs | Assertions, claims, descriptions | The words fit the world ("outside" world) | Speaker |
| **Commissives** | Commit the speaker to some future course of action | Promises, threats, vows | The world will fit the words | Speaker |
| **Directives** | Get the addressee to carry out some action | Commands, requests, dares, entreaties | The world will fit the words | Hearer |
| **Declarations** | Themselves bring about a state of affairs | Marrying, naming, blessing, arresting | The words change the world | Speaker |
| **Expressives** | Indicate the speaker's psychological state or mental attitude | Greeting, congratulating, thanking, apologizing | The words fit the world ("psychological world") | Speaker |

## 4. Formulating rules

In the study of English, we can work out many kinds of rules. To begin with, we may distinguish between rules of structuring and rules of use. For example, we are referring to a rule of phonological structuring when we talk about the following rule governing the clustering of consonants at the initial position in English: The first consonant must be /s/, followed by /p/, /t/, /f/, or /k/, and the last consonant must be /l/, /r/, or /w/, as diagrammed below:

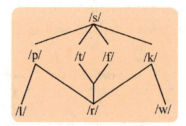

**Figure 1　Sequential rule in English**

By contrast, when we talk about the felicity or appropriate conditions for performing a speech act like promising (again refer to Unit 8), we are tackling a rule of language use. Even for rules of use, a subtle distinction can be drawn between constitutive rules and regulative rules, as in the case of the Chinese chess. While there are restrictions as to how a horse moves (like what makes a basic invitation), there are strategies directing how to move it in order to win the game (like what makes a successful invitation). Constitutive rules are by nature prescriptive. For example, traditional Latin-based grammar had the prescriptive rule that a grammatical sentence must not end with a preposition. Prescriptive rules are often arbitrary, whereas regulative rules are generally motivated, for biological, socio-cultural or other reasons such as the need for economy of effort, visual symmetry, and politeness.

For a given language phenomenon, we must not posit redundant rules. That is, if two statements converge or overlap with each other, refinement of one and abandonment of the other need to take place. Also, when we state the rules for it, we must abide by the principles of economy and clarity; given two rules that account for a given body of data, the briefer one is to be preferred. The following table illustrates how we work step by step towards a neat rule for the use of reflexives in English:

Appendix II  Conceptual Studies of English

Table 2  Rules of English reflexives

| Sentences | Rules | Rule selection |
|---|---|---|
| John hurt him. ("him" refers to Jack)<br>John hurt himself. | a. The reflexive must be co-referential with the subject. | Keep (a) only because (b) is redundant. |
| *John hurt herself.<br>*John hurt themselves.<br>*John hurt myself. | b. The reflexive must agree with the subject in number, gender and person. | |
| *Himself hurt John.<br>John himself went there.<br>John went there himself. | c. The reflexive can't fill the subject position alone. When used as subject appositive, its position is flexible.<br>d. The reflexive must have an antecedent to the left of it. It is bound by the antecedent. | Drop (a) and keep (c) and (d), because (a) is not descriptive enough; i.e. it does not cover all cases. |
| John thought Mary respected him.<br>*John thought Mary respected himself.<br>*John thought himself respected Mary. | e. The reflexive is bound by the subject of the clause in which it occurs. | Keep (e) and (c) but drop (d), which is not restrictive enough. |
| John expected Mary to respect him.<br>*John expected Mary to respect himself.<br>John promised Mary to elect himself.<br>John's sister saw him.<br>*John's sister saw himself.<br>The photo of himself in the newspaper upset John. | f. The reflexive is bound by an accessible subject in the local domain which includes the accessible subject, the governor and the reflexive. | Keep (f) and (c) but drop (e), which is not inclusive enough. |
| | g. The reflexive is bound in its governing category. | Keep (c) and redefine (f) as (g) because (f) is not economical. |

To achieve economy, we commonly resort to technical terms that embody fragments of linguistic expertise. In the above example, "a governing category" is used in rule g to replace the long descriptive expression "the local domain which includes the accessible subject, the governor and the reflexive", which also makes it possible to delete "by an accessible subject" in rule f. Thus, an accompanying requirement for rule description is the use of technical terms whenever we can, although non-technical language is preferred in giving reader-friendly explanations. When writing out the sequential rule for English consonantal clusters in the initial position, we might have stipulated the following: The first consonant must be the voiceless fricative alveolar, followed by a voiceless plosive or a voiceless fricative labiodental; the last one must be a liquid or a glide.

## 5. Constructing models

"Model" in this context refers loosely to any pattern pertaining to a body of apparently messy linguistic facts and an explanatory framework that serves to capture the generating mechanism of some linguistic facts or provides an account of the motivation behind certain linguistic facts.

The first type of model reminds us of the turn-taking system (refer to Unit 5) proposed to describe and explain how conversation is organized and developed. The following model, which originates with Rod Ellis (1997a), belongs to the second type. It explains how L2 learning takes place, with special attention to such key factors as noticing (which converts input into intake) and integrating (which serves to develop the intake into part of the interlanguage system for future output).

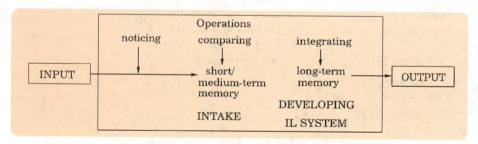

Figure 2　Rod Ellis' (1997a) model of L2 learning

Another second-type model is manifested by the Cooperative Principle (see Unit 9). Although it is sometimes used to describe how people talk in conversation, it is primarily designed to reveal and calculate conversational implicatures. That is, the intentional violation of one or more maxims will suggest that the speaker is intending to convey a certain non-literal meaning or implicature. Considering other factors like the context and the speaker's willingness to cooperate at a basic, deep level, the hearer will be capable of deriving the implicature.

A well-known generating model is Noam Chomsky's Transformational Generative Grammar (TG Grammar for short), built on a lot of assumptions. For example, the distinction between the deep structure and surface structure of a sentence helps, in the first approximation, to make a syntactic difference between "Jane is easy to please" and "Jane is eager to please". Next, the phrase structure rules like "S→NP VP" (for details see Unit 4) and the transformational rules can, to a satisfactory extent, explain how we can make an infinite number of sentences out of a finite set of words and syntactic rules as well as why the two sentences above are fundamentally different.

A further purpose for constructing a model is to seek functional explanations for why a certain pattern exists and why a certain constraint works on some linguistic facts. For that purpose, we need to exercise our cause-effect reasoning, by taking into account cognitive, biological, and socio-cultural processes. For instance, in explaining why the phonological process of sound assimilation takes place (see Unit 2), we might resort to the model of interaction between phonology and biology: the pronunciation of a sound is affected by its following sound in the way that reflects biological conditioning, which is subject to the constraint of the principle of least effort. Thus, we pronounce "love to" (/ˈlʌvtə/) as /ˈlʌftə/, presumably because some effort can be saved: the feature [+voiced] becoming [-voiceless] means making no vibration of the vocal bands at the moment.

To construct a model, we may take the following steps:
(1) study the known facts carefully;
(2) come up with a hypothesis that can explain the known facts;
(3) test the hypothesis with more facts and modify it, when necessary, to better accommodate the facts;
(4) refine the hypothesis (to be further modified or replaced in the future, as happened to Chomsky's early versions of TG Grammar).

# References

Akmajian, A., et al. (1979). *Linguistics: An Introduction to Language and Communication*. Cambridge: The MIT Press.

Austin, J. (1962). *How to Do Things with Words*. Cambridge: Harvard University Press.

Bellugi, U. (1970). Learning the language. *Psychology Today*, 4: 32-35.

Bolinger, D. (1968). *Aspects of Language*. New York: Harcourt Brace Jovanovich.

Brown, P. & Levinson, S. (1987). *Politeness: Some Universals in Language Usage*. Cambridge: Cambridge University Press.

Chomsky, N. (1957). *Syntactic Structures*. The Hague: Mouton.

Chomsky, N. (1965). *Aspects of the Theory of Syntax*. Cambridge: The MIT Press.

Chomsky, N. (1995). *The Minimalist Program*. Cambridge: Cambridge University Press.

Cook, C. (2000). *Second Language Learning and Language Teaching*. Beijing: Foreign Language Teaching and Research Press. [1996. London: Edward Arnold Ltd.]

Corder, S. P. (1973). *Introducing Applied Linguistics*. Harmondsworth: Penguin.

Crystal, D. (1985). *Linguistics*. Harmondsworth: Penguin Books Ltd.

Ellis, R. (1990). *Instructed Second Language Acquisition*. Oxford: Basil Blackwell.

Ellis, R. (1994). *The Study of Second Language Acquisition*. Oxford: Oxford University Press.

Ellis, R. (1997a). *SLA Research and Language Teaching*. Oxford: Oxford University Press.

Ellis, R. (1997b). *Second Language Acquisition*. Oxford: Oxford University Press.

Eschholz, P., Rosa, A. & Clark, V. (1974). *Language Awareness*. New York: St. Martin's Press, Inc.

Fasold, R. (2000). *The Sociolinguistics of Language*. Beijing: Foreign Language Teaching and Research Press. [1990. London: Blackwell Publishers Ltd.]

Ferguson, C. (1959). Diglossia. *Word*, 15: 325-340.

Fromkin, V., et al. (2003). *An Introduction to Language* (7th edition). Boston: Heinle.

Goatly, A. (2012). *Meaning and Humor*. Cambridge: Cambridge University Press.

Green, G. (1989). *Pragmatics and Natural Language Understanding*. Hillsdale, NJ: Laurance Erlbaum Associates.

Gregory, H. (2000). *Semantics*. London: Routledge.

Grice, P. (2002). *Studies in the Way of Words*. Beijing: Foreign Language Teaching and Research Press. [1989. Cambridge: Harvard University Press.]

Grundy, P. (1995). *Doing Pragmatics*. London: Edward Arnold.

Hall, R. (1968). *An Essay on Language*. New York: Chilton Books.

Halliday, M. A. K. (1994). *An Introduction to Functional Grammar*. London: Edward Arnold.

Halliday, M. A. K. & Hasan, R. (1976). *Cohesion in English*. London: Longman.

Hayes, C., et al. (1987). *The ABC's of Languages and Linguistics: A Practical Primer to Language Science*. Chicago: Voluntad Publishers, Inc.

Holmes, J. (1992). *An Introduction to Sociolinguistics*. London: Longman.

Jaszczolt, K. (2004). *Semantics and Pragmatics: Meaning in Language and Discourse*. Beijing: Peking University Press. [2002. London: Pearson Education Ltd.]

Knowles, G. (1987). *Patterns of Spoken English*. London: Longman.

Krashen, S. (1981). *Second Language Acquisition and Second Language Learning*. Oxford: Oxford University Press.

Krashen, S. (1982). *Principles and Practice in Second Language Acquisition*. New York: Pergamon Press.

Krashen, S. (1985). *The Input Hypothesis: Issues and Implications*. Oxford: Pergamon Press.

Langacker, R. (1987). *Foundations of Cognitive Grammar, Vol.1, Theoretical Prerequisites*. Redwood, CA: Stanford University Press.

Larsen-Freeman, D. & Long, M. (2000). *An Introduction to Second Language Acquisition Research*. Beijing: Foreign Language Teaching and Research Press. [1991. London: Blackwell Publishers Ltd.]

Leech, G. (1969). *A Linguistic Guide to English Poetry*. London: Longman.

Leech, G. (1983a). *Style in Fiction*. London: Longman.

Leech, G. (1983b). *Principles of Pragmatics*. London: Longman.

Leech, G. (2014). *The Pragmatics of Politeness*. Oxford: Oxford University Press.

Levinson, S. (1983). *Pragmatics*. Cambridge: Cambridge University Press.

Lyons, J. (1968). *Introduction to Theoretical Linguistics*. Cambridge: Cambridge University Press.

Lyons, J. (1981). *Language and Linguistics*. Cambridge: Cambridge University Press.

Lyons, J. (2000). *Linguistic Semantics: An Introduction*. Beijing: Foreign Language Teaching and Research Press. [1995. Cambridge: Cambridge University Press.]

Martinet, A. (1964). *Elements of General Linguistics*. London: Faber and Faber Limited.

Mey, J. (1993). *Pragmatics: An Introduction*. Oxford: Blackwell.

O'Malley, J. M. & Chamot, A. (2001). *Learning Strategies in Second Language Acquisition*. Shanghai: Shanghai Foreign Language Education Press. [1990. Cambridge: Cambridge University Press.]

Palmer, F. (1981). *Semantics*. Cambridge: Cambridge University Press.

Peccei, J. (2000). *Pragmatics*. Beijing: Foreign Language Teaching and Research Press. [1999. London: Taylor & Francis Ltd.]

Poole, S. (1999). *An Introduction to Linguistics*. London: Macmillan Publishers, Ltd.

Quirk, R., Greenbaum, S., Leech, G. & Svartvik, J. (1985). *A Comprehensive Grammar of the English Language*. London: Longman.

Ratford, A. (2000). *Syntax: A Minimalist Introduction*. Beijing: Foreign Language Teaching and Research Press. [1997. Cambridge: Cambridge University Press.]

Richards, J., Platt, J. & Weber, H. (1985). *Longman Dictionary of Applied Linguistics*. London: Longman.

Robins, R. H. (1978). *General Linguistics: An Introductory Survey*. London: Longman.

Robins, R. H. (2001). *A Short History of Linguistics*. Beijing: Foreign Language Teaching and Research Press. [1997. London: Addison Wesley Longman Ltd.]

Robinson, P. & Ellis, N. (2008). *Handbook of Cognitive Linguistics and Second Language Acquisition*. New York: Routledge.

Rosch, E. (1973). Natural categories. *Cognitive Psychology*, 4: 328-350.

Saeed, J. (2000). *Semantics*. Beijing: Foreign Language Teaching and Research Press. [1997. London: Blackwell Publishers Ltd.]

Sampson, G. (1980). *Schools of Linguistics: Competition and Evolution*. London: Hutchinson.

Sapir, E. (1921). *Language*. New York: Harcourt Brace.

Saussure, F. de. (2001). *Course in General Linguistics*. Beijing: Foreign Language Teaching and Research Press. [1983. London: Gerald Duckworth & Co. Ltd.]

Schmidt, R. (1990). The role of consciousness in second language learning. *Applied Linguistics*, 11: 129-158.

Schmidt, R. (1993). Awareness and second language acquisition. *Annual Review of Applied Linguistics*, 13: 206-226.

Searle, J. (2001). *Expression and Meaning: Studies in the Theory of Speech Acts*. Beijing: Foreign Language Teaching and Research Press. [1979. Cambridge: Cambridge University Press.]

Simpson, J. (1979). *A First Course in Linguistics*. Edinburgh: Edinburgh University Press.

Sinclair, J. (1999). *Corpus, Concordance, Collocation*. Shanghai: Shanghai Foreign Language Education Press. [1991. Oxford: Oxford University Press.]

Sperber, D. & Wilson, D. (1995). *Relevance: Communication and Cognition*. London: Blackwell Publishers.

Spolsky, B. (1998). *Sociolinguistics*. Oxford: Oxford University Press.

Swain, M. & Lapkin, S. (1995). Problems in output and the cognitive processes they generate: A step towards second language learning. *Applied Linguistics*, 16: 371-391.

Swain, M. (1985). Communicative competence: Some roles of comprehensible input and comprehensible output in its development. In S. Gass & C. Madden (Eds.), *Input and Second Language Acquisition*. Rowley, MA: Newbury House, 235-253.

Swain, M. (1993). The Output Hypothesis: Just speaking and writing aren't enough. *The Canadian Modern Language Review*, 50: 158-164.

Taylor, J. (2001). *Linguistic Categorization: Prototypes in Linguistic Theory*. Beijing: Foreign Language Teaching and Research Press. [1995. Oxford: Oxford University Press.]

Thomas, J. (1995). *Meaning in Interaction: An Introduction to Pragmatics*. London: Longman.

Traugott, E. & Pratt, M. (1980). *Linguistics for Students of Literature*. New York: Harcourt Brace Jovanovich, Inc.

Trudgill, P. (1974). Linguistic change and diffusion: Description and explanation in sociolinguistic dialect geography. *Language in Society*, 3: 215-246.

Ungerer, F. & Schmidt, H. J.(2001). *An Introduction to Cognitive Linguistics*. Beijing: Foreign Language Teaching and Research Press. [1996. London: Addison Wesley Longman Ltd.]

Wardhaugh, R. (1977). *Introduction to Linguistics* (2nd edition). New York: McGraw-Hill Book Company.

Wardhaugh, R. (2000). *An Introduction to Sociolinguistics*. Beijing: Foreign Language Teaching and Research Press. [1998. London: Blackwell Publishers Ltd.]

Watts, R. (2003). *Politeness*. Cambridge: Cambridge University Press.

Widdowson, H. G. (2003). *Linguistics*. Shanghai: Shanghai Foreign Language Education Press. [1996. Oxford: Oxford University Press.]

Yule, G. (1996). *Pragmatics*. Oxford: Oxford University Press.

Yule, G. (2000). *The Study of Language*. Beijing: Foreign Language Teaching and Research Press. [1996. Cambridge: Cambridge University Press.]

陈新仁.（2009）.新编语用学教程.北京：外语教学与研究出版社.
戴炜栋,何兆熊.（2002）.新编简明英语语言学教程.上海：上海外语教育出版社.
丁言仁,郝克.（2001）.英语语言学纲要.上海：上海外语教育出版社.
何自然.（1997）.语用学与英语学习.上海：上海外语教育出版社.
何自然,陈新仁.（2004）.当代语用学.北京：外语教学与研究出版社.
胡曙中.（1993）.英汉修辞比较研究.上海：上海外语教育出版社.
胡壮麟.（2001）.语言学教程(修订版).北京：北京大学出版社.
李延福.（1988）.英语语言学基础读本.济南：山东大学出版社.
梁锦祥.（1995）.语言学研究的通用方法.广州：广东科学技术出版社.
王佐良,丁往道.（1987）.英语文体学引论.北京：外语教学与研究出版社.
文军.（1992）.英语修辞格词典.重庆：重庆大学出版社.
文秋芳.（1995）.英语语言学导论.南京：江苏教育出版社.
杨信彰.（2005）.语言学概论.北京：高等教育出版社.

# Glossary

## A

accent　重音，口音
acculturation　文化适应
accuracy　准确度
acoustic phonetics　声学语音学
acquisition　习得
acronym　首字母拼读词
addition　增添
adjacency pair　毗邻对子
adverbial　状语
affixation　词缀法
African-American Vernacular English (AAVE)　非裔美国人本地英语
Afro-Asiatic Family　亚非语系
agent　主格
Agreement Maxim　一致准则
alliteration　头韵
allomorph　语素变体
allophone　音位变体
Altaic Family　阿尔泰语系
alternative question　选择疑问句
ambiguity　歧义性
American English　美国英语
analogy　类推法
anapestic　抑抑扬格/短短长格
anaphora　前指
anaphoric reference　前指照应
anomaly　语义不规则，变则

ANOVA　方差分析
antecedent　先行词
antepenultimate　倒数第三个音节的
antonym　反义词
antonymous　反义的
antonymy　反义关系
Approbation Maxim　赞誉准则
appropriateness condition　得体条件
arbitrariness　任意性
argot　隐语，黑话
argumentation　议论文体
articulatory phonetics　发音语音学
assimilation rule　同化规则
assonance　谐音，准押韵
attrition　耗损
auditory phonetics　听觉语音学
Australian English　澳大利亚英语
Austro-Asiatic Family　亚澳语系
avoidance　回避

## B

baby talk　儿语
back-formation　逆成法
backsliding　倒退
bar graph　柱状图，柱形统计图
behabitive　行动类（以言指事）
bilingualism　双语现象
Black English　黑人英语
blending　混成法

bridging　语用照应
British English　英国英语

## C

calculability　可推导性
camaraderie　同志情谊
Canadian English　加拿大英语
care-takerese　保姆式语言
case　（语义）格
case study　个案研究
cataphoric reference　后指照应
Caucasian Family　高加索语系
change of state verb　状态变化动词
child directed speech(CDS)　针对孩子的话语
China English　中国英语
Chinglish　中国式英语
chunk　语块
class dialect　阶级方言
class interval　组距
clause　小句,从句
clipping　截断法
closed class　封闭类
coda　音节尾
code-mixing　语码混用
code-switching　语码转换
coding time　编码时间
cognitive strategy　认知策略
coherence　连贯
cohesion　衔接
co-hyponym　同属下义词
coinage　新造法
collocation　搭配
comment　评价

commisive　承诺类(以言行事)
communication strategy　交际策略
communicative competence　交际能力
competence-related error　能力引起的失误
complement　补语
complementary antonym　互补性反义词
complementary distribution　互补分布
complex sentence　复合句
complexity　复杂程度
componential analysis　语义成分分析
composition　合成法
compounding　合成法
conative　意动的
conceptual metaphor　概念隐喻
conceptual research　理论研究
concordance check　共现关系检测
consonant　辅音
constative　表述句
constituent　成分
constituent structure　成分结构
constitutive rule　构成规则
construction　构块,结构
construction grammar　构块语法
context　语境,上下文
contraction　缩略
contrastive distribution　对比分布
control variable　控制变量
conventional implicature　规约含意
conversation　会话
conversational implicature　会话含意
converse antonym　对立性反义词
conversion　转类法,转化法

Cooperative Principle 合作原则
coordinate sentence 并列句
copying 复制
corpus 语料库
corpus linguistics 语料库语言学
corpus planning 主体规划
correlational analysis 相关分析
co-text 上下文
creativity 创造性
creole 克里奥语
critical period 关键期
cross-association 交叉联想
cross-sectional study 横截面研究,横断研究
cultural transmission 文化传播性

## D

dactylic 扬抑抑格/长短短格
data 数据
data analysis 数据分析
data collection 数据收集
dative construction 与格构块
declaration 宣告类(以言行事)
declarative knowledge 陈述性知识
declarative sentence 陈述句
deep(or underlying) structure 深层结构
defeasible 可取消的
deference 尊敬
deictic expression 指示语
deixis 指示现象,指示语
deletion 删除
deletion rule 删除规则
denotation 外延
dependent variable 因变量

description 描写文体
descriptive data 描述性数据
descriptive grammar 描写语法
descriptive statistics 描述性统计
developmental pragmatics 发展语用学
dialect 方言
diglossia 双语体现象
diglossic 双语体的
dimeter 二音步
directive 指令类(以言行事)
discourse 话语,语篇
discourse deixis 语篇指示
discourse-completion test (DCT) 语篇补全测试
displacement 不受时空限制的特性
distance 距离
distinctive feature 区别性特征
ditransitive construction 双及物构块
doer 动作执行者
Dravidian Family 达罗毗荼语系
duality of structure/double articulation 结构二重性

## E

echo probe 回声探究
elision 省音
ellipsis 省略
embedded sentence 内嵌句
emotive 情感的
empirical research 实证研究,实验法研究
endophoric reference 内照应
English globalization 英语全球化
entailment 蕴涵

error analysis　错误分析
Esperanto　世界语
essential condition　基本条件
ethnography of communication　交际民族学
euphemism　委婉语
exclamatory sentence　感叹句
exercitive　行使类(以言指事)
exophoric reference　外照应
exposition　说明文体
expositive　表达类(以言指事)
expressive　表达类(以言行事)
external feedback　外部反馈
external validity　外部效度
extraneous variable　随机变量,无关变量

## F

face　面子
face-enhancing act　面子提升行为
face-threatening act (FTA)　面子威胁行为
factive verb　叙实动词
family resemblance　家族相似性
felicity condition　适切条件
field of discourse　语场
field work　田野工作
floor　讲话机会
fluency　流利程度
focus　(话语)中心
foot (*pl.* feet)　音步
foreigner talk　外国人话语
form class　形式类
form of writing　体裁

formal style　正式语体
formulaic sequence　程式化词语
fossilization　石化
fossilize　石化
free variation　自由变异
frequency　频率,频次
frequency check　频次检测
functional shift　功能转换法
fuzziness　模糊性
fuzzy　模糊的

## G

generalized conversational implicature　一般会话含意
generative　生成
generative grammar　生成语法
Generosity Maxim　慷慨准则
genre　语类
gradable antonym　可分等级的反义词
grammatical competence　语法能力
grammatical meaning　语法意义
grammatical subject　语法主语

## H

Hawthorne effect　霍索恩效应
hedge　模糊限制语
hesitation marker　迟疑标记
hierarchical structuring　层级结构组织
homography　同形异义关系
homonymy　同形/同音异义关系
homophony　同音异义关系
hyperbole　夸张
hyponym　下义词
hyponymy　上下义关系

hypothesis 假设

## I

iambic 抑扬格/短长格
iambic pentameter 五部抑扬格
iconicity 象似性
ideational function 概念功能
idiolect 个人言语风格
idiom 习语
idiomaticity 符合表达习惯的程度
illocutionary act 以言行事/施为性行为
Immediate Constituent 直接成分
Immediate Constituent Analysis (IC Analysis) 直接成分分析法
imperative sentence 祈使句
impersonalization 非人格化
implicative verb 含蓄动词
independent variable 独立变项
independent variable 自变量
indeterminacy 不确定性
indexical expression 指示语
indirect speech 间接言语
indirect speech act 间接言语行为
Indo-European Family 印欧语系
inferential statistics 推断统计
infix 中缀
inflection 屈折变化
informal style 非正式语体
initialism 首字母缩略法
initiation 话语始发
Innate Hypothesis （语言）内在假设
input 输入
input hypothesis 输入假设
intake 摄入

interaction hypothesis 互动假设
interlanguage 中介语, 语际语
interlanguage grammar 中介语语法
internal validity 内部效度
interpersonal function 人际功能
interrogative sentence 疑问句
interval scale 区间尺度
intervening variable 介入变量
interview 访谈
intonation 语调
intonation unit 语调单位
inversion 倒装
It-cleft construction It-断裂构块

## J

jargon 行话, 黑话

## L

L1 acquisition 第一语言习得
labeled tree diagram 加标记的树形图
language acquisition device (LAD) 语言习得机制
language acquisition planning 语言习得规划
language diffusion policy 语言扩散政策
language education policy 语言教育政策
language family 语系
language policy 语言政策
language policy and language planning (LPLP or LPP) 语言政策与语言规划
language standardization 语言标准化
language type 语言类型

lapse  失误
learner error  学习者错误
learner strategy  学习者策略
learning  学习
learning strategy  学习策略
left dislocation construction  左移位构块
lexeme  词素,词位
lexical gap  词汇空白
lexical pragmatics  词汇语用学
lexical rule  词汇规则
lexicogrammatical structure  词汇语法结构
lexicon  词汇,词典,词库
liaison  连诵,连音
linearization problem  线性化排列问题
lingua franca  通用语,混合语
locutionary act  以言指事/表述性行为
logical subject  逻辑主语
London Cockney  伦敦土话
longitudinal  纵深研究,跟踪研究

## M

Malayo-Polynesian Family  马来-波利尼亚语系
Manner Maxim  方式准则
marked  有标记的
maturation  (语言的)自然发展或成熟
mean  平均值
meaning  意思,意义
mental grammar  心智语法
meronymy  部分整体关系
metacognitive strategy  元认知策略
metafunction  元功能

metalanguage  元语言
metalingual  元语言的
metaphor  隐喻
metaphorical extension  隐喻性扩展
metaphorical reasoning  隐喻性思维
meter  韵律,音步
metonym  转喻
metonymic reasoning  转喻性思维
mime  模仿
minimal pair  最小对立体
mirror maxim  镜像准则
mode of discourse  语式
model  模型
moderator variable  调节变量
Modesty Maxim  谦虚准则
morpheme  语素,词素
mortality  (受试的)流失
motherese  母亲语言
motivation  动机

## N

narration  叙述,记叙文体
national language  国民语言
negative  反义词
negative, directional hypothesis  反向的定向假设
negative face  消极面子
negotiated input  协商性输入
neologism  新词
new information  新信息
New York English  纽约英语
Niger-Congo Family  尼日尔-刚果语系
nominal scale  名目尺度
non-directional hypothesis  非定向假设

nonsense word 无意义词
normativism 规范主义
noticing 注意
noticing hypothesis 注意假设
nucleus （音节）核心
null hypothesis 零假设
numeric data 数字性数据
nursery names 保姆式用语

## O

object 宾语
obligatory role 必要角色
official language 官方语言
officialese 官样语言，官腔
old information 旧信息
onomatopoeic word 拟声词
onset （音节）首音
open class 开放类
optional element 可选成分
optional role 可选角色
ordinal scale 顺序尺度
orientational metaphor 方位隐喻
output 输出
overextension 过度扩展
overgeneralization 过度概括

## P

paragraph 段落
paraphrase 同义阐释
particle 小品词
particle movement 小品词移动
particularized conversational implicature 特殊会话含意
passivize 被动化

pentameter 五音步
penultimate 倒数第二个音节的
performance-related error 使用引起的失误
performative 施为句
perlocutionary act 以言成事/成事性行为
person deixis 人称指示
perspective 视角
phatic communion 寒暄
phone 音素
phoneme 音位
phonetic environment 语音环境
phonetics 语音学
phonology 音系学
phonotactics 音位配列学
phrase 短语
phrase structure rule 短语结构规则
pidgin 皮钦语，洋泾浜
pie chart 圆饼图
pilot study 试点研究
pitch 音高，声调高低
place deixis 地点指示
poetic 诗学的
point of departure 出发点
point of view 观点
politeness 礼貌
Politeness Principle 礼貌原则
polygon 多边图
polysemy 多义性
population 总体，母体，群体
positive, directional hypothesis 正向的定向假设
positive face 积极面子

possible world　可能世界
pragma-linguistic failure　语用语言失误
pragmatic competence　语用能力
pragmatic failure　语用失误
pragmatics　语用学
Prague School　布拉格学派
predicate　谓语
predicate verb　谓语动词
pre-emptive usage　（指示语的）先用现象
prefabricated chunk　预制语块
prefix　前缀
preparatory condition　预备条件
prescriptive grammar　规定语法
prescriptivism　规定主义
presupposition　预设,前提
presupposition trigger　前提触发语
pre-test effect　前测效应
procedural knowledge　程序性知识
production strategy　表达类策略
productive　能产的
productive vocabulary　用于表达的词汇
productivity　能产性
projection problem　投射问题
proposition　命题
propositional content condition　命题内容条件
prototype　原型
psychological subject　心理主语

## Q

qualitative research　定性研究
Quality Maxim　质准则
quantitative research　定量研究
Quantity Maxim　量准则

questionnaire　问卷

## R

ready-made expression　现成表达
Received Pronunciation（RP）　标准发音
receiving time　接受时间
receptive vocabulary　用于理解的词汇
recipient　受事格
recursion　递归性
recursive syntax　递归句法
reduplication　重叠,重复
reference　指称,照应
referent　指称对象
referential　指称的
referential expression　指称表达
regional or geographical dialect　地区或地理方言
register　语域
register theory　语域理论
regulative rule　调节规则
relation maxim　相关准则
relational opposite　关系反义词
reordering　重排
repair　修正
repertoire　交际语库,全部语言变体
representational metaphor　表征隐喻
representative　阐述类（以言行事）
research design　研究设计
research question　研究问题
response　话语回应
resultative construction　结果式构块
rheme　述位
rhetorical question　修辞问句
rhyme　押韵

rhythm 节奏

## S

sample 样本
sampling 抽样
scalar implicature 梯度含意
schema 图式
schwa [ə] 非重读央元音
SE (standard English) 标准英语
second language acquisition (SLA) 第二语言习得
segment 音段
semantic categorization 语义范畴化
semantic compositionality 语义组合性
semantic extension 语义扩展
semantic feature 语义特征
semantic field 语义场
semantic property 语义属性
semantic role 语义角色
semantics 语义学
semiotics 符号学
semi-structured 半组织的
semivowel 半元音
sense 意义
sentence 句子
sentence semantics 句子语义学
sequential rule 序列规则
shortening 缩短法
significance level 显著水平
simple sentence 简单句
sincerity condition 真诚条件
Sino-Tibetan Family 汉藏语系
situational context 情景语境
slang 俚语

slip of the tongue 口误
sloppy speech 不地道的言语
social deixis 社交指示
social dialect 社会方言
social mediation strategy 社会中介策略
social-class dialect 社会方言
socioaffective filter 社会情感过滤
sociolect 社会方言
sociolinguistic competence 社会语言能力
socio-pragmatic failure 社交语用失误
speech act 言语行为
speech community 言语社区
speech error 口误
speech organ 发音器官
spoonerism 首音互换(口误)
standard deviation 标准差
standard language 标准语言
status planning 地位规划
strategic competence 策略能力
strategies of second language communication 第二语言交际策略
stress 重音
strong syllable 强音节
structural subject 结构主语
structured 有组织的
style 语体
sub-genre 次语类
subject 主语, 受试
suffix 后缀
superordinate 上义词
supporting sentence 支撑句
surface structure 表层结构

syllable 音节
Sympathy Maxim 同情准则
synecdoche 提喻
synonymous 同义的
synonymy 同义关系

## T

taboo 禁忌,塔布
Tact Maxim 得体准则
tag question 附加疑问句
tautology 同义反复,冗辞
temporal dialect 时间性方言
teacher talk 教师话语
tenor of discourse 语旨,基调
terms of address 称呼语
testing effect 测试效应
tetrameter 四音步
text 篇章,语篇
textual function 语篇功能
texture 语篇组织
thematic progression 主位进程
thematic role 主位角色
theme 主位,受事
theorizing 理论研究
think-aloud 有声思维
time deixis 时间指示
token 标记
tone 声调,音调
topic 话题
topic sentence 主题句
topicalization construction 话题化构块
transfer 迁移
Transformational Generative Grammar (TG grammar) 转换生成语法

transformational rule 转换规则
treatment 处理
tree diagram 树形图
trimeter 三音步
trochaic 扬抑格/长短格
truth condition 真值条件
truth value 真值情况
t-test t-检验
turn 话轮
turn taking 话轮转换
type 类型

## U

Universal Grammar (UG) 普遍语法
universals （语言）普遍性
unmarked 无标记的
unstructured 无组织的
Uralic Family 乌拉尔语系
utterance 话语

## V

vague predicate 模糊谓词
validity 效度
variety of English 英语变体
verbal probe 语言探究
verb of judging 评价动词
verdictive 裁决类(以言指事)
vernacular 本地语,土话
vocal tract 发音器官,声道
voiced 浊音的
voiceless 清音的
voicing 浊音化,振动声带情况
vowel 元音

# W

weak syllable　弱音节
weakening　弱化
Whorfian Hypothesis　沃尔夫假设
WH-question　特殊疑问句

word　词
word class　词类

# Y

Yes-No question　一般疑问句